TEAM-BASED ORGANIZING

ADVANCES IN INTERDISCIPLINARY STUDIES OF WORK TEAMS

Series Editor: Michael M. Beyerlein

ADVANCES IN INTERDISCIPLINARY STUDIES
OF WORK TEAMS   VOLUME 9

TEAM-BASED ORGANIZING

EDITED BY

MICHAEL M. BEYERLEIN

Department of Psychology, University of North Texas, USA

DOUGLAS A. JOHNSON

Department of Psychology, University of North Texas, USA

SUSAN T. BEYERLEIN

Department of Psychology, University of North Texas, USA

2003

JAI

An Imprint of Elsevier Science

Amsterdam – Boston – London – New York – Oxford – Paris
San Diego – San Francisco – Singapore – Sydney – Tokyo

ELSEVIER SCIENCE Ltd
The Boulevard, Langford Lane
Kidlington, Oxford OX5 1GB, UK

First edition 2003

Library of Congress Cataloging in Publication Data
A catalog record from the Library of Congress has been applied for.

British Library Cataloguing in Publication Data
A catalogue record from the British Library has been applied for.

ISBN: 0-7623-0981-4

⊗The paper used in this publication meets the requirements of ANSI/NISO Z39.48-1992 (Permanence of Paper).
Printed in The Netherlands.

CONTENTS

LIST OF CONTRIBUTORS

Michael M. Beyerlein	Center for the Study of Work Teams, University of North Texas, USA
Karen Blansett	4545 Highridge, The Colony, TX, USA
Lori Bradley	Center for the Study of Work Teams, University of North Texas, USA
Toni L. Doolen	Industrial and Manufacturing Engineering, Oregon State University, USA
Erik R. Eddy	24 Hampshire Way, Schenectady, New York, USA
Samer Faraj	Robert H. Smith School of Business, University of Maryland, USA
Marla E. Hacker	Industrial Engineering, Business/Management, Oregon State University, USA
Terry Halfhill	Department of Psychology. University of North Texas, USA
Cheryl L. Harris	Center for the Study of Work Teams, University of North Texas, USA
Joseph W. Huff	Department of Psychology, University of North Texas, USA
Frances Kennedy	Clemson University, SC, USA

Gerald D. Klein	Rider University, NJ, USA
Steven J. Lorenzet	College of Business Administration Rider University, NJ, USA
Tjai M. Nielsen	RHR International, Atlanta, GA, USA
Henry P. Sims, Jr.	Robert H. Smith School of Business, University of Maryland, USA
Sarah K. Soulen	Department of Psychology, University of Tennessee, USA
Eric Sundstrom	Department of Psychology, University of Tennessee, USA
Duane Windsor	Jones Graduate School of Management, Rice University, TX, USA
Yan Xiao	School of Medicine, University of Maryland, USA
Seokhua Yun	Department of Management, Montclair State University, NJ, USA

ACKNOWLEDGMENTS

The papers in this volume grew out of presentations given at the ninth Annual University of North Texas Symposium on Individual, Team, and Organizational Effectiveness. However, another key part of the Symposium consisted of the discussant remarks by representatives of business. Discussants typically talked with the authors and often read early drafts of their papers before the Symposium. Discussants were charged with sharing ways in which their companies were applying the concepts presented by the authors. The Center for the Study of Work Teams has always considered bridging of the gap between the worlds of research and practice a goal of each conference event. The success of that bridging is primarily due to the efforts of the discussants. Therefore, we acknowledge their important contribution to the Symposium and to the authors' thinking about the concepts in their papers from a practical frame of reference.

The discussants and their affiliations at that time for the Ninth Symposium were:

Fred Asher, Thomson Corporation
Sue Freedman, Knowledge Work Associates
Karon Hoban, Hoban and Associates
Ronald Shenberger, Well-Formed Outcomes

We want to acknowledge the outstanding help and support of Nancy Gorman. She has been responsible for communicating with authors and editors, arranging for flow of manuscripts back and forth among these people, educating all of us on manuscript format, maintaining the relationship with the publisher, arranging for proofing, catching the errors the editors miss and bringing the chapters, introduction, and preface together in a final assembly for the publisher. A more conscientious and courteous style than Nancy's would be hard to find. It is particularly notable that Nancy maintained the quality of her work at the highest levels on this volume and the calm and patient demeanor that makes her a joy to work with while completing manuscripts for three other books at the same time.

Melanie Bullock organized the symposium. With assistance from Erica Lopez, she organized and oversaw all of the logistics of the Symposium event. She arranged for discussants and provided opportunities for the presenters and discussants to share ideas before the symposium. Melanie established effective relationships with each presenter and provided them with a level of support and information that many found so exceptional that they went out of their way to comment on it. The symposium and the book series would not have achieved the level of quality it did without the dedication that Melanie brought to the work.

ABOUT THE EDITORS

Michael M. Beyerlein is Director of the Center for the Study of Work Teams (*www.workteams.unt.edu*) and Professor of Industrial/Organizational Psychology at the University of North Texas. His research interests include all aspects of collaborative work systems, organization transformation, work stress, creativity/innovation, knowledge management and the learning organization, and complex adaptive systems. He has published in a number of research journals and has been a member of the editorial boards for *TEAM Magazine, Team Performance Management Journal*, and *Quality Management Journal*. Currently, he is senior editor of this JAI Press/Elsevier annual series of books *Advances in Interdisciplinary Study of Work Teams* and the Jossey-Bass/Pfeiffer *Collaborative Work Systems* series. In addition, he has been co-editor with Steve Jones on two ASTD case books about teams and edited a book on the global history of teams, *Work Teams: Past, Present and Future*. His most recent books are *Beyond Teams: Building the Collaborative Organization*, and *The Collaborative Work System Fieldbook*. He has been involved in change projects at the Center for the Study of Work Teams with such companies as Boeing, Shell, NCH, AMD, Raytheon, First American Finance, Westinghouse, and Xerox, and with government agencies such as Veterans Affairs, DCMAO, EPA, and the City of Denton.

Douglas A. Johnson is professor of the Industrial/Organizational psychology program, professor of psychology, and associate director of the Center for the Study of Work Teams, University of North Texas. Doug has published research in a variety of areas, ranging from leadership and job satisfaction to operant conditioning and interpersonal attraction. He co-founded and served as president of the Dallas-Fort Worth Organizational Psychology Group, and participated in the creation of the Dallas office of the I/O psychology consulting firm, Personnel Decisions International, with whom he works on a part-time basis.

Susan T. Beyerlein has taught undergraduate and MBA management courses at Our Lady of the Lake University and Texas Woman's University in the Dallas area. Susan has served as a research project manager with the Center for the Study of Work Teams and as a research scientist with the Center for Public Management at the University of North Texas. She continues to be an ad hoc reviewer for the *Academy of Management Review*. She is currently working on several edited book projects.

INTRODUCTION

This introduction of Volume 9 in the annual series *Advances in Interdisciplinary Studies of Work Teams* provides some historical context for the series and a preview of each of the chapters in this volume. The chapters presented here are based on presentations in the team track at the ninth Annual University of North Texas Symposium on Individual, Team, and Organizational Effectiveness. Each volume focuses on a specific topic in the study of teams. This volume focuses on the issue of team-based organizing. Prior volumes focused on:

(1) Theories of Self-Managing Work Teams.
(2) Knowledge Workers in Teams.
(3) Team Leadership.
(4) Team Implementation Issues.
(5) Product Development Teams.
(6) Team Performance Measurement.
(7) Team Development.
(8) Virtual Teams.

Each of these topics has represented an area of vital interest for both researchers and practitioners over the past decade. The theme for this volume, Team-Based Organizing, represents the evolution of these themes, as the focus shifts away from the team, a rather micro level focus, and toward the organization, a more macro level focus. There are two primary reasons for that shift. First, most team failures have apparently been caused by problems in the teams' larger environments, especially the lack of alignment of support systems with team needs. Second, the payoff from using teams as a solution to the organizing problem may be larger from focusing between-teams and on the team system rather than on isolated teams.

The chapters in this volume address these macro issues but also include micro level chapters focused on little-studied areas of teaming, such as research teams and medical emergency room teams. Taken as a whole, the chapters point to potential that has yet to be realized in practice. The research-based frameworks the authors provide can aid the decision making of managers and change leaders. Hopefully, it will also raise the level of research a notch, so we continue to explore the use of teaming principles and designs in new settings and the value of integrating micro and macro perspectives in understanding how teams can add value to organizations.

CHAPTER OVERVIEWS

(1) In the opening chapter of this volume, Cheryl Harris and Michael Beyerlein have provided an overview of the process of team-based organizing which they abbreviate as TBO*ing*. The "ing" indicates that the transformation to a team-based system is a continuous process. The process benefits from following the general principles of organizational development and change, but also from paying attention to some specific critical factors, including a careful determination of whether the large investment TBO*ing* is appropriate or worthwhile.

(2) The environments that organizations are now embedded in are turbulent. Change is constant and comes from a variety of sources. For organizations to cope with such turbulence, they must be continually adapting. Research on the critical success factors for organizational change has begun to provide some guiding principles. Transformation to team-based organizing represents one of those changes. Duane Windsor has reviewed and critiqued that research and organized it into a framework that can guide both researchers and practitioners. He has focused on the use of the principles in creating collaborative organizations. It becomes clear that choices must be made between such approaches as the GE method and the Motorola method and those choices depend on the strategic goals of the organization.

(3) Toni Doolen and Marla Hacker have also examined the role of context in team success. From careful review of the literature and interviews with managers, they have identified a number of the context factors that directly or indirectly influence the performance of the teams. The dimensions of the resulting instrument include: management processes, organizational culture, and organizational systems. Each of these is complex in itself and a challenging target for change.

(4) Isolated teams are common and they often fail. Managers frequently attribute the failure to the personalities of the team members. Perhaps, they should look at a bigger picture. Frances Kennedy presents a model for tracking the return-on-investment (ROI) of teams. She focuses on three components; team dynamics is only one. The second component is the alignment of support systems with the teams. For example, do team members have the training or the information they need for achieving their work goals? The combination of the team and the support

systems is presented as the team system – a complex component of the organization that needs direction from the top. The third component is the feedback of team performance information and development needs to the strategic decision makers at the top. If such information is unavailable, top managers are likely to undernourish or abandon the teaming initiative.

(5) Shifting from the macro perspective to the micro, Steven Lorenzet, Erik Eddy, and Gerald Klein suggest that a clear understanding of the team-level tasks is an essential prerequisite for high performance. Based on a thorough review of the job analysis literature, they argue that the team task analysis (TTA) approach is most appropriate. They critique other approaches as focusing on the tasks of individuals, so critical teamwork behaviors like interdependence, coordination, and cooperation are simply not measured by those methods.

(6) Work team effectiveness is the focus of all of the chapters in this volume. The approaches vary from the macro to the micro, from context factors outside the team to dynamics within the team. In such a complex landscape, the personal characteristics of the team members must be considered a beginning point. Team composition has been related to team effectiveness in a number of students, particularly the factor of personality. Terry Halfhill, Joseph Huff, Eric Sundstrom, and Tjai Nielsen review the empirical studies that examine the relationship of personality to team effectiveness. They conclude the paper with seven best practices derived from the studies, including the importance of assessing the conscientiousness and agreeableness of potential team members.

(7) High levels of performance do not occur when people merely conform to standards; or metaphorically, the letter of the law falls short of the spirit of the law. The term for capturing the behavior of people who go beyond the minimum requirements of their job role is organizational citizenship behavior (OCB). Tjai Nielsen, Eric Sundstrom, Sarah Soulen, Terry Halfhill, and Joseph Huff examine the literature on this topic and find that OCB plays a pivotal role in performance. For example, when one team member readily helps another for the overall benefit of the team, a new resource is being created – a leveraging of the talents available. OCB can be increased through the practices of team member selection, training, and measurement and can lead to increased competitive advantage.

(8) Teaming has spread to many forms of work. The key factor has been whether or not people must depend on each other to perform at high levels. One of the less obvious but most critical locations for such teaming

is the emergency room (ER) in hospitals. Seokhwa Yun, Samer Faraj, Yan Xiao, and Henry Sims present a study of trauma resuscitation teams working in the ER. They find that team work is a key to the performance of these groups. But, they also find that there are interesting variations in the team's organization and process depending on who has the expertise needed. Urgent, multiple, and concurrent tasks are tackled in an environment with high time pressure and high uncertainty. Empowerment, flexible boundaries, a goal focus, and shared experience all aid in saving lives in the ER.

(9) New product development begins with research. Because of the complexity of the intellectual work involved in original research, collaboration among scientists is essential. Does the collaborative capability of the scientists or the system they work in impact the quality of the results? Karen Blansett has examined the question in relationship to creativity in research. She finds that creative research begins only with creative individuals. The role of the team manager and the organization context are equally critical for breakthroughs on a project.

(10) Most team performance literature focuses on the contribution to a single company. In some circumstances, the contribution crosses company boundaries. Virtual product development teams represent one such example. Teaming across company boundaries during mergers and acquisitions (M&As) represents another. Lori Bradley reviews the literature on mergers and acquisitions and suggests a number of techniques for reducing the high number of M&A failures, including transition teams. M&As impact the business and the employees. Methods that include performing cultural assessments, engaging in transition planning, improving communication, recognizing and addressing separation anxiety, offering stress management programs or workshops, and offering outplacement services to displaced employees can reduce the stress, disruption, and destruction that occur during M&As. Integration teams can be a tool for making that work.

CONCLUSION

This volume highlights a shift in thinking about team-based work toward a focus on the larger organizational system – the context for the team or collaborative group. It also identifies an increase in attention to informal types of collaboration. We believe these shifts represent emerging trends in practice and research. The in-depth literature reviews published in this series on collaborative work systems will aid researchers and practictioners in broadening their perspectives on ways of organizing that enable effective collaboration. Future volumes will continue this tradition, because collaborative capacity is one of the cornerstones we have to build on in trying to shape our world so all peoples can survive and thrive in the 21st Century.

Michael M. Beyerlein
Douglas A. Johnson
Susan T. Beyerlein
Editors

NAVIGATING THE TEAM-BASED ORGANIZING JOURNEY

Cheryl L. Harris and Michael M. Beyerlein

ABSTRACT

Teams often fail to achieve expected levels of high performance. The primary cause of failure is context. The team-based organization (TBO) focuses on creation of a context that enables teams to achieve their potential. The challenge is the transition from a traditional, hierarchical organization based on command-and-control management to a TBO organized around teams, empowerment, and involvement. This chapter focuses on the steps involved in a successful transformation process. The TBO change initiative is complex and requires years of learning and redesign to reach maturity.

INTRODUCTION

Today's fast-paced world requires flatter organizations with more connections to customers and the ensuing quicker customer response and flexibility to changes in the environment. Many organizations implement teams to achieve these ends. However, the benefits of teams are minimized when the team context, specifically, the organizational structure, systems, and culture, does not support those teams. Team-based organization (TBO), where the core organizational unit is some form of team and the organization is designed to support the logic of teams, is one form of organization being pursued in this effort.

Team-Based Organizing, Volume 9, pages 1–29.
ISBN: 0-7623-0981-4

The journey to TBO is complex, continuous, and never-ending. Many organizations have made the effort and failed. Some may have reached high performance for a brief time, only to lose focus on the effort and revert to earlier habits. To emphasize the need for a continuous development focus, we use the verb form of the term – "team-based organizing" in this chapter (Beyerlein & Harris, in press).

To gain a real-time, more practically-oriented view of TBO, we created a qualitative study of professionals in the area. From March to July 2001, phone interviews were conducted with 20 participants, who each had a minimum of five years of experience with TBO, and a mean of 13 years experience. The majority of participants held doctoral degrees, with degree areas in a wide variety of fields, the majority being organization development related. The majority of participants were external consultants, with the next largest group being internal consultants/human resources, then professor/researchers. Given their educational credentials, organizational level focal point, combination of theoretical and implementation focuses with a leaning towards the implementation side, years of experience with TBO, and proportion of current TBO clients, this subject population can be considered a credible source of data for the topic of TBO. Illustrative excerpts from the interview study will be used throughout this chapter. "Interview study" in parentheses will indicate the excerpts.

The team-based organizing (TBO*ing*) journey is a major transformational process. In many ways, the process of change is more important than the content of the change. In this chapter, we will focus on that process of change, by describing some of the components of that process and ideas for establishing the change infrastructure for the transformation to TBO*ing*. Please note that many of these ideas relate simply to good change practices, but we will gear them towards TBO*ing*. First, we present our definition of TBO*ing*. Second, we share some things to consider before taking on the effort. Third, we make suggestions for managing the change to TBO*ing*. Fourth, we share some types of transition methodologies to consider in the change. Finally, we convey some ideas for utilizing the foundational principle for successful TBO*ing*, alignment. We combine literature and interview data with our own conceptual thinking to focus on what the *organization* needs to do to better support teams.

WHAT IS A TEAM-BASED ORGANIZATION?

In a nutshell, a TBO is an organization that uses teams as the basic unit of accountability and work when the task is appropriate; the organization is structured and designed to support teams, and support systems are deliberately aligned to serve teams. A TBO may use a variety of team types to meet the needs of each particular work situation. Teams are prevalent at all hierarchical levels in the organization, not just at the work level. For example, teams of managers oversee teams of production workers or teams of new product development workers. Organizational systems must be flexible enough to support the variety of team types, used as well as the individual contributors when they represent a better fit with the task than teams.

The key tenets to our definition of TBO*ing* are listed below (for more detail, see Harris & Beyerlein, in press):

(1) Teams are the basic units of accountability and work.
(2) Only use teams when teams are appropriate.
(3) Teams lead teams.
(4) Use an array of teams.
(5) Recognize that it is a never-ending, continuous process.
(6) Design in flexibility for adaptability (connect to the environment).
(7) Design the organization to support teams.
(8) Hold it all together with alignment.
(9) Organization leaders must have TBO-compatible philosophy.
(10) Implementation requires intentional effort.

These tenets represent a radically different form of organizing. Consequently, significant change is required throughout the organization that commits to the transformation. Guidelines for that change are described below.

BEGINNING THE TRANSITION TO TEAM-BASED ORGANIZING

The decision to begin a TBO*ing* effort should not be taken without some forethought. This section briefly reviews some things to consider before taking on the effort, including who starts the change effort, carefully make the decision to start the initiative, and where to start.

Who Starts the Change Effort?

Change starts with someone making the effort to speak up and put actions behind their words. The initiative for change can come from many places; we characterize them as: bottom-up, middle-out, and top-down.

Bottom-up. Grassroots efforts, where someone at the worker level initiates the change to TBO*ing*, are unusual, though some examples exist.

> There have been some grassroots efforts where somebody in a work group took the initiative to do a team which spread through the organization, so the TBO grew from the bottom up. There's some literature that argues that is the best, but that's still pretty rare, because it's tough to survive in the company's immune system (Interview Study).

If the change effort does begin at the bottom, it is imperative that management commitment is achieved quickly, so the initiative is not stopped before it builds momentum.

Middle-out. It is more likely that a movement to transform an organization comes from someone in middle management than from a bottom-up beginning. In fact, one interview participant believes that, "most of the successful innovations started in the middle with a department head or a plant manager (who) wants to do something and just starts doing it, and that creates good results, then others follow" (Interview Study).

Top-down. Often, the initiative begins with top management, with a mandate to start the transition to TBO. Unfortunately, sometimes the mandate comes as a memo from an executive that says something to the effect of "Monday you will be in teams," with no real change occurring to back the use of the "team" label. However, when the words are supported by action, top-down change can be highly successful. Especially in large organizations, where real transformation requires complicated change in multiple systems across the organization, it seems that top-down change is the only realistic way to achieve success. "Evidence shows clearly that programs are most successful when they are led by the top, not when they are a bottom-up operation" (Lawler, Mohrman & Ledford, Jr., 1998, p. 138).

> The transition to say, OK, we are going to make a successful transition to a TBO, it really requires that the senior management say that we can support the kind of flexible system; that we can create a structure that is designed to support teams; and that we can do the core of our work in teams (Interview Study).

Carefully Make the Decision to Start the Initiative

As with any major business change, the decision to transform to a TBO must be weighed carefully. There should be a clear idea of the goals of the transformation and of the costs. Seventy to eighty percent of the cost is the time employees spend training and meeting. There is additional cost for materials, physical changes to the work place, expert help, and so on. The question is: is it worth the investment required?

There is a fairly substantial literature delineating the benefits from using teams and from implementing a TBO to create a context within which those teams can achieve high levels of performance. Most of that literature consists of anecdotal and case evidence. A major source of quantitative data consists of the series of survey results that Lawler and his associates publish every three years (e.g. Lawler, Mohrman & Ledford, Jr., 1998). They report the significant return-on-investment from investing in participative designs and employee empowerment.

A TBO changes many facets of an organization, including information flow, decision making processes, accountability structures, mechanisms for building intellectual and social capital, and feedback systems. As a consequence, we expect improvements in cost, innovation, speed, safety, morale, responsiveness to customers, etc. Work to establish the systems for capturing the value of those improvements has only recently begun (e.g. Kennedy, in press; Levenson, in press).

If the decision is made to go forward with the transformation, commitment and communication must be emphasized. Commitment to the change initiative begins with careful decision making to allocate the resources needed for successful transition. The decisions must be conscious and deliberate. In many examples, the decisions are made too haphazardly, so the launch of the initiative rests on a shaky platform. Substantial resources must be invested over a long period of time to sustain the teaming effort, including time, money, and people.

> The first question an organization should address is whether it makes sense to establish a team organization. The organization should clarify its goals and articulate why it feels that teams will help accomplish them. It should decide whether the benefits to be derived from redesigning for teams outweigh the costs of the transition. It should determine where in the organization it makes sense to establish teams, and for what purposes (Mohrman, Cohen & Mohrman, Jr., 1995, p. 6).

It is important not to underestimate changes needed in the transition to TBO. "This is exactly why I'm such a stickler for identifying whether you are going towards TBO. I don't want you to underestimate the changes needed" (Interview Study). One way to build the case for change is to prove that TBO works by showing business results.

> As you go through those top level discussions about what are the big building blocks that you need for the organization. They say things like they want a more flexible organization, a more fluid organization, something where everyone works together. And when you start structure conversations about the characteristics of the organization, it emerges that what they are really looking for is going to be team based (Interview Study).

A final initial step is an educational process whereby everybody in the organization, whether or not they're going to be involved in a team, understands

why the teams are being implemented and what the change represents"
(Interview Study). This represents a wide dissemination of the vision and goals
for the transformation and begins the process of building an organization-wide
shared mental model of what the future looks like.

Where to Start?

There are a number of places where the change can begin. A few variations
are listed below:

Pilot site. Many organizations choose a pilot site as a way of testing the design,
controlling risk, and testing training and assessment materials. The site may be
chosen for convenience or lack of visibility or a high level of readiness. The
advantage is that failure on a small scale is less damaging to the whole organization and there is greater ease in managing a small implementation. The
disadvantage is transitioning out of the pilot site without premature leakage or
excessive delay.

> Start it small and prove it and then let it catch like wildfire approach. It's where you get
> some leader who is interested in this on a local level and they start doing some great things
> and getting great results. Then, other people in the organization say, maybe our department
> ought to be comprised of teams also instead of comprised of individuals in a hierarchical
> organization chart (Interview Study).

Change the whole system at once. Changing the whole system at once through
the use of search conferences, future search, open space, and other change
technologies (see more on this in a subsequent section) has some advantages,
such as increased commitment to the customized plans that are created by a
large number of people who then take the lead for change. However, it is
extremely difficult to achieve in a large organization due to the logistics of such
an approach.

Create new organization and migrate

> We've certainly found it easier if you are building from scratch. Changing an existing orga-
> nization we have found almost impossible. So, we tend to create a new organization and
> then migrate existing people into a new organization. The downside that we have encountered
> where staff are uncomfortable in moving and where they just don't apply for new jobs.
> Then you are left with staff that you don't have a role for anymore. The upside is that you
> end up with people who have actually asked to be in the organization, so they come in to
> it feeling very positive. It's been part of a choice that they have made . . . and you get a
> very high commitment to make it work (Interview Study).

Find natural teams and build

> Work with a part of the organization that you're closest to developing team working anyway, naturally. And you work through the problems they have and you assist them, pretty much in an action research way (Interview Study).

MANAGING THE CHANGE TO TEAM-BASED ORGANIZING

The change process may last for years. There are usually stages in the TBO process, although a lot of concurrent engineering also takes place. Stages may include: planning, launch, development, sustaining the initiative, and transformation to the next level, such as the self-managing organization (Purser & Cabana, 1998), and the collaborative organization (Beyerlein, Freedman, McGee & Moran, 2002). Some suggestions for managing the change to TBO*ing* are listed below.

Integrate Initiatives

Organizations often have multiple change initiatives underway, such as re-engineering, TQM, lean manufacturing, leadership development, performance appraisal, etc. Ulrich (1997) gives the example of one company that listed 17 such initiatives that were concurrent. Each of those initiatives may have been under the direction of a different team, which makes conflict likely. A team may suboptimize through competition for resources and contradictory design decisions that undermine other teams' initiatives. One study found that when the organization change effort consisted of a series of unrelated initiatives, this correlated negatively with all employee involvement (EI) outcomes (Lawler, Mohrman & Ledford, Jr., 1998).

Intentional, Planned Effort

Major projects benefit from careful planning. This dictum is widely known in organizations but is not so widely practiced. It seems to be practiced with technical projects, but ignored around the introduction of major people-oriented projects. TBO*ing* is a major change project. It requires long-term commitment, resources, expertise, and coordination for success. As one interviewee said, "Very intentional, very planned effort" (Interview Study). Another interviewee said, "No shortcuts!"

> In this organization, the transition happened before I worked here, but it was very well thought out. They did have a consultant who helped them. They had a long-term strategic plan, did training and development, steering committee, transition committee made up of

cross-section of organization. They really did it right here, but I don't think that is the norm. Treat it like a change initiative, that's what it is (Interview Study).

It is an error to ignore the work that a successful transformation takes. "Most of them wave a magic wand and say now you are a team. I think that is one of the biggest issues of TBO. People don't really understand what it means, and they don't do a good job of making the transition" (Interview Study).

For a successful transition, organizations should "take more of a controlled approach, and approach it as an organizational structural change, and move the teams around and get them established" (Interview Study). However, some "take such a controlling approach, they never get to the point of having enough detail to feel confident that they can [trust the] teams – they're always micromanaging them, their development. They spend a lot of time focusing on the plan and no time, really, focusing on the real issues" (Interview Study). There is a need to shift from planning to action or to cycle back and forth between them continuously. Mohrman et al. (1995) describe the convergence-divergence cycle of brainstorming alternatives and then shifting to the selection of an alternative and the decision to focus on it in new product development; the same process applies to change programs.

Not Every Component Has To Be Changed
One way to approach the difficult reality of organizational transformation is to realize that not every component has to be changed. According to one participant, you can "Leave many components of structure in place and integrate using teams. You don't have to change every component of your organizations structure to make it a team. You may want to leave many components of your structure in place, but do more integrating by using teams. I think one of the powerful applications of teams is to integrate highly differentiated functions."

Deal with Reality of Enterprise Systems

Enterprise systems (systems mandated by the larger corporate entity) are less flexible and more difficult to modify. So, instead of assuming that every component must change, look for the bits of individual organization that you can change (Interview Study).

A Few Simple Rules
Rules form a basic control system within bureaucratic organizations. Rules and hierarchy remain as important organizing tools in a TBO. However, releasing the creative power of a team requires empowerment which means discretionary space within the bounds of the rules. The principle of minimal critical specifications means use a few simple rules that all know and understand. Exceptions

to the rules require special permission. Everyone follows the rules. The rules deal with ethics, customer satisfaction, performance, etc. (Beyerlein, Freedman, McGee & Moran, 2002).

Tailor, Not Cookie Cutter

The plan for implementing TBO depends on basic principles of change, design, and involvement, but it also depends on tailoring to the local situation. This might be called the "practice level" (Brown & Duguid, 2002).

> And that comes to what I call the cookie cutter phenomenon where people will take one thing and say this applies to me, and there may be some principles that we can generalize, but the specifics are not generalizable (Interview Study).

A Successful Transition Requires Significant Resources

The scope of the transformation effort tends to exceed the imagination of people responsible for planning it. It is not uncommon for managers to expect the initiative to be completed within six or eight months. Using the development of a new car design or a new chip design or a new pharmaceutical product as comparisons might help managers understand the development time and resources that must be invested in TBO.

> That whole process, which I'm calling the initial transition, could be anywhere from 2–3 year process. It's not an overnight process, and that would be another major mistake that a lot of organizations make (Interview Study).

> Time wise, if not a Greenfield (creation of a startup site in contrast to the redesign of a 'brownfield'), if you're doing a transition from a different culture to a team-based culture, I think you're still looking at something over five years for it to be fully integrated (Interview Study).

> It is a huge transition, takes a long time – estimates are varied, but probably 7–11 years. It takes a lot of training time, meeting time, etc., so there's a lot of money tied up because of that. At a local plant, they estimated $5 million after 2.5 years. Most of that was employee time as opposed to cashing out (Interview Study).

> Three years . . . [at the] end of three years, we had gotten to a point where TBO was implemented 40%. Still learning. It would have taken another 2–3 years. Definitely not quick changes (Interview Study).

Using Consultants

The TBO initiative is a complex and dynamic change program. It depends on information, learning, and expertise. The members of the steering team will have considerable expertise about the organization and some expertise about teams and change management. They will need to work hard to learn more. However, they will probably need the guidance of someone with extensive

experience with change initiatives and TBO*ing*. Consequently, they will work
with consultants from inside or outside their organization or both.

> Company X hired an outside consulting firm, and I happened to work for that firm at the
> time . . . they hired the firm to implement the formal team development with all of their
> teams and they continue to use the outside consultants to provide team development on an
> on-going basis. They also provided them with, what I would call 'needed team skills,' like
> conflict resolution and things like that, skills that teams need to have (Interview Study).

> People who run a business often are not the best people to draw the structure and that's rec-
> ognized. So, they will go call on some of the people within head office, from either my own
> team, or our HR function does work in this area, as well, to help them do that (Interview Study).

Develop Internal Resources

Consultants play a vital role in facilitating the change to TBO. However,
consultants cannot, and should not, do it alone. Eventually, consultants should
be able to leave the situation and feel confident that it will continue without
them. It is crucial to develop internal resources, such as internal change agents,
team sponsors, team trainers, etc., to provide the backbone for change.

> When we go into an organization trying to go to collaborative teams, we take a group of
> people and start training them as team facilitators. At the point that the teams begin to
> operate, because we have to have some way to work ourselves out of the team, so we have
> to have some people there who are skilled enough to be able to facilitate when other teams
> break down: people within the team to meet with the team, not someone who's external to
> the organization, or out of HR (Interview Study).

Share Best Practices

The issue of technology transfer applies to the development of the TBO
initiative. Best practices must be identified through assessment and then shared
with other parts of the organization, so adoption or adaptation of the practices
is effective. This process involves the practices of both knowledge management
and the learning organization. The practices must be disseminated, so the
organization develops into a whole system based on teams, but also to manage
the corporate immune system reaction. Each level of the organization is
embedded in a higher level that can act as an immune system (Pinchot, 1985)
– seeking out and destroying whatever does not fit with standard practices, so
effective dissemination of information and best practices across the organization
and up the organization reduces the threat to the initiative.

> The final one is monitoring progress, disseminating best practices, diffusing. The challenge
> is how to move it to other parts of the organization (Interview Study).

Start Where They Are

> Then it is typically a matter of looking at what they are doing. You're typically not blowing
> up what they have; you're looking at what they have and trying to move from there toward

something different. For example, in one place, we put together a group to do that in the second year of the innovation, and they went out and benchmarked what organizations were doing in terms of gain sharing and skills-based pay, and things like that. They benchmarked some places, and that is not our consulting specialty, so we got them in contact with someone who was going to design a skill-based pay system and then overlay some sort of a team bonusing plan related to plant-wide metrics. So we hooked them up with a consultant who designs pay systems. That same client, we did a lot of the work to help them redesign their hiring system, to move to a more behavioral interview process, and to add a simulation which would assess certain critical teamwork skills. So we helped them design those inter-view formats and the assessment, and we trained assessors who were team members from around the organization who were involved in the hiring process. So it is taking the systems they've got and figuring out how to adjust them (Interview Study).

Educate Management and Change Team

Management and the change team have a responsibility for leading the change, so they need to become educated on TBO*ing*. This can be done in many different ways, including reading, attending workshops, benchmarking, and site visits.

I work with the plant manager or general manager. They do some benchmarking. They would look at what is happening elsewhere at other plants. They might get some educa-tion. They might have some of their own experience on a small scale. There might be some dissatisfaction with business results. And that leads to some sort of search process. Out of that comes the formal effort to move in this direction (Interview Study).

Continuous Assessment and Renewal

Does the TBO add value? This is the key question for top management in determining whether the investment should be continued. The answer depends on two things: assessment of the current outcomes and investments and benchmarking others for predicting the future. Appelbaum, Bailey, Bergy and Kalleberg (2000) have presented a strong case about general payoffs from empowerment and participation that complements the work of Lawler et al. (1998) that the investment is worthwhile in the general sense. For the specific situation, rely on assessment. Kennedy (this volume) has outlined how that can be conducted. Her model includes a feedback loop to top management for delivering the financial contribution that teaming generates. The goal is sustained support from the top.

Develop Change Champions

Change champions, who are formal or informal leaders of change, are vital to the change effort. Look for natural leaders to help lead the effort.

You also need folks who have passionate energy for it . . . you engage them in the process so you have early adopters of it, who can help you in making that successful (Interview Study).

Align to Environment

When making a change to TBO, or any other organization change initiative, focus tends to shift internally. This is a problem, since the world continues outside of the organization. Often, change leaders become so focused on internal change, that they forget the outside world. Whatever methodology you choose, it is important to keep a constant link to the customer and business environment. Become aware of external changes that cause need for internal changes, and quickly adjust accordingly. Most change initiatives fail due to changes in their external environment, and lack of ability to adjust accordingly.

Deal With Traditional Corporate Entity

In reality, there is often a dichotomous environment between the TBO business unit and the more traditional system of the larger organizational entity. This reality must be addressed in the organizational change, and mechanisms put in place to deal with the dichotomy.

TYPES OF TRANSITION METHODOLOGIES

Whole systems organization change interventions are rooted in socio-technical systems (STS) theory. STS, a theory developed out of work in the 1950s by Fred Emery, Eric Trist, and the Tavistock Institute, approaches organizational development from at least three levels: the outside environment that affects the organization, the technical system (business processes), and the social system (the people side). After all this data is collected, one has a view of the "whole system" (Filipczak, 1995).

When planning and implementing TBO, it is crucial to have this view of the whole system. Key characteristics of the whole systems approach to organization design include "purpose/results driven, future-focused, custom-designed, systemic, objective, value-based, and procedural" (Lytle, 1998, pp. 47–48). Looking at the entire system as a whole helps designers prevent piece-meal, simplistic, short-term solutions that could ultimately do more harm to the organization than good. For example, a solution to a problem in one department may cause a problem in another. Without a whole systems view, these mismatches of solutions occur quite often.

Many different change methodologies exist to help the organization examine the whole system when planning and implementing change. These vary in the time required for execution and level of involvement of those working in the system. One of the goals of TBO*ing* is to increase involvement and participation of organizational members, and therefore gain the benefit of the intellectual capital of all members. Methods of planning and implementation should be aligned to that goal and emphasize involvement and participation whenever possible.

The next two sections examine representative group involvement, which is a category of transition methodology that requires a representative group to lead the change; and whole system involvement, which requires that members from a critical mass of the affected system be involved in the transition. An overview, different variations of the methodology, and the benefits and problems of each will be summarized. Then we share some hybrid combinations of the two categories.

Representative Group Involvement

In this category, group of individuals (usually a steering committee or design team) is fully responsible for planning and implementation of the change effort. The group is responsible for assessing and analyzing the organization to make the decision whether the organization is ready for TBO*ing*, and whether TBO*ing* is the best method to meet the business strategy. Once the decision is made to go forward, the group needs education on TBO*ing*, some of which may come from site visits to other organizations, reading relevant materials, attending conferences, and participating in training courses. The group should become grand communicators of the initiative, supporters of the process, and resources for others in the organization.

Since this group leads the change to teams, they must model team behavior, and put significant time into their own team development. Part of this team development is developing a mission statement and charter, which then becomes the guiding force for the group.

People to include. Members may be involved in the group for many years, and may need full-time involvement for the first 6–12 months. It is a huge commitment of time and effort, and requires a special kind of person. Some of the characteristics needed by members are listed below (Manion, Lorimer & Leander, 1996, p. 93):

(1) Ability to tolerate high levels of ambiguity.
(2) Self-directed behavior and demonstrated initiative.
(3) Good communication skills.
(4) Creative thinker and continuous learner.
(5) Great curiosity.
(6) Ability to interact effectively with people from all levels of the organization
(7) Demonstrated belief in the concepts of employee involvement and empowerment

In addition, it is helpful if the member is a respected, natural leader in the organization.

Time required. Initial assessment, analysis, and planning of the change effort usually takes at least six months to a year. Some form of guiding group will continue in existence throughout the life of the change initiative, though their roles will change slightly, and less time may be needed.

Variations of representative group involvement. The steering committee is responsible for assessing the organization to determine whether TBO*ing* is a viable option. Once the decision has been made to go forward, the steering committee oversees the planning and implementation of the initiative. The steering committee "educates themselves, and then begins to lay out a plan on how to roll out the transition. The steering team sets up design teams to become the champions and support structure for implementation at the local level" (Interview Study). In smaller organizations or business units embarking on the TBO journey, the steering committee and design team may be the same.

> The design team's mandate is to, first of all, clarify the organization's core mission, competitive advantage, and strategy. Then to understand where in the organization there are interdependencies that represent key linkages among units or individuals, and those interdependencies, again, are what are required in order to accomplish the core mission of the organization. If there isn't a design team that represents the various parties that could potentially be involved in the teaming effort, you might get an isolated pocket of teaming here or there, that really doesn't take into consideration the big picture of what's required to reach the organization's goal (Interview Study).

Steering committee membership may be comprised of the management group or a representative cross-section (in terms of hierarchical levels and functions, and, if applicable, union members) of the affected group. The benefit of limiting membership to management or executives is that they have the power and authority to make the required changes to the organization. However, management often does not have real access to information at all levels of the organization, so they may not have the amount and depth of information needed for a successful TBO effort. The opposite situation occurs when membership is comprised of a cross-section of the organization – information can be collected and disseminated at many levels, but the group may have to go outside its boundaries to ask permission to make changes necessary for the effort. A combination of both worlds is a vertical slice of the organization with key decision makers involved. The difficulty with this arrangement is the power differential that may stifle the contributions of members from the lower levels of the hierarchy – a problem that requires strong group norms and trust to enable open discussion. Some organizations solve the dilemma by using management in the steering committee, and emphasizing a cross-section of representation at the design team level.

Benefits of involving representative groups. Using representative groups as a change mechanism may be the best fit for traditional hierarchical organizations with stable environments. These organizations are used to incremental change, and may not have a pressing need for accelerated change. Also, having representative groups with full time members dedicated to the change effort ensures continuity of the change effort.

Problems with involving representative groups. Members of the steering committee or design team are responsible for all data collection, which usually comes in the form of focus groups and interviews. Especially with large organizations, this methodology simply takes too long – often a year to complete. After such an extended period of time, the data is often ineffective, because the organization has changed in that time.

Additionally, members of the design committee often become insulated from the "real world" around them. The people creating the changes are not always the ones recommending the changes, which causes lack of ownership of both the problems and the suggested adjustments, and therefore hinders the possibility of a completed implementation. Furthermore the whole process drains energy from the change effort and demoralizes participants, as recommended changes are not always implemented. The analysis phase often takes all the energy, and leaves none for the final, crucial step – implementing the change.

Other problems that occur include excessive data analysis as the group becomes immersed in data, and a loss of credibility among peers (Lytle, 1998).

Whole System Involvement

As our complex, technology-driven business environment changes at an ever-increasing pace, so does the need for organizations to create accelerated change. These accelerated change methodologies are often called "critical mass," because they require the whole system, or at least a minimum percentage, of the part of the organization undergoing change to be in the room during the intervention event (see Holman & Devane, 1999, for detailed coverage of all the critical mass approaches). These methods capitalize on several assumptions: (1) people support what they create; and (2) with everyone in the room, all the critical information is available.

People to include. The key premise behind critical mass interventions is to bring the whole system being affected by the change into the room for the meetings. This incorporates all stakeholders in the process, possibly comprising, but not limited to: employees and managers from all affected departments and at all levels, internal and external customers, and community members. While having everyone in the system in the room is ideal, it is not always feasible, especially in large-scale change efforts. A good rule of thumb for minimum participation is to include ten percent of the people undergoing the change (Filipczak, 1995). Whoever participates should represent the system you are changing; in other words, you must include members of all constituencies and stakeholder groups, and attempt to have a representative sample of that population.

Another crucial aspect of participation is that members comprise a common database of information. In other words, all the information needed to make a decision should be in the room. Every viewpoint and area of expertise, from front-line worker to supplier to customer to executive to stockholder, should be present (Filipczak, 1995).

Time required. A common length of time for critical mass events is three days (Filipczak, 1995). However, some interventions require multiple sessions of three days each. The rule of thumb is to match the time required with the scope and the magnitude of the change needed.

Task force to plan event. Before the critical mass event, a task force or steering committee from the organization works with one or more consultants to set up the event to ensure maximal probability of success. The planning is thorough and essential and may take three to six months of work. This committee is responsible for planning the scope and magnitude of the changes to be addressed, the ensuing range of participants to be present, and logistics for the meeting. In this way, critical mass events are very similar to traditional OD efforts.

Variations of critical mass interventions. Many variations on the critical mass intervention theme exist, with the crucial point being to match the intervention to the purpose, number of people involved, and expected outcome. The amount of structure utilized in these techniques for organizing meetings ranges from no structure (Open Space) to a good deal of structure (Future Search). Six of the most popular critical mass techniques are Open Space, large-scale interactive process, real-time strategic change, participative work redesign, Conference Model, and Future Search.

Open Space (Owen, 1997; Owen & Stadler, 1999) is the least structured event, and is a technique for holding better meetings, not just large-group events.

In Open Space meetings, diverse, often conflicted groups of up to 1000 people manage hugely complex issues in minimal amounts of time, with no advance agenda preparation, and little to no overt facilitation. The strength of Open Space is its utilization of emergent self-organization, which ensures that participants are discussing what needs to be discussed regarding a particular issue. Facilitation of such events requires expertise about the method and about large group dynamics.

Whole-scale change, also known as large-scale interactive process (Dannemiller, James & Tolchinsky, 1999; Dannemiller Tyson Associates, 2000), is used to implement organization-wide changes, and usually lasts three days. Real-time strategic change (Jacobs, 1994) change grew out of work on the large-scale interactive process, and is also used to implement organization-wide changes. The key difference between large-scale interactive process and real-time strategic change is that real-time strategic change is an approach to work, rather than just an event. The Conference Model is a comprehensive system created by Dick Axelrod that is used to accomplish a top-to-bottom redesign of the organization. It consists of up to four separate two or three day events (Filipczak, 1995).

Future Search conferences (Weisbord & Janoff, 1995) have the goal of finding an ideal future and aiming for it. The strength of Future Search is its structured approach for incorporating multiple perspectives to develop a shared vision of the future.

Participative work redesign, created by Fred Emery, emphasizes a democratic approach to job design, and involves a three-day event (Filipczak, 1995). One example of how participative work redesign is used for TBO*ing* is described below.

> To conduct a series of briefings and workshops whereby you teach people how to organize themselves into self-managed teams. You conduct those workshops and then they are off and running. The briefings are pretty much educational: what the environment is going to look like in post-team. You would tend to try and run 100% of the people in the organization through those. Where they are going to design the teams. Where they are going to determine what their goals are as teams. What skills they will need to have to make sure that things go well for the teams. Determining any other type of support they may need as far as information technology. Figuring out what other teams they need to negotiate with because they need to provide or receive an output from them. So, those are some of the things that we would go over in a workshop (Interview Study).

Benefits of involving the whole system. Critical mass models have several advantages over the traditional design committee. First, critical mass models gain from the premise that successful implementation is most likely when "the people who do the work are the ones engaged in the redesign of both the technical and social systems" (Levine & Mohr, 1998, p. 305). People tend to support what they create, thus reducing resistance to change (Bunker & Alban, 1997). Second, since critical mass models utilize methods of including the "whole system" in the room to consider change, they are faster and encompass more viewpoints. Third, the diversity of knowledge utilized through such large-scale involvement leads to greater creativity and innovation in both the technical and social system arenas (Bunker & Alban, 1997).

> The argument is that in environment of rapid change, you need a different kind of approach like conferences. Each conference is a meeting . . . where everyone comes to the room together, and in an intense few days of work, they figure out where they've been, where they are and where they're going, and to launch the change process as whole systems approach. That appears to fit better in systems with rapid pace of change (Interview Study).

By participating in the design of the organization's future, participants begin to evolve necessary attitude, skill, and belief changes concurrently. By structuring critical mass intervention activities to prompt the use of new skills and behaviors, the participants cannot help but be changed by the experience (Levine & Mohr, 1998). Thus, the intervention begins immediately in the meeting, as opposed to the traditional design committee approach of waiting to begin changes until the full assessment process is completed and recommendations made.

The scope of the changes to be addressed in the critical mass meeting can be from as small as developing a work group mission to as large as attempting to create ways to impact society. One of the attractions of the critical mass meeting is that they can be used for many different purposes, as long as a critical mass and representation of the system to be affected are present.

To sum it up,

> As a general rule, the more people in the organization affected by change, the more that they participate, the better the ideas, the better the design, the more sense of ownership, and the more support the people give the design, the faster the organization will be implemented and up and running (Interview Study).

Problems with involving the whole system. Critical mass techniques are not suitable for small changes, because they are rather time-consuming and involve lots of people. Rather, they are for alterations that are large in magnitude and scope, such as to "change business strategies, develop a mission or vision about where the company is headed in the next century, or foster a more participative environment . . ." (Filipczak, 1995, p. 36). Critical mass interventions are also often used to kick off other popular initiatives that require lots of thought and participation from many people, such as Total Quality Management or TBOing.

Whole system involvement methods must be planned carefully so that data is collected and distributed, action plans are reviewed and renewed, and the change effort implementation is continued in between meetings. If everyone waits to do all the work in the meetings themselves, the acceleration gained by this approach is lost. Although change occurs during the meetings, the follow-up actions generate the most significant and lasting change.

Finally, involving the whole system in the planning and implementation of change requires managers to relinquish some control over the decisions being made. If management continuously "vetoes" decisions made in the meetings, eventually energy for the effort will be lost. However, some decisions will need to remain in the control of management. The key is to identify those decisions upfront so that the members attending the meeting understand their limits. Working with managers before the meeting prepares them for the problem of reduced control – a trade-off for significant results.

Hybrid Methodologies

When creating TBO*ing* change, the most appropriate methodology will be a combination of the approaches discussed here. Each has its own strengths and weaknesses; combining them contributes a stronger, holistic process. The time-line for change in TBO*ing* is so long that the critical mass events can function as launch points, mile stones, or re-energizing gatherings. Lytle (1998) suggested a few different combinations, each of which will be discussed briefly below.

The modified traditional systems approach. In this approach, the steering team and design teams remain in place, but they develop methods of speeding up the process. For example, they may collect data in parallel, and use whole system involvement conferences, but strictly for the purposes of collecting data. Decision-making power remains in the steering and design teams (Lytle, 1998).

The cascading, micro-design approach. In this approach, the level of involvement of the whole system is increased slightly about that of the modified traditional systems approach. The steering team serves as the design team. Key design features are decided by the steering team, and then further design and implementation occurs simultaneously by all units in the organization (Lytle, 1998).

The sequenced, multiple-conference approach. This approach utilizes a combination of the whole system involvement conferences listed in the previous section. Different parts of the system are involved in each conference. Conferences are spread over 3–5 months, and each conference lasts 1–3 days. A conference support team is responsible for collecting and distributing data generated in the conference, but no steering team is required (Lytle, 1998).

Align Planning and Implementation Process with Desired Outcome

There is no "one right way" to create change in organizations. Before you select a change methodology for your organization, consider the following:

- *Think about the tradeoff between cost of involvement and benefit of commitment*: Whole system representation in change efforts is costly in terms of time and money. However, commitment increases dramatically due to involvement in planning and implementation of changes. Consider the tradeoff and act accordingly.
- *Consider the direct control desired by management*: Using whole system representation in change efforts means giving more decision making control to the workforce. Do you have regulations in place that prevent this? Is management comfortable with empowering their workforce with decision making authority and responsibility?
- *Align change methodology to desired change*: If you want to create a more empowered, involved work force, it makes sense to involve them in planning and implementation.
- *Match the degree of radicalness of the method with the openness of the organization to new approaches* (Lytle & Rankin, 1996): Lytle and Rankin described one failed attempt at using a radical method with a conservative organization. Given the chance to do it over, they would have used a more conservative method – matching tool and culture.
- *Involve all key players*: Regardless of your situation, include the input of all key players in the change process. If you have a union, you must include them.
- *Combine the best parts of each methodology to meet your needs*: Change methodologies are not mutually exclusive – use different tools for different situations.

ALIGNING FOR TEAM-BASED ORGANIZING

Alignment is the foundation for successful TBO*ing*. The dictionary defines alignment as "the process of adjusting parts so that they are in proper relative position." In the organization, "alignment is the degree to which an organization's strategy, design, and culture are cooperating to achieve the same desired goals" (Semler, 1997, p. 23). When all the parts are cooperating instead of conflicting, people in the organization receive consistent messages about what they are supposed to do, which removes barriers to collaboration, enhances performance, and focuses human capital. Alignment theorists suggest that the more the various components of the organization are aligned, the better performance will be (Nadler & Tushman, 1989; Semler, 1997).

Alignment is characterized by four factors: (1) congruence – extent to which systems are compatible, in accord, consistent, and parallel with each other; (2) synchronization – extent to which progress or initiatives within the system are sequenced appropriately; (3) direction – extent to which systems support the organization's overall goals, vision, values, mission, and strategies; (4) accessibility – effort required by teams to obtain the support, including overcoming hurdles and translating information from one language to another (Van Aken, 1997).

As with any organization design, organizational structure, systems, and culture should be aligned with each other. Therefore, if the organization is comprised of teams, the organization context and systems must be congruent with teams.

The major components of the organization that must be aligned when transitioning to TBO are listed below. This list of components was developed over years of observation and research, and was used in the interview study. The interview participants confirmed this as a comprehensive list of organizational components that must be aligned to teams in a successful TBO. A few additional components that they found to be important will be discussed later.

- *Reward and recognition systems*: Methods of rewarding and recognizing performance and other desired behaviors.
- *Goal setting system*: Methods of establishing aligned goals.
- *Performance measurement system*: Methods of identifying and measuring appropriate performance.
- *Performance appraisal system*: Methods of reviewing and appraising appropriate performance and other desired behaviors associated with performance.
- *Team design system*: Methods of looking at the organization as a whole and determining appropriate places for teams. At the team level, making sure the team has the inputs it needs to get the work done.
- *Communication and information systems*: Methods for teams to get the information it needs to perform effectively, and methods for communication throughout the organization.
- *Culture*: A pattern of shared organizational values, basic underlying assumptions, and informal norms that guide the way work is accomplished in an organization.
- *Training system*: Methods for teams and individuals to identify and get the skills needed to perform.
- *Knowledge management system*: Processes for acquiring, organizing, and sharing, and utilizing knowledge.
- *Strategy*: Methods for creating a well-thought-out "game plan" for the organization affected by the change to TBO. (*Note:* this definition proved to

be difficult for many participants. Instead, strategy was considered to be the organizational means for achieving success in the business environment. As such, TBO is one possible method of many.)

- *Leadership system*: Formal and informal processes for creating leadership conducive to teamwork, including shared leadership.
- *Between-teams integration systems*: Methods for ensuring that teams do not become the new silos, and instead are pieces of an integrated whole.
- *Resource allocation system*: Processes for ensuring that teams get the resources they need to get the work done.
- *Physical workspace*: The actual space in which the team works. If it is a virtual team, then the "space" created by technology.
- *Renewal system*: Methods for periodically reevaluating and changing organizational design and systems, when necessary.
- *Selection system*: Processes for bringing new and transferred employees with the right skills into the right teams.
- *Work process design*: Methods for analyzing and changing, if appropriate, the work process. Often used in conjunction with team design.

To test the idea that changing these components to align to teams led to the success of the TBO*ing* effort, interview participants were asked to give examples of their TBO*ing* efforts, and rate the level of change that occurred in each of these components. These ratings were compiled into an overall change score. This overall change score was then related to the overall success of the change effort. The resulting correlation ($r = 0.74$, $p < 0.01$) supports our idea that these components must be changed to support teams in order for successful TBO*ing* to occur.

These component ratings were then individually related to the rating of the overall success of the change effort. The correlations were the most statistically significant ($p < 0.01$) for team design system ($r = 0.85$), training system ($r = 0.67$), leadership ($r = 0.68$), and renewal system ($r = 0.69$). Correlations were slightly less statistically significant ($p < 0.05$) for performance measurement system ($r = 0.52$), culture ($r = 0.53$), between-teams integration systems ($r = 0.58$), and resource allocation system ($r = 0.56$). While the sample size was small ($n = 20$) and simplistic statistics were used in analysis, these results shed light on possible areas of emphasis in the TBO transition. However, we acknowledge that the emphasis may shift as the TBO change initiative matures. For example, integration of the organization by creating linking mechanisms that tie teams together across boundaries may emerge as a critical focus in a more mature initiative.

Interview participants were also asked to give their opinions on the top three most important components to change for the ultimate success of a TBO. The majority of participants named leadership (70%) and culture (50%) as the most crucial TBO components. Team design (30%), communication and information systems (23%), goal setting system (22%), and work process design (20%) were the next most often named components.

Comparing the two sets of results (see Table 1), a few patterns emerge. Leadership and culture are clearly indicated by both sets of results as crucial components to be changed for the success of the TBO effort. Interestingly, though training was highly correlated to the success of the effort, the participants did not frequently mention it as a crucial TBO component. Kennedy (2001) found that team members did not consider training important, either, although their managers did. Similarly, between-teams integration systems correlated highly, and no participants mentioned it as a crucial component. Perhaps "between-teams integration systems" is not seen as a formal component, merely as a byproduct of other pieces, or few mature TBO's have been observed by the select group of interviewees.

Finally, these results suggest that goal setting, performance appraisal, knowledge management, strategy, physical workspace, and selection are not as central as the other components to a successful TBO*ing* effort. Perhaps these systems

Table 1.   Comparison of TBO Measures.

TBO Component	Correlation Between Component Change and Overall Success of Change Effort	% Participants Who Indicated As One of the Three Most Crucial TBO Components
Reward and recognition system	0.28	13%
Goal setting system	0.06	22%
Performance measurement system	0.52*	15%
Performance appraisal system	0.40	0%
Team design system	0.85**	30%
Communication and information systems	0.31	23%
Culture	0.53*	50%
Training system	0.67**	7%
Knowledge management	0.45	7%
Strategy	0.45	0%
Leadership	0.68**	70%
Between-teams integration systems	0.58*	0%
Resource allocation system	0.56*	7%
Physical workspace	−0.17	0%
Renewal system	0.69**	13%
Selection system	0.23	0%
Work process design	0.48	20%

* indicates $p < 0.05$; ** indicates $p < 0.01$.

change as a byproduct of other changes, or simply are not as important as the others. Given the expanded definition of strategy as the overall business strategy as opposed to the original definition (the "game plan" for transitioning to TBO), most participants indicated that TBO is a means to the strategy, and therefore strategy was not a crucial component to TBO. If we define strategy as methods of aligning the organization with its environment, then TBO becomes a form of strategic change that contributes through the redesign of the organization.

Additional TBO components suggested by interview participants are listed below. These components were not included in the previous statistical discussion, as each participant did not consider them in the ratings. The quotes below come directly from interview participants.

- *Accounting systems*: Methods of connecting between successful implementation of TBO and business success. "Outcome measures include: customer acquisition – sales and getting new customers, customer retention, innovation, and quicker and more effective in implementing new things (e.g. ERP). Those are the reasons to put TBO in place." "The point being, how do you assess the value of intangibles and create a feedback system to strategic decision-makers so they can take that into account to make the decisions."
- *Union-management relationships*: "By definition, (TBO) radically redefines power in ways that are threatening to traditional union views." "Need to design collective agreement to be aligned with the TBO so it is much more flexible than the traditional agreement."
- *Planned people movement*: "Something that links selection and training and resource allocation . . . to reinforce the team philosophy. It is an effort to really say, if you've got teams, then the team needs to have some say in when someone can leave and when someone can come and those kinds of things. So, how do we match the business needs that we have to be dynamic because we need more resources and fewer resources there and respond to changing business needs? We have teams that dynamics of their own in terms of what people need to learn and grow and then we have individuals that have their own career and growth plans. And, how do you marry those so that individuals moving can map to the business needs but also honor the team requirements?"
- *External sensors and channeling*: "Setting up sensors for the marketplace and then channeling that into the appropriate strategic planning body so that what is going on outside actually gets incorporated into what is going on inside and if it needs to react quickly, it can."
- *Continuous improvement*: Research shows that "organizations that were doing a significant amount of, what they called in their study, self-directed work teams or empowered work teams, the significant difference in terms of

measurable results was their rate of improvement over the past five years . . ..
Then what's critical to that process is having your people trained and giving
them dedicated time in the work schedule to apply process improvement and
problem solving skills."

- *Adaptation component*: "Both leadership and management functions looking
  at what are we doing; how well is this process working; how does it need
  to be changed, does the whole process need to be thrown out and redesigned
  or do we just need to adapt it here. What is happening in our industry? Are
  we still doing things in a way that we're going to see viable in the industry?
  So we're gradually adapting as a part of how we're in the world."
- *Citizenship*: "The individual's relationship with the company. Somehow the
  employment contract changes as TBO is implemented."
- *Larger community*: "Once you start thinking about collaboration, and start
  thinking systematically, even mapping processes, you don't go very far down
  that path without including community as a whole."
- *Orientation*: "That might be separate from training. Mostly in terms of new
  hires – getting new people to understand what the team-based system is all
  about. It is not enough to tell people in the orientation that we're a team-
  based organization and here's parents or partners, blah, blah, blah. Try to
  prevent the 'five-year wall' where all of a sudden they've made the easy
  gains, they've had turnover, and the new people don't really get it. And they
  focused a lot on doing their 'real work' instead of attending to the team
  culture, and things start to unravel."
- *Business acumen*: "I think the fact that we have the teams has resulted in
  people being better informed on business and how it operates."
- *Career planning and management*: "Lateral movement and skills acquisition
  as opposed to climbing the ladder. How do we get more money now that
  we have fewer hierarchical levels?"
- *Personal development*: "A lot of TBOs, all the development is focused on
  teams, and there is another piece there, those teams are made up of people and
  whatever you can do to strengthen each individual's person, you are strengthening the team. When we put an hourly person in a leadership class, they walk
  out with a much better understanding of why some management decisions are
  made. And that just has ripple effects all the way through the organization."
  "People have to grow in this environment or they can't survive. That is different
  than training. I can sit in a training class and absorb a lot of knowledge and not
  really put it to work anywhere. And in this environment, I have to be able to put
  my KSAs in the world, and that's personal and professional growth. We see
  people who have absolutely no courage go from timidity and inability to speak
  in a group being able to be very assertive and right out there."

CONCLUSION

The journey to TBO*ing* is a long and complex one. This chapter presented just the tip of the iceberg. First, we presented our definition of TBO*ing*. Second, we shared some things to consider before taking on the effort, including who starts the change effort, carefully make the decision to start the initiative, and where to start. Third, we made suggestions for managing the change to TBO*ing*. A summary of that list can be found in Exhibit 1. Fourth, we shared some types of transition methodologies to consider in the change, including representative group involvement, whole system involvement, and hybrid combinations. The key is to align the planning and implementation process with the desired outcome, and some suggestions for managing that were given. Finally, some ideas for utilizing the foundational principle for successful TBO*ing*, alignment, were shared. A list of components that should be aligned for a successful TBO is summarized in Exhibit 2. Our research shows that leadership and culture are the two most important components to be changed.

If the change to TBO is so complex and difficult, why would organizations pursue it? When done well, results include higher quality and productivity, increased innovation, higher flexibility and adaptability, and greater speed and better response to the needs of customers. But, the bottom line is that it is a difficult process and the decision to undertake it must be carefully made. In the words of one of the interview participants, organizations pursue TBO "because it is worth the effort. If what they are doing in the world can be done better in teams, then it is worth the effort to go the collaborative route. If not, then it is not the best decision to make, because teaming is incredibly hard. I would say that organizations make the effort because they believe that the payoff is greater than the cost and that it will contribute to their long-term health, and help them become more stable and productive and adaptable over time. And that's what they truly believe that there has to be a payoff, because it's incredibly costly" (Interview Participant).

ACKNOWLEDGMENTS

Thanks to the Center for Creative Leadership for supporting the interview study data collection. Special acknowledgement goes to colleagues Judith Steed and Gina Hernez-Broome for their help conceptualizing the study. Thanks to David Loring for supporting the idea.

Special appreciation goes to the interview participants who gave from 1–4 hours of their busy schedule to share their thoughts on this exciting topic. Thank you!

(1)	Integrate initiatives.
(2)	Intentional, planned effort.
(3)	Not every component has to be changed.
(4)	Deal with reality of enterprise systems.
(5)	A few simple rules.
(6)	Tailor, not cookie cutter.
(7)	A successful transition requires significant resources.
(8)	Using consultants.
(9)	Develop internal resources.
(10)	Share best practices.
(11)	Start where they are.
(12)	Educate management and change team.
(13)	Continuous assessment and renewal.
(14)	Develop change champions.
(15)	Align to environment.
(16)	Deal with traditional corporate entity.

Exhibit 1. Summary of Suggestions for Managing Team-Based Organizing Change.

(1)	Reward and recognition systems
(2)	Goal setting system
(3)	Performance measurement system
(4)	Performance appraisal system
(5)	Team design system
(6)	Communication and information systems
(7)	Culture
(8)	Training system
(9)	Knowledge management system
(10)	Strategy
(11)	Leadership system
(12)	Between-teams integration system
(13)	Resource allocation system
(14)	Physical workspace
(15)	Renewal system
(16)	Selection system
(17)	Work process design
(18)	Union-management relationships
(19)	Planned people movement
(20)	External sensors and channeling
(21)	Continuous improvement
(22)	Adaptation component
(23)	Citizenship
(24)	Larger community
(25)	Orientation
(26)	Business acumen
(27)	Career planning and management
(28)	Personal development

Exhibit 2. Components to Be Aligned to Teams in Team-Based Organizing.

REFERENCES

Appelbaum, E., Bailey, T., Berg, P., & Kalleberg, A. L. (2000). *Manufacturing Advantage: Why High-Performance Work Systems Pay*. Ithaca, NY: Cornell University Press.

Beyerlein, M. M., Freedman, S., McGee, C., & Moran, L. (2002). *Beyond teams: Building the collaborative organization*. San Francisco: Jossey-Bass/Pfeiffer.

Beyerlein, M. M., & Harris, C. L. (in press). Critical success factors in team-based organizing. In: M. Beyerlein, C. McGee, G. Klein, J. Nemiro & L. Broedling (Eds), *The Collaborative Work Systems Fieldbook: Strategies for Building Successful Teams*. San Francisco: Jossey-Bass/Pfeiffer.

Brown, J. S., & Duguid, P. (2002). *The Social Life of Information*. Cambridge, MA: Harvard Business School Press.

Bunker, B. B., & Alban, B. T. (1997). *Large Group Interventions*. San Francisco: Jossey-Bass.

Dannemiller, K. D., James, S. L., & Tolchinsky, P. D. (1999). *Whole-scale change*. San Francisco: Berrett Koehler Publishers.

✓ Dannemiller Tyson Associates (2000). *Whole-scale change: Unleashing the magic in organizations*. San Francisco: Berrett-Koehler Publishers.

✓ Filipczak, B. (1995). Critical mass: Putting whole-systems thinking into practice. *Training, 32*(9), 33–41.

Harris, C. L., & Beyerlein, M. M. (in press). Team-based organization: Creating an environment for team success. In: M. A. West, K. Smith & D. Tjosvold (Eds), *International Handbook of Organisational Teamwork and Cooperative Working*. West Sussex, England: John Wiley & Sons, Ltd.

Holman, P., & Devane, T. (1999). *The change handbook: Group methods for shaping the future*. San Francisco: Berrett-Koehler.

✓ Jacobs, R. W. (1994). *Real time strategic change: How to involve an entire organization in fast and far-reaching change*. San Francisco: Berrett-Koehler Publishers.

Kennedy, F. (in press). Return on teaming initiative (ROTI): Measuring teaming outcomes to optimize their performance. In: M. Beyerlein, C. McGee, G. Klein, J. Nemiro & L. Broedling (Eds), *The Collaborative Work Systems Fieldbook: Strategies for Building Successful Teams*. San Francisco: Jossey-Bass/Pfeiffer.

Lawler, E. E. III, Mohrman, S. A., & Ledford, G. E., Jr. (1998). *Strategies for High Performance Organizations – The CEO Report: Employee Involvement, TQM and Reengineering Programs in Fortune 1000 Corporations*. San Francisco: Jossey-Bass.

Levenson, A. (in press). ROI and strategy for teams and collaborative work systems. In: M. Beyerlein, C. McGee, G. Klein, J. Nemiro & L. Broedling (Eds), *The Collaborative Work Systems Fieldbook: Strategies for Building Successful Teams*. San Francisco: Jossey-Bass/Pfeiffer.

Levine, L., & Mohr, B. J. (1998). Whole system design (WSD): The shifting focus of attention and the threshold challenge. *Journal of Applied Behavioral Science, 34*(3), 305–346.

Lytle, W. O. (1998). *Designing a high-performance organization: A guide to the whole-systems approach*. Clark, NJ: Block Petrella Weisbord.

Lytle, W., & Rankin, W. (1996). *Fast-paced change*. Workshop given at the 1996 Strategies and Skills Conference for Effective Teaming, Dallas, Texas.

Manion, J., Lorimer, W., & Leander, W. J. (1996). *Team-based health care organizations: Blueprint for success*. Gaithersburg, MD: Aspen Publishers.

Mohrman, S. A., Cohen, S. G., & Mohrman, A. M., Jr. (1995). *Designing team-based organizations: New forms for knowledge work*. San Francisco: Jossey-Bass.

Nadler, D. A., & Tushman, M. L. (1997). *Competing by design: The power of organizational architecture.* New York: Oxford University Press.

Owen, H. (1997). *Open Space Technology: A User's Guide.* San Francisco: Berrett-Koehler.

Owen, H., & Stadler, A. (1999). Open space technology. In: P. Holman & T. Devane (Eds), *The Change Handbook: Group Methods for Shaping the Future.* San Francisco: Berrett-Koehler.

Pinchot, G. (1985). *Intrapreneuring.* New York: Harper & Row.

Purser, R., & Cabana, S. (1998). *The self-managing organization: How leading companies are transforming the work of teams for real impact.* New York: The Free Press.

Semler, S. W. (1997). Systematic agreement: A theory of organizational alignment. *Human Resource Development Quarterly, 8*(1), 23–40.

Ulrich, D. (1997). *Human resource champions: The next agenda for adding value and delivering results.* Cambridge, MA: Harvard Business School Press.

Van Aken, E. (1997). Aligning support systems with teams. Unpublished manuscript.

Weisbord, M. R., & Janoff, S. (1995). *Future search: An action guide to finding common ground in organizations and communities.* San Francisco: Berrett-Koehler Publishers.

CHANGE MANAGEMENT COMPETENCIES FOR CREATING COLLABORATIVE ORGANIZATIONS

Duane Windsor

ABSTRACT

This conceptual chapter addresses identification, development, and appli-cation of change management competencies directed at creating more collaborative work systems through transformation of existing businesses. The chapter draws on, and assesses, selected key ideas and works in the available literatures on change management and collaboration (applied both internally and externally), including reported cases of revealing successful and failed change efforts. Improved collaboration is posited to be desirable and feasible, in certain circumstances. Change management and organizational transformation are big and broad topics, with large conceptual and empirical literatures, as is the topic of collaborative work systems. There is here a deliberate narrowing of focus on how to obtain more collaboration in and between existing organizations, where desirable but not occurring naturally. Attention is explicitly directed to transforma-tion of existing businesses as distinct from the relative managerial freedom afforded in startup situations and the almost natural change processes inherent in successful innovation firms. Any shift from conventional to collaborative work approaches is a transformational problem drawing on change management competencies. A fundamental difficulty is the absence

Team-Based Organizing, Volume 9, pages 31–65.
ISBN: 0-7623-0981-4

of empirically verified theories immediately relevant to management practice. Useful knowledge on these important matters has been built up piecemeal and experientially.

INTRODUCTION

This chapter addresses identification, development, and application of change management *competencies* directed at creating more collaborative organizations through transformation of existing businesses. Collaboration is posited to be desirable, at least in certain circumstances. (Attempts to increase collaboration may be undesirable in other circumstances.) The focus here is on how to obtain more collaboration in and between existing organizations, where desirable. The intermediate objective (collaboration) must be distinguished from the approach (change management competencies); the ultimate objective is sustained profit growth.

What do we know about change management competencies applied to improving collaboration within and between existing businesses – improvement necessarily involving some form of transformation of existing activities? Any shift from conventional to collaborative work approaches is a transformational problem drawing on change management competencies. Change management, organizational transformation, and work collaboration are big and broad topics, each with large, growing, and internally disagreeing conceptual and empirical literatures. (There is a specialty resource: *Journal of Organizational Change Management.*) In this chapter, the broad topic is deliberately narrowed to focus on creation of more collaborative organizations through identification, development, and application of relevant change management competencies. Attention is explicitly directed to transformation of existing organizations as distinct from the relative managerial freedom afforded in startup situations and the almost natural change processes inherent in successful innovation firms. A new stand-alone organization (such as AES, in electricity generation, see Wetlaufer, 1999b), effectively an entrepreneurial venture, can be partly "designed" (or at least deliberately oriented) at the outset with respect to strategy, structure, management, personnel, compensation, and so on – in large measure. Innovation firms (such as 3M or Intel) have natural internal change processes at work. Change management is precisely about problems of business process reengineering or renewal (BPR), business transformation or repositioning, continuous improvement (CI), evolutionary strategic change (Wetlaufer, 2001), innovation, total quality management (TQM), and so on – in greater or lesser degree.

The approach of this chapter is conceptual and interpretive. The chapter draws on, and assesses, selected key ideas and works in the available conceptual and empirical literatures on change management competencies and collaborative work approaches (defined both internally and externally), as well as reported cases of revealing successful and failed change efforts. The *Harvard Business Review* has pioneered in publishing interviews with executives who have successfully (or not) pioneered startup, innovation, and change processes.

The basic approach is that of a *critique* rather than being intentionally critical (in an explicitly negative sense) of particular authors or approaches. A critique searches for both strengths and weaknesses (the latter being the exclusive target of critical work) in existing knowledge (hence it is a form of scholarly inquiry analogous to competitive benchmarking) in order to identify likely paths of progress (or dead-ends) beyond that knowledge base. Systematic critique is an appropriate and desirable procedure in "organizational science" and change management practice.

The relationship between "theory" and "practice" should be remarked briefly. There is arguably a profound gap between the discipline (or theory) and the practice (or field experimentation) of management (Drucker, 1999, p. 4). Chandler et al. (1998) addressed the widening gap between changing practices and existing theories of the firm, with the former racing ahead of the latter. The unifying theme of the volume is that often conflicting interaction among technology, strategy, organization, and geography must be the core of a new dynamic theory of the firm (see Zahra, 1999). Joyce (1998) emphasizes the danger that management research will be insulated not only from practice but from its constituent intellectual disciplines (see Kilduff & Dougherty, 2000). Much of the empirical testing in "organizational science" depends on comparison of cases resulting from managers' quasi-experiments. (The term "quasi-experiment" means simply that one-time conditions cannot be repeated with precision elsewhere. Benchmarking of best practices, even for purposes of leapfrogging competitors, involves the risk that necessary conditions and activities are not understood sufficiently for transfer.) Much of conceptualization or theorizing in "organizational science" either draws on current practice (best or otherwise) or develops new (and relatively untested) ideas for influencing future practice – often invoking analogies and metaphors for explication. The matter is arguably compounded by the phenomenon of management gurus, who now rapidly develop and market new (and relatively untested) ideas. There are highly experienced consultants to assist change management, as at McKinsey (Katzenbach et al., 1996) and Price Waterhouse (1995).

To reiterate, none of these observations are meant to be critical (in the sense of being intentionally negative). Rather, as Micklethwait and Wooldridge (1996) characterize the matter, "management theory" is an immature "discipline" that as a result provides conflicting advice to managers on practical action.

Immaturity is simply a condition, such that academic empiricists, academic theoreticians, consultants, employees, executives, and managers will (under-standably) have quite different views (and experiences) concerning what to do in particular circumstances. Shapiro (1997) recommends that managers proceed by adapting theories as they make decisions – that is, that they experiment (cf. Joyce, 1998, on the differing interests of academics and managers; LaBianca et al., 2000, on stability and change as simultaneous organizational experiments). One should note the phenomenon (pioneered at the *Harvard Business Review*, and drawn on here) of interviews with executives who have successfully (or not) pioneered startup and change processes. Hence, sometimes practice (occurring under differing conditions) leads lagging theories (often conflicting); sometimes theories (often conflicting) lead lagging practice, but practitioners most likely adapt as they go along. (Hence, according to Schaffer & Thomson, 1992, managers may be "prey" to any plausible solution to modern competitive conditions.) We simply do not have reliable theories or models (amounting to useful practice manuals) of business process reengineering, business renewal and transformation, change management, employee compensation and motivation, empowerment inter-organizational networking, mergers and acquisitions, organizational learning and redesign, teambuilding, work process redesign, and so on. Indeed, a literature highly critical of "orthodoxy" (defined here as praising change approaches) has developed and is growing in each of these areas.

While the chapter is strictly conceptual, and based on an interpretive reading of literature (academic, case, consulting, and executive), the guiding intent here is to be practical, defined as explicit pragmatism with respect to possibly complex matters. The author presumes that managers will have to experiment in the face of considerable uncertainty. The chapter presumes a simple ultimate goal of sustained profit growth (within ethical and legal norms) to which collaboration and change management are both subordinate (like other aspects of business). Pragmatism must cope with two circumstances. The received tradition in science is simple theorizing tested against empirical data. Complex explanations are presumed less likely to be valid. However, this tradition ("Ockham's Razor") implicitly assumes simple phenomena. A theory, hypothesis, or explanation must always be sufficiently complex to explain the phenomena under study (cf. Glynn et al., 2000). Managers think of themselves as practical (and they are action-oriented and problem solving), but practice may be acceptance of an ideology (including buzzwords and fads) legitimating a highly experimental course of action in the face of uncertainty concerning the likely outcomes of choices. This formal language is simply another way of describing managerial judgment. An actuarial record (i.e. history) is a statistical predictor of the future only for reasonably stable phenomena: fundamental changes in cause-and-effect relationships are far less predictable, much less controllable.

It has been suggested that change management is emerging as a new profession (Farias et al., 2000; Lyneham-Brown, 1997; Worren et al., 1999). Change can also be a mantra (as with collaboration) – on the abstract admonition of "change or die" (which is always true, in a sense, in the very long run; but in the very long run, how many firms will survive in any case?). Colby (1996) lists among five management myths that one cannot stick with the status quo (i.e. change is mandatory) and that one must change urgently (i.e. one cannot take time to think carefully). Colby argues that new paradigms seldom work better, although innovation and improvement are always desirable. (Colby's other "myths" are that mergers always demonstrate significant savings, that downsizing always improves efficiency, and that cost-effectiveness can be measured.) An abstraction, even if often valid, does not tell (cf. Campbell & Alexander, 1997) a manager how to go about change and development (Van de Ven & Poole, 1995), defined here as what to do and when so as to improve and sustain profit growth. Innovation should generally (but not always) outperform imitation even where the latter is based on best-practice benchmarking (Higgins, 1996; Wilmot, 1987). But innovation can also fail, as in Motorola's recent apparent error in digital cellular technology, now dominated by Nokia (a transformed Finnish company).

COLLABORATIVE WORK SYSTEMS

The concept of *collaboration* embraces both how *internal* work processes are conducted among employees and how an organization networks *externally* with stakeholder (or constituency) groups and other organizations (such as distributors, partners, and suppliers). Internal collaboration likely connotes cross-functional team building to many readers, but the concept necessarily covers inter-unit (i.e. intra-organizational) interaction and communication as well, regardless of how work processes are in fact handled within each unit. Hence, collaboration could occur within a complex matrix of organizations, units, teams, and individuals – at different levels of analysis from organization to individual. (Inter-unit collaboration could occur between a cross-functional team and a conventionally structured staff office, for example.)

The chapter begins with a presumption that the ultimate goal in business is sustained profit growth. Such profit growth (i.e. real profits rising over time) is a function of revenue growth drivers (i.e. rising customer demand in relationship to improving products-services) and expense growth restraint drivers (i.e. more productive – efficient and effective – business processes and employees), both resting on steadily better strategy and organization. Given changing environmental conditions (especially markets and technologies), there is a sound case for continuous improvement (CI) in revenue growth drivers, expense growth restraint drivers, strategy, organization, and management (see Wetlaufer, 2001).

Yet Garvin (1993, p. 78) noted: "Continuous improvement programs are sprouting up all over as organizations strive to better themselves and gain an edge. . . . Unfortunately, failed programs far outnumber successes, and improvement rates remain distressingly low." Garvin attributes a high failure rate to a lack of understanding of "a basic truth": "Continuous improvement requires a commitment to learning" (see Senge, 1990). Otherwise, "Change remains cosmetic, and improvements are either fortuitous or short-lived."

There are of course success stories of true learning organizations and knowledge-creating companies that have achieved a link between learning and continuous improvement. (Garvin cites Analog Devices, Chaparral Steel and Xerox.) Baldwin et al. (1997, p. 47) note, for instance, that "Although reports of new corporate initiatives appear daily, and rhetoric abounds, there has been little synthesis of the underlying logic of recent learning initiatives."

One of the great continuous improvement (CI) stories is simply that of Lincoln Electric (founded 1895 in Cleveland), long regarded as one of the world's best manufacturing firms (making arc welding equipment). The company was based on the human motivation theory of its founder. It practiced empowerment (without the term or formal teamwork) in a piecemeal-with-performance bonus compensation setting (bonuses up to 100% of pay) operating virtually without hierarchical supervision and with a job guarantee policy after probation (Fast, 1975). Yet Lincoln Electric was caught at one of Andy Grove's (CEO of Intel) "strategic inflection points" (Fuffer, 1999) when it went global from 1987 through acquisitions (O'Connell, 1998). At least initially, the human motivation approach did not translate well abroad. (In 1995, the closely held firm put 40% of its equity in the public market, shares to acquire voting rights in 2005.) The stumble put pressure to move toward a more traditional pay scheme and forced use of temporary debt one year (1992, due to the first loss, on a consolidated basis, in the firm's history) to meet bonuses (Chilton, 1993; Schiller, 1996). Donald Hastings, the CEO, told the annual meeting (May 26, 1992): "We miscalculated the time it would take [to 'turn around' our new associates]. The tenacity of foreign cultures to hang on to their unprofitable ways is startling to me. They seem to have no sense of urgency to make profits, and don't seem to hurt when they lose" (Chilton, 1993, p. 1). Pascale et al. (1997) relate successful culture changes at Sears, Shell, and the U.S. Army, and attribute failures not to change programs but to their dependence on too few individuals.

Schein (1999), who "virtually invented and defined the field" (Schein, 1985, revised 1992) of corporate culture (see Spector, 2000), is highly critical that culture has become a fad, oversimplified and misunderstood. Schein argues that culture is very complex and not particularly malleable. It must be understood before intervention to alter it can succeed. (The standard interpretation of Johnson & Johnson, discussed below, focuses on the important role of its organizational culture.) Indeed, failure of activity-oriented change programs is perhaps often attributed to difficulties of changing "strong" (i.e. well-entrenched) cultures (Schaffer & Thomson, 1992, cite an anonymous executive to this effect).

Innovation has been traced to promotion of appropriate capabilities, structures, competencies, and especially cultures by Tushman and O'Reilly (1997; see Katz, 1997). Duncan (1989) observes that "corporate culture" – a notion adopted from anthropology – is an elusive notion. (Duncan and his team of researchers used "triangulation" – multiple methods – to get at culture in a study site, and then discovered different subcultures within the organization, one of which was innovative by deviating from the "central" culture and hence presenting various difficulties for top management.) While emphasizing the importance of strong culture, Goffee and Jones (1996) identify four different types of corporate culture (as combinations of sociability and solidarity), recognize that firms are not homogeneous, and caution that culture must fit the environment for competitive advantage. "Networked organizations [high sociability, low solidarity] are characterized not by a lack of hierarchy but by a profusion of ways to get around it" (1996, p. 137), because highly political. Unilever is cited as an example, where cooperation is difficult to obtain. The *mercenary* culture (low sociability, high solidarity) is focused on business matters and directed to beating the competition, as at General Electric. The *fragmented* culture reflects low sociability and low solidarity (Goffee & Jones cite the academic context); the *communal* culture reflects high sociability and high solidarity. The Linux software development community (Malone & Laubacher, 1998), operating virtually, cannot be readily located in this typology.

While a large literature certainly supports the usefulness of collaborative work approaches such as internal team building, cross-unit communication, and external organizational and constituency networking, there is also an important critical literature – and one that is likely to grow. As a broad generalization, this critical literature addresses two fundamental difficulties in the theory and practice of collaboration. The first difficulty is that much of "organizational science" should be regarded as dealing with poorly understood and possibly complex as well as contingent relationships that are themselves subject to changing environmental conditions about which knowledge is also relatively poor. Hence, "organizational science" tends to be highly abstract and prone to error. The second difficulty is that managers often lack the change management competencies (i.e. capabilities and skills) appropriate to handling the transformation of organizations from conventional to collaborative work approaches. In other words, scientists do not have sound theories and managers do not know what they are doing – as a broad generalization.

For the purposes of this chapter, collaborative work systems may be considered in terms of four key dimensions: (a) empowerment; (b) teams; (c) inter-personal and inter-unit cooperation; and (d) ultimately global inter-firm networks. (Closeness to markets communicates external pressures more rapidly and effectively within organizations.)

As Segol, an R&D scientist with Bechtel (Wetlaufer, 1999b), comments: teamwork is a business expediency and not a philosophy of business. Cooperation, empowerment, networking, and teamwork are purely instruments; the purpose of any (and all in combination) is sustained profit growth of the firm; they have no independent purpose, even if they work to profit growth through employee morale and capabilities. This view accords with Schaffer and Thomson's (1992) dictum that "Successful Change Programs Begin with Results." They argue that change efforts often mistakenly focus on activities or means, that is on process (characterized as a "ceremonial rain dance)"; when the true purpose is to achieve particular ends or outcomes, that is results. Activity-oriented change may involve analysis of complex conditions; results-oriented change permits both measurable short-term gains and employee initiative. (The Japanese approach of "Hoshin" planning attempts to combine long-term visioning with annual improvement targeting of one major barrier to progress and continuous improvement throughout an organization; see Cowley & Domb, 1997.) AlliedSignal, after some false starts, evolved by trial and error (with Price Waterhouse assistance) a multidivisional account-team structure to work with customers (Hendershot, 1996). These teams set priorities for each division; worked within flexible measures of success for compensation purposes (25% division, 25% corporate revenue benchmarks, 50% customer satisfaction measures); and shifted inter-divisional competition for customers to common purpose. Hendershot attributed an 11% increase in revenues and increased customer satisfaction ratings to better marketing (including the team account approach).

Teamwork is desirable in some situations, and undesirable in others. A *team* is a set of interdependent individuals who (voluntarily or unavoidably) share responsibility for outcomes. Teambuilding and maintenance is sufficiently expensive (in various ways) that there should be a good reason, rather than adoption of a fad. (Football, basketball, and baseball by definition are played by teams, but in quite different ways. Tennis can be played singles or doubles. Golf can be played only individually, although group scores can be aggregated, if desired for some reason.) A recent study of 114 teams in four organizations (Kirkman & Rosen, 1999) found that success was a function of four factors: (a) external leadership; (b) acceptance of responsibilities; (c) human resource policies; (d) social structure of the team.

It has been reported that in just four previous years, nearly 30,000 articles about *empowerment* (on definition and measurement, see Herrenkohl et al., 1999) had appeared in print media (Wetlaufer, 1999b, p. 111). Argyris (1998) concluded that empowerment is largely an illusion, because CEOs undermine it, employees are either unprepared or unwilling to assume new responsibilities (quite possibly for good reasons), and change management professionals themselves arguably inhibit empowerment. Argyris argues that the chief difficulty is generating internal (i.e. personal) commitment, as distinct from the appearance of external compliance within a command and control hierarchy (see Randolph, 2000, for reinforcement of how difficult empowerment may be to accomplish in practice). While empowerment is undoubtedly a potent idea, its practice needs rejuvenation (Forrester, 2000). Empowerment must be closely linked to mission and measurement (Galagan, 1992). Empowerment has the difficulty that it must be undertaken by those in authority (Hardy & Leiba-O'Sullivan, 1998), or wrested from those in authority (Hamel, 2000a, b, c, d) – for that is what revolutionary change from the bottom of an organization is (at least temporarily). There may be a balancing of power between authority and empowerment (Lucas, 1998). Recent empirical studies include Kirkman and Rosen (1999) and Koberg et al. (1999).

Johnson & Johnson fits Handy's (1989, 1994, 1996) notion of corporate federalism and concept of subsidiarity for decentralization of power (Kelly, 1998). It is a modern kind of holding company (directed by an executive committee supported by central staff offices) that today owns nearly 200 operating companies (defined on product-service, technology, geographic principles) – each with its own president and board (Aguilar & Bambri, 1986a). More than 50 operating companies have been added (by mergers, acquisitions, startups, and so on) over the past 15 years or so. These wholly owned operating companies (structured into groups) send dividends to the holding company. (J&J stock price has risen dramatically since the mid-1980s with expansion.) What is essentially a network of operating groups and companies (further networked to customers, distributors, and suppliers) faces a set of issues and problems in inter-company collaboration as well as intra-company collaboration (Aguilar & Bambri, 1986b). The network is united (in addition to ownership) by adherence to the Johnson & Johnson "Credo" (defining responsibilities to key stakeholders) and common management principles and strategic planning practices. In theory, at least, one J&J company might embrace internal team building while another J&J company might utilize conventional work processes; and the two companies (however different internally) might need to collaborate. At J&J, management is empowered; but there may be no particular justification for formal team building within or across these operating companies. How does one coordinate and improve collaboration in such a firm?

THEORIES AND EXAMPLES OF CHANGE MANAGEMENT

There has been a shift over "The past decade of organizational research" from "an investigation of organizational statics to an investigation of organizational dynamics" (Boeker, 1997, p. 152). Change, development, innovation, learning, transformation, and turbulence are central themes of now modern classics such as Kanter (1983), Handy (1989, 1994, 1996), Senge (1990), and D'Aveni (1994). Handy (1996) argues that we live in an uncertain world of discontinuous change characterized by managerial experimentation (see Carey, 1996). The literature is, however, fundamentally divided over the ability of organizations to adapt to environmental changes vs. their tendency (i.e. inertia) to preserve strategy and practices, likely defining poles on an empirical continuum of organizations (Boeker, 1997, p. 152). Some prominent scholars have issued cautions concerning various popular change management approaches (as with other aspects of recent experimentation). "Despite all the rhetoric surrounding transformation and major change programs, the reality is that today's managers have not yet encountered change programs that work" (Argyris, 1998, p. 104). Organizational handling of "paradox" (that is, resolving tension between two apparently conflicting considerations) is becoming a motif in recent literature (Handy, 1994; Lewis, 2000; Nooteboom, 1989; Price Waterhouse, 1996; see Vroman, 1996). One way of viewing the paradox notion is that it conveys that management is less a matter of common sense and more a matter of dealing with complexity (Vroman, 1996). The Price Waterhouse Change Integration Team (1996) argues five paradoxes about change (Vroman, 1996):

(1) successful positive change requires stability (cf. Leana & Barry, 2000);
(2) enterprise development requires individual focus;
(3) the critical role of culture requires indirect approaches;
(4) forceful leadership is essential to true empowerment (and power must be used in order to surrender it through empowerment); and
(5) you must tear down to build up.

In other words, employee freedom operates within limits set by leadership prepared to intervene. (The book is also critical of the classical "forming, storming, norming and performing" model of teamwork.)

Assessing theories and practices of change management should take account of both successes and failures and the circumstances in which change management was undertaken. A set of selected revealing case experiences lies along the continuum illustrated in Fig. 1 below. The chapter distinguishes between two different kinds of modern successful change cases (illustrated more or less at the same time historically): (a) the steady (or continuous) investment model (the term is the author's) illustrated at Motorola by Bob Galvin; and (b) the burning platform model (the term is Lawrence Bossidy's) illustrated at General Electric (GE) by Jack Welch, and imitated or adapted subsequently at AlliedSignal by GE alumni Lawrence Bossidy (formerly head of GE Capital, see Tichy & Charan, 1995) and at PerkinElmer (formerly EG&G, see Heimbouch, 2000) by Greg Summe (who had previously worked at McKinsey, then GE, and then AlliedSignal), and at the merged Swedish-Swiss firm Asea Brown Boveri (ABB) by Percy Barnevik (Taylor, 1991; Uyterhoeven, 1996). The steady investment approach can be thought of as the Motorola model. The burning platform approach can be thought of as the GE model.

The steady investment model captures some of what we think of as product-service innovation companies such as Intel (in hardware), Microsoft (in software), Priceline (in on-line purchasing, Maruca, 1999), and 3M (in consumer and industrial products); Motorola is an innovation firm of this type. (It must be noted, however, that EG&G was an innovation company whose government sector work was discarded during the transformation into PerkinElmer, a commercially oriented firm. EG&G was a holding company for 31 diverse

Steady Investment Successes (Motorola Model)	Failures	Burning Platform Successes (GE Model)
Motorola	Levi Strauss	General Electric
Lincoln Electric	(offshore)	AlliedSignal
AES (startup)	Vickers, Inc.	PerkinElmer
3M (innovation)	Navistar	ABB merger
Johnson & Johnson	(IH breakup)	Lockheed Martin
Nestlé		(merger)
Unilever		Continental Airlines
		(turnaround)

Fig. 1. Approaches to Change Management.

businesses.) There is a difference between steady product-service innovation and business renewal or transformation accomplished by radical shift in products-services and markets or internal organizational practices.

The essential story at Motorola is well detailed in the case literature (Gogan et al., 1994a, b). In the late 1970s, at a management meeting, someone (correctly) criticized the quality of Motorola products relative to those of Japanese competitors and called for action. Bob Galvin, the CEO (and son of the firm's founder) heeded the warning. There was an effort to introduce quality improvement (leading to a Six Sigma program for dramatic reduction in defects.) The effort early encountered the difficulty that many employees were simply not sufficiently educated (much less trained) to implement the desired changes. Motorola undertook a company-wide educational and training effort that became today's Motorola University (Wiggenhorn, 1990). Flattening and decentralizing occurred. The then existing employee participation process, modeled on Japanese quality circles and tied in the United States to a bureaucratically complex bonus procedure, was abandoned (late 1980s). Some 4,000 total consumer satisfaction teams were formed (1989) and an annual team competition organized. Then Motorola began to address employee empowerment (1989). Learning approaches (Baldwin et al., 1997) have also been emphasized at Ford Motor (Wetlaufer, 1999a) and Bell Atlantic (Kanter, 1991) as the foundation for transformation efforts. Motorola rose from $5.443 billion in 1985 to just over $27 billion in 1995. (By 1995, foreign business was 64% of sales.) Subsequently, and about the time Chris Galvin became CEO, Motorola apparently missed the turn in digital cellular technology, and the firm has reorganized and downsized under heavy competitive pressure. In 1998, 15,000 workers (15%) were laid off; stock price dropped from $90 in 1997 to $50 in 1998.

At GE, Welch (taking over in 1981) transformed the firm in at least two phases (Tichy & Charan, 1989). Phase 1 built a new "business engine" by restructuring the business portfolio (acquiring and divesting to meet a business-unit standard of #1 or #2 in global market share), delayering management levels, reducing corporate staffs, downsizing employee count significantly, and focusing on the three "strategic circles" of core manufacturing units, technology-intensive businesses, and services. Phase 2 focused on shaping a new "human engine" to energize employees by simplifying procedures, providing feedback (including participative "Work-Out" sessions), and providing rewards to desired qualities. (Desired business characteristics were stated as: lean, agile, creative, ownership, reward. Desired individual characteristics were stated as: realism, leadership, candor/openness, simplicity, integrity, dignity.) It is important to note that at GE, much of the profit driver has been due to GE Capital (lending) and services, with traditional products earning much lower returns. (A detailed study of the redesign of GE Canada is provided in Applegate & Cash, 1989.) From 1988 to 1997, earnings per share (EPS) rose from $0.94 to $2.50, sales from $39 to $49 billion, net profit from $3.4 billion to $8.2 billion, while long-term debt fell from $4.3 to $0.7 billion. In later stages, GE Capital was about 39% of net income.

AlliedSignal (Tichy & Charan, 1995), a firm of $13 billion in sales (aerospace systems, automotive parts, and chemical products), was in trouble. During 1991–1994, under Bossidy's leadership, net income rose from $359 to $708 million, market valuation from $4.5 to nearly $9.8 billion, and operating margin from 4.4% to 8.5%. Bossidy characterized the burning platform theory of change management as either deliberately setting the firm on fire, or taking advantage of the fact that it is on fire already. He then used three tactics:

(1) develop support and active participation from the bottom to drive the middle;
(2) do not worry about changing culture, but simply "coach people to win" with unification accomplished through vision and values statements that achieve clarity about business issues of customers and organizational process ("centralize people, decentralize people"); and
(3) use TQM to drive change.

He also emphasized that leadership can affect three common core processes: (a) strategy (execution being the difficult dimension); (b) operations; and (c) human resources ("you bet on people, not on strategies"). Lobby monitors permitted employees company-wide to track stock price. (AlliedSignal merged in 1999 with Honeywell, which was to be acquired in early 2000 by GE, with Jack Welch to handle the makeover of Honeywell. The European Union halted the acquisition.)

Abrahamson (2000) argues that while GE began with creative destruction, it shifted to far less disruptive and more incremental change efforts: "the idea of change itself is changing. Companies are increasingly aware of the need to combat chaos, cynicism, and burnout by using change tools that are less disruptive. [Timed] Oscillation between big changes and small changes helps ensure dynamic stability in organizations. More critically, it paves the way for change that succeeds."

The formal academic version of this point is punctuated equilibrium theory, see Gersick, 1991, drawn from evolutionary biology, arguing that:

(1) most organizational transformations occur in rapid, discontinuous change – "punctuated" – and over most domains of organizational activity, followed by long periods of stability or statis – "equilibrium";

(2) with small changes not accumulating to such fundamental transformations; and

(3) major environmental changes and CEO succession are important influences.

Lichtenstein, 1995, is critical of the approach. Romanelli and Tushman (1994) tested the model against data for U.S. microcomputer producers, with supportive results. They noted that at the time "To date . . . few aspects of the model have been tested formally." Peter Brabeck, CEO of Nestlé, rejecting revolutionary transformation for his firm, argues that it is important, in evolutionary strategic change, to determine what to hold stable or constant. (Beer & Nohria, 2000a, b, also advise a blend of timed large-scale changes and small adjustments. Stoddard & Jarvenpaa, 1995, argue that while reengineering design should be radical, reengineering change implementation need not be. Design is a "blueprint for change" but implementation can be much less revolutionary and accomplish much. Labianca et al., 2000, address stability and change as simultaneous experiments in organizational life. They argue that employee resistance is typically less self-interest than failure of cognitive understanding of proposed changes.)

The GE model does not necessarily work everywhere, even with a GE alumni transplant as CEO. A reported failure case occurred at Vickers, Inc., a manufacturing firm in Ohio (Helyar, 1998). A GE manager (with McKinsey background and Harvard MBA) took over and applied the GE model. He was reportedly met by "Gandhian resistance." Helyar argues that part of the GE secret was the firm's resources and like-minded managers, so that different cultures at other firms may prove more resistant (consider in contrast Summe's more successful efforts at PerkinElmer).

The author contrasts these success stories with failures of change management efforts at Levi Strauss, Navistar, and Vickers. Levi Strauss reflects response to anticipation of and Navistar reflects response to fundamental deterioration of market conditions. Vickers reflects failure in transferring the GE model.

Levi Strauss is an interesting example of a failed change management process followed by global repositioning (sourcing and production) to outside the U.S. in order to reduce costs. The firm was privatized in 1985 (Hamilton, 1985) by Robert Haas (a member of the Strauss family). Essentially, two phases in change management followed: the "Levi's Aspirations Statement" (see Hill & Wetlaufer, 1998), and a reengineering effort, from 1993, hailed as "the most dramatic change program in American business" (Sheff, 1996; see Stopper, 1998). The aspirations statement highlights participation, diversity, account-ability, teamwork, and open communication. The change effort can be described as carefully prepared. Two hundred change agents were assembled on the "Third

Floor" of the San Francisco headquarters building (cf. Havelock, 1995). The change process then effectively dissolved all job descriptions and employment "contracts" so that everyone (outside manufacturing) had to re-apply for work on the principle of "can you add value to the firm" (in some "hiring" authority's view). The focus of the effort was redesign of the supply chain (and doubtless important improvements were achieved). But the change process had to be slowed due to widespread resistance. Then, as Levi's market share fell dramatically, the white-collar workforce was downsized. Manufacturing facilities have steadily been reduced in the U.S. and moved overseas. Teamwork was introduced into the piecemeal factories by the device of putting stronger and weaker workers together on teams, so that the compensation of the former fell and the compensation of the latter rose. Productivity fell, and internal conflict rose.

Navistar had the distinction of being rated by the *Wall Street Journal* as the worst stock-market performer over 10 years in the 1980s (Rose, 1996). Shares worth $34 in 1981 were worth about $2 in 1996 (arguably doubled in "true" value due to a 10-for-10 reverse stock split above 1993). In fairness to Navistar's management (James Cotting was CEO, 1987 to 1995, succeeded by John Horne), the firm's woes came initially from the breakup of International Harvester (IH) (Hamermesh & Christiansen, 1980). Horne tied pay of 430 managers to company performance on several measures, including stock price and return on equity. IH was a market share and production-oriented firm, with difficult union conditions (UAW). Essentially, it was broken up into pieces when nothing else would evidently work, although considerable progress in the 1970s had been made. The International Harvester name went with the farm machinery business (purchased by Tenneco). Navistar (trucks and diesel engines) wound up ultimately with 15,000 employees (down from some 110,000 at IH). Most of the IH pension liabilities (the retiree-to-active employee ratio was 33 to 1) went to Navistar. Cotting certainly attempted to make employees the core of the business (Borucki & Barnett, 1990; Byrne, 1988; Gilson & Cott, 1994; MacIsaac, 1989). As Roxanne Decyk (Senior VP, Administration) described the situation at Navistar: "If you ask me to name one change in the last decade, I couldn't do it. I don't know where one change ends and the next begins. All we seem to do is manage change" (MacIsaac, 1989). Managed health care became the contention point between management and others. The solution was to obtain concessions in return for stock (diluting, of course) (Williams, 1993).

Miles (1997, analyzing six organizations), a distinguished academic consultant highly experienced in change interventions (see Joyce, 1998), identifies four types of large-scale transformations: Type I, repositioning a successful firm (e.g. Southern Corp.); Type II, revitalizing a firm in crisis (e.g.

National Semiconductor); Type III, merging different businesses and cultures (e.g. Norrell); Type IV, managing the process of leadership development (e.g. PGA Tour). Joyce criticizes the four "scenarios" as "not much of a typology" and notes that no sharp distinction is drawn within the broad rubric of organizational change and transformation that explicitly defines a transformation, presumably a large-scale and discontinuous (or punctuated) change as distinct from more continuous and incremental change. Flamholtz and Randle (1998; see Evink, 1999) use a phase approach (three kinds of organizational transformation) in the history of a company: (a) transition from entrepreneurship to professional management (not studied in this chapter); (b) revitalization out of necessity (Miles' Type II); and (c) radical business redesign for future advantage (Miles' Type I).

One can posit logically a two-by-two matrix: one stub distinguishes incremental (or evolutionary) from revolutionary change, the latter being transformation or reinvention or repositioning; the other stub distinguishes continuous from episodic or punctuated change. In principle, there can be continuous transformation, as could occur in explosive growth or under rapid succession of change-oriented leaders. Innovation or hustle firms may be of this type; they, like startups, are excluded from more detailed examination here (except as Motorola is an innovation company). A third dimension to the matrix would consider whether the change process is undertaken by choice (Type I) or necessity (Type II). Peter Brabeck, CEO of Nestlé, makes the case for evolutionary change except in the face of crisis (Wetlaufer, 2001). The survival through transformation of Lockheed Martin (Augustine, 1997) is a Type II necessity story; with U.S. defense establishment downsizing, the industry market was reduced by more than 50%. There was a consolidation process (Lockheed combining with Martin Marietta, GE Aerospace, Loral, and General Dynamics' aerospace defense unit). Hence, Type II overlapped with Type III. Lockheed Martin's survival involved: (a) preparing contingency plans; (b) preparing a road map; (c) moving expeditiously on that road map; (d) making megachanges; (e) getting outside the box to think outside the box (while airplanes are long-lived, electronics are short-lived); (f) benchmarking; (g) maintaining day-to-day business despite change chaos; (h) focusing on the customer; (i) being decisive; (j) creating one culture; (k) recognizing that people are the real assets; and (l) communicating. Continental Airlines similarly was failing when subjected to rapid turnaround efforts; Greg Brenneman, president and COO (1998), reported that "In a turnaround situation you don't have the luxury of time to try out solutions. You just find the most leveraged plan of action and take it" (p. 9). The momentum of urgency favored success of the Go Forward Plan (p. 12).

Boeker (1997) examined (limited to 67 firms in the semiconductor industry in Silicon Valley) strategic change (defined operationally as annual percentage change in degree of product-market diversification) as a function of the combined effects of managerial characteristics and organizational performance (defined as revenue growth, with controls, accounting for 11% of variance in one model, for industry sales, firm size, firm age, time – a span of 14 years, public-private ownership). Statistical significance was limited (positively) to larger firms and public ownership. Poor performance (Miles, Type II scenario) makes strategic change more likely. CEO and top management team tenure and homogeneity of tenure make strategic change less likely. Success and tenure promote inertia and resistance to change. There was an interaction effect between performance and tenure. Poor performance signals need for strategic change (and/or CEO change), but the effect on strategic change is mediated by managerial characteristics. (There was not a statistically significant effect for CEO succession.) One would expect that earlier success would reinforce inertial strategic persistence in the face of radical environmental change, as found in the airline and trucking industries and a laboratory study by Audia et al. (2000).

Miles (1997, as cited by Joyce) argues that change across all dimensions of the organization is necessary (p. 34) but must be "deliberately orchestrated to maintain dynamic alignment" (p. 48), so that the role of leadership is not simply release of change but direction of change. Miles' theory of change intervention emphasizes generating "energy" (i.e. support) for transformation, developing a vision for the future (i.e. a purpose for transformation), aligning organization and culture with that vision, and then orchestrating (i.e. implementing) the transformation process. Given sufficient resources and employee readiness for change, successful transformations generate energy from vision and transformational leadership, but involve a systemic understanding and a comprehensive implementation system.

The sense of Miles' "typology" is that transformation may occur in successful firms (presumably out of choice to maintain success) and deteriorating firms (presumably out of necessity). Navistar and Levi Strauss represent change failures in the latter scenario. One may possibly disaggregate the successful firm scenario into explosive growth, steady (i.e. low-rate-of-change) growth, and stagnation conditions. Explosive growth involves continuous but likely extreme change by its nature. The problem becomes keeping up with and sustaining growth. (AES represents this situation.) Steady growth involves continuous but incremental change. Motorola represents this situation, once change was deliberately undertaken. Stagnation involves little change and management intervention or rebellion from below is needed. GE, AlliedSignal, and PerkinElmer represent this situation. Welch's rationale was always that the future would compel change, better undertaken immediately. Mergers and acquisitions may or may not dictate full integration. J&J tends to leave its operating companies alone, for example. But acquisition-specialist firms like Newell Rubbermaid (Gordon, 1999) and Emerson Electric (Knight, 1992) tend to remake acquisitions for the practical business purpose of improving their profitability through what amounts to business process reengineering and new management drawn from the new parent firm. Miles also draws attention to leadership development as a change management scenario (cf. Siebert et al., 1995). One variant is bringing in new leadership from the outside (as occurred at AlliedSignal and PerkinElmer); another variant is handpicking a successor from outside the top ranks (as occurred with Welch's elevation at GE).

CHANGE MANAGEMENT COMPETENCIES

Prahalad and Hamel (1991) introduced the now popular notion of core competence of the corporation. (They thought in terms of a small set, say four or five, of competencies at the core of a firm.) Competencies are specialized and economically valuable skills, constituting collective learning. The Prahalad and Hamel argument is that firms should invest in competencies that make growth possible. A competency, definitionally, (a) provides potential access to a wide variety of markets; (b) makes a significant contribution to perceived customer benefits of end products; and (c) is difficult for competitors to imitate. This chapter applies the basic notion to change management competencies. However, it must be noted that core competency theory has been criticized. "While much has been written on what it is, there is little information on how to apply the concept" (Javidan, 1998, p. 60). Coyne et al. (1997) hold that the tangible impact on corporate performance has been mixed (at best). Corporate competence has been characterized as a myth in practice, resulting in frustration and bewilderment among managers attempting to apply competency theory (Turner, 1997).

Clemmer (1996) cautioned that "change management" is an oxymoron: "A dubious consulting industry and 'profession' has developed, claiming to provide 'change management' services." His view holds that "Change can't be managed" although it can be "ignored, resisted, responded to, capitalized on, and created." Clemmer emphasizes instead personal improvement as the relevant change management process.

The basic conceptual approach for identifying, developing, and applying change management competencies is sketched in Fig. 2 as a set of five key and interacting dimensions (cf. Smith's, 1996, 10 principles). The figure relates the approach to the McKinsey 7-S™ framework (see Higgins, 1995, 1996, discussed

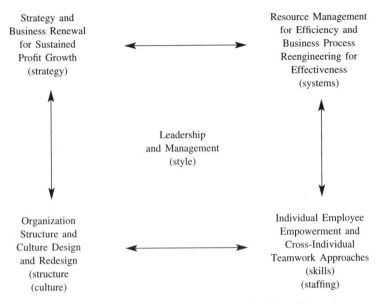

Fig. 2. Change Management Competencies in Relationship to the McKinsey 7-S™ Model (shown parenthetically).

shortly). The labels are in the nature of broad rubrics: each dimension is likely a complex of competencies, which are bundled together here as closely linked in practice. Leadership lies at the center of the model. The other four key change management competencies, in addition to leadership, are: sound strategy and business renewal for sustained profit growth; organization structure and culture design and redesign; resource management for efficiency (including both acquisition and allocation) and business process reengineering for effectiveness in functional operations; individual employee empowerment and cross-individual teamwork building. A critical problem in effective change management is understanding that the five competencies (or certainly some set of competencies) likely work together in success cases, and do not come together in failure cases (whether one or more necessary competencies are missing). At the present state of knowledge, we must accept that the change management competencies are necessary but not necessarily sufficient to successful change programs.

Quinn (Loren, 1998) urges that core competencies are a matter of managing intellect (i.e. talent) through aligning corporate and individual goals. He also argues that innovation limits the usefulness of teams, because innovation in complex situations is necessarily turning to voluntary cooperation, often accomplished virtually, among specialists. Amabile (1998) points out that change may interfere with creativity, while radical change may be needed in some circumstances. In her view, creativity (which was more often stifled than stimulated), involving expertise, motivation, and creative-thinking skills, is a function of challenge, freedom, resources, work group features, encouragement, and support. Higgins (1995) views innovation (strongly linked to profitability, Higgins, 1996), as *the* core competence accomplished through an "Innovation Equation" in which Creativity + Organizational Culture = Innovation. Creativity must occur in the right culture. Higgins provides 49 characteristics of innovative organizations: 7 in each of the McKinsey 7-S™ model dimensions (strategy, structure, systems, skills, staffing, style, superordinate goals = culture). However, Pavitt and Patel (cited by Rheem, 1995) question whether there are such things as core competencies with respect to technology (as at Motorola).

Bartlett and Ghoshal (1994; Ghoshal & Bartlett, 1995; Bartlett & Ghoshal, 1995) may be read, reasonably enough, as a criticism of some elements of Fig. 2. They view organizational transformation in terms of changing the role of top management to move beyond strategy to purpose, beyond structure to processes, and beyond systems to people (cf. Conference Board, 2000). And Fig. 2 is admittedly somewhat traditionalist in this regard. Their fundamental approach, however, is to release human energy (cf. Miles, 1997). The author believes that Fig. 2 is somewhat richer than its surface appearance, so that purpose can be married to strategy and renewal, that the organizational dimension is explicitly broader than structure (while placing processes in a different location), and that the important role of people is recognized (both as leaders and employees). The dimensions can be relabeled, perhaps more effectively. But Barlett and Ghoshal emphasize top management, and leadership is at the center of Fig. 2.

"The problem for most executives is that managing change is unlike any other managerial task they have ever confronted" (Duck, 1993, p. 109). Leadership need not be hierarchical, in the sense of the chief executive officer or top management team. On the contrary, the revolution at IBM was evidently led from below (Hamel, 2000a, b, c, d); and empowered teams or networked organizations reflect distributed leadership. While there has been an emphasis on consensus building in change management, Franco Bernabè at Eni (Italy, some 135,000 employees and 335 companies operating in 84 countries) states the case for making executive decisions alone in a transformational situation against intense resistance to change (Hill & Wetlaufer, 1998).

There is a distinction between transformational and transactional leadership (Jung & Avolio, 1999; Pawar & Eastman, 1997, review the transformational literature in detail). Transformational leadership is associated with vision and charisma, in the context of organizational change. (Transactional leadership is focused on negotiating or exchange with followers.) Pawar and Eastman postulate that change is possible, results from various mechanisms of which transformational leadership is important, such leadership functioning through articulation and followers' acceptance of leaders' vision and creation of congruence between followers' self-interests and this vision. There must be a correspondence between transformational leadership processes and transformational leaders' capabilities; the authors find this correspondence unaddressed in the literature. (They also argue that transforming leaders can either confront or harness the existing organizational context.)

In a study of 347 students of different cultural backgrounds (153 Asians, 194 Caucasians, mostly college juniors and seniors, mostly business majors) separated into experimental brainstorming tasks (to generate recommendations to support the business school's application for re-accreditation within a fixed time period) handled by individuals (50%) or groups (50%), Jung and Avolio tested transformational and transactional leadership styles against task conditions. They found that (within groups) collectivists generated more ideas with a transformational leader, while individualists generated more ideas with a transactional leader. While group performance was generally higher than that of individuals working alone, collectivists generated more ideas that required fundamental organizational changes when working alone.

Pasternack and Viscio (1998, p. 264), of Booz-Allen & Hamilton Strategic Leadership Practice, give a specific approach for successful transformation, in which leaders (a) create vision and values; (b) create conditions of empowerment; and (c) and overcome resistance to change – so as to create disciples (i.e. followers) who in turn (d) reward appropriate behavior (e.g. initiative and responsibility), (e) build capabilities, and (f) encourage others to lead change – so as to achieve continual organizational renewal. In the authors' view (p. 272), vision shapes integration of content, process, and people to achieve successful transformation.

Goss et al. (1993) observed that after the 1980s, CEOs have knowledge of cross-functional teaming, TQM, BPR, and stretch goals (Thompson et al., 1997, report the term may have been coined by Welch) implemented to reduce costs and improve performance. They argue, however, that this knowledge is of incremental change management, and that CEOs lack knowledge of, and motivation or courage for, fundamental reinvention. The difference lies between becoming better and becoming different: they cite British Airways, Europcar, and Häagen-Dazs as instances of fundamental change in "context" that as a result alters culture, improves performance dimensions, and creates the ability to weather future changes in the business environment. (They characterize Ford Motor as a firm that almost succeeded in reinvention.)

This author adheres to the view that strategy will remain important, even if changed in content and process. (As Porter, 1996a, points out, Japanese companies may not use strategy.) Galpin (1996; see Karl, 1996) directs attention to both the strategic and grassroots levels in change management handled through team process. At the strategic level, senior management creates the improvement of team infrastructure, creates the open two-way communications strategy (i.e. a complete information process), integrates the change process into the organizational culture, and cultivates key leadership attributes throughout the organization. Galpin recommends an organizationally representative steering committee and an integration team (whose leader is on the steering committee) comprised of the leaders of the various improvement teams. At the grassroots level, managers design specific change goals and progress measurement systems, provide feedback and coaching, and provide generous rewards and recognition.

Strategic thinking may *not* be a "core managerial competence at most companies" because it is rarely practiced (Christensen, 1997). There is increasing emphasis on strategy decentralization (Whitney, 1996) and participative planning (Gendron, 1998). Porter (1996b, p. 61) characterizes current views on operational effectiveness – a term embracing many of the dimensions of change management – as "dangerous half-truths" that "are leading more and more companies down the path of mutually destructive competition." Operational effectiveness (when accomplished) is necessary but not sufficient to constitute strategy for sustainable competitive advantage. (Schaffer & Thomson, 1992, state that in a 1991 survey of over 300 electronics firms by the American Electronics Association 73% reported a TQM program; but only 63% of those programs had improved quality defects by as much as 10%). Andrew Grove, CEO of Intel (Fuffer, 1999), views fundamental change in business strategy as arising from "strategic inflection points" due to major changes in competitive environment (new technologies, regulations, demand, and so on).

The literature on strategic change (understood as alignment with external environment) remains divided between content and process schools of thought not well integrated (Rajagopalan & Spreitzer, 1997). The former examines statistically the antecedents and consequences of change in samples; the latter examines, using qualitative case studies, the role of managers in change situations. The statistical findings are characterized as contradictory: (a) firm size is positive (a source of resource flexibility) or negative (a source of inertia); (b) changes in environmental conditions lead to firm change or lead to firm inertia (presumably mediated by managers); (c) strategic change leads to improved performance or leads to firm failure. (The authors attempt a multi-lens integrative framework drawing on rational, learning, and cognitive interpretations. Fundamentally, they apprehend pressures for change outweighing inertial dampening forces; and difficulties in relating variations in outcomes to antecedent changes in strategic content, managerial actions, and both organizational and environmental conditions.) A sense of the problem is conveyed below in an "equation" form postulating that outcomes are some function (with a constant term "a") of specific changes given conditions (themselves changing) treated as controls and subject (statistically) to errors. (a, b, c, and errors must account for 100% of variance in outcomes.) The more multi-dimensional the outcomes, changes, conditions, and errors, the more difficult the statistical analysis will be. Unanticipated consequences must be expected (McKinley & Scherer, 2000).

$$\text{Outcomes} = a + b \text{ Changes} + c \text{ Conditions} + \text{errors}$$

Disaggregation of a complex set of causal factors is arguably difficult. Dennis Bakke (CEO, AES) attributes the firm's success (started in 1991, and recently operating 90 electricity plants in 13 countries with 40,000 employees arranged as empowered teams) to a holistic explanation: "It has to do with our structure and our practices – hiring, compensation, information flow, and so on. They're like an ecosystem. Everything about how we organize gives people the power and the responsibility to make important decisions, to engage with their work as business people, not as cogs in a machine" (Wetlaufer, 1999b, p. 112).

Organization design or redesign is an implementation of strategy, in change management situations (see Howard, 1992, on Paul Allaire's approach to organizational architecture at Xerox). The McKinsey 7-S™ framework gives an indication of the possible complexity of dealing with multiple, interacting dimensions of what constitutes an "organization." Organization design now focuses heavily on team approaches (including virtual teaming) and inter-organizational networking, and is becoming in a profound sense relatively fluid. The key issue in organization design is how to foster and reward collaboration among individuals, units, and organizations.

Resource management – both acquisition and allocation – is where concrete decisions are crafted through determinations of who gets what. Business process reengineering (BPR) can be viewed as directed at resource management issues. Business process reengineering has moved from massive companywide efforts to local actions in departments or units (Harvard Management Update, 2000). "Reengineering is made necessary by changes in technology and markets . . . . What seems more common now is a kind of do-it-yourself reengineering . . . residing in a single department or business unit." Hill & Collins (1999) comment:

From the perspective of practising managers, especially those in small and medium-sized enterprises (SMEs) which proliferate in Northern Ireland, the literature on BPR and TQM is not particularly helpful, as it very often raises more questions than it answers. Considerable debate surrounds the very nature of BPR . . .; the circumstances in which the use of BPR is most appropriate . . .; the most effective mode of implementation . . .; the role of IT . . .; and what, if anything, BPR is likely to achieve . . . Another interesting aspect of the literature concerns the differences between TQM and BPR, and whether or not they may be used to complement one another.

Empowerment is both the decentralization of organizational structure and resource management, within strategic guidelines, and the preparation of individuals and teams to cope with their business responsibilities within such contexts. Beer et al. (1990) attributed failure of change programs to top-down companywide change efforts, whereas successful programs began locally with the line management. "Successful change efforts focus on the work itself, not on abstractions like 'participation' or 'culture' " (p. 5). George Tooker, CEO of Motorola (between Bob Galvin and his son Chris Galvin) stated (p. 9): "Empowerment is a powerful strategy for improving business performance. But I don't think you can mandate empowerment. Wouldn't that be an oxymoron?"

SOFT CHANGE MANAGEMENT

"While the notion of radical change is intuitively appealing to fix organizational woes, it has not always met with the degree of success originally claimed by its many proponents" (Grover, 1999, p. 37). Much of the problem lies in lack of knowledge and skills (i.e. competencies) and in failing to deal appropriately with realities of human motivation and reaction.

Kotter (1995, 1996) defines a sequential model of successful transformation involving eight steps: (a) sense of urgency; (b) powerful guiding coalition; (c) clear, compelling vision; (d) communication of that vision; (e) empowerment to act on the vision; (f) obtaining short-term wins; (g) consolidating those wins as a basis for further change; (h) institutionalizing new approaches. Beer & Nohria (2000a, b) argue that change managers must integrate short-term economic value creation (i.e. material incentives to stakeholders) and investment in long-term capabilities (i.e. building up the corporate culture). The authors compare the two poles along six dimensions of change: (a) goals; (b) leadership; (c) focus (hard structure and systems vs. soft culture); (d) process; (e) reward system; (f) use of consultants (analysis vs. support). Integration involves: (a) embracing value-capability paradox; (b) setting direction top-down while engaging employees; (c) focusing simultaneously on hard-soft elements; (d) planning for spontaneity; (e) using incentives to reinforce rather than drive change; (f) using consultants as expert resources to empower employees.

In Fig. 2 above, one may roughly group the top panels (strategy and resource management) as constituting the "hard" aspects of change management, and group the lower panels (organization design and empowerment) as the "soft" aspects (cf. Galpin, 1996). We know more about "hard" change than "soft" change: the latter deals with human behavior in work settings. Reactions to change in existing organizations vary across a continuum defined by the following possibilities: (a) commitment; (b) grudging compliance; (c) tacit resistance; (d) open defiance; and (e) exit. Change management efforts typically focus on compelling employees to choose between commitment and exit, while neglecting the intervening possibilities for employee reactions. Reichers et al. (1997) distinguish among employee cynicism, skepticism, and resistance. Skepticism doubts success but hopes for it, and hence skeptics will not resist change; they can be recruited to change. Cynicism is a loss of faith in change leaders and responds to a history of non-successful change efforts (see Rothstein et al., 1995); hence cynics will fail to support change and may additionally lose organizational commitment and/or work motivation. Cynicism may result as well from lack of adequate information and personal predisposition (cf. Morrison & Milliken, 2000).

Resistance to change (cf. Piderit, 2000; Strebel, 1996) reflects some combination of self-interest (who loses from change), misunderstanding of change and its benefits, and personal limited tolerance of change; ambivalence may need to be added to this typology (Piderit, 2000). (The authors' analysis requires either that the change be objectively necessary or beneficial, or at least within the formal authority of leadership without respect to objective necessity. Otherwise, cynics, skeptics, and resisters might be right, if not strategically rational in conduct with respect to survival of change. Lord, 1990, reports that a Right Associates annual survey of the financial services industry found that downsizing had a positive financial effect but a negative effect on morale of remaining employees, that could be minimized through "effective severance policy.")

A 1993 survey (Anonymous, 1994) was made of 160 U.S. and European organizations (private and public sector) undertaking some form of change management initiative (at least being a major change), two-thirds of the respondents being human resource managers (the remainder from other functions). Nearly 60% had begun the initiative in 1989 or later; only 20% before 1986. Over 50% reported strong progress in stock value, product-service quality, productivity, employees' customer awareness, and employees' quality awareness. In direct contrast, only one-third reported marked progress in enabling employee adaptability or winning employee commitment; 15–20% reported low levels of progress in these dimensions. The firms also reported difficulties with implementing changes in vision, values, and culture.

Goss et al. (1993) focus attention in reinvention on the employees, a critical mass of whom must be the key stakeholders in change. It is this critical mass of employees that must uncover the true competitive situation in an organizational audit, create urgency in discussing that situation (which is typically subjected to a code of silence as undiscussable), harness conflict to jump-start the creative process, and then engineer organizational breakdowns revealing of weak points (as in Nordstrom's use of extraordinary customer service practice to stress its business processes).

Halal (1998) argues (see Beam, 1998) that 21st century organizations will operate on three principles (or assumptions) fundamentally different from those found today:

(1) entrepreneurial freedom will succeed hierarchical control – because increasing complexity will lead to the decline of hierarchy;
(2) cooperation (externally as well as internally) will succeed conflict (including market competition) – because such cooperation will prove more efficient; and
(3) knowledge and spirit will succeed wealth as measures of performance – because knowledge (an inexhaustible resource) increases when shared (presumably resulting in observable productivity gains).

Fig. 3 characterizes the conventional vertical organization (whether functionally or divisionally subdivided) as involving two key problems that must be addressed simultaneously in change management: command-and-control hierarchy degrading individual initiative and responsibility; and organizational-silo independence degrading inter-unit cooperation. This conventional vertical organization is commonly depicted as a pyramid (shown in dotted outline in Fig. 3). The prediction here is that "hierarchy" – in the sense of some final authority – is unlikely to disappear any time soon. The general goal in recent change management initiatives is to configure the optimal conditions for empowered employees – defined in the center of Fig. 3 as some best-practice combination of strategic and resource guidance in relationship to individual initiative and responsibility vertically, and of conflict vs. autonomy, resulting in both collaboration and innovation. These relationships are pictured as likely "paradoxes" to be resolved by tailoring in each firm or situation. It is not clear that empowered employees must be deployed in teams. Communication, incentives, knowledge, and motivation are the basic elements of individual and team action. Command-and-control will be increasingly replaced by strategic and resource guidance (hierarchy does not fully disappear with empowerment but rather changes), involving a two-way interaction with subordinate initiative

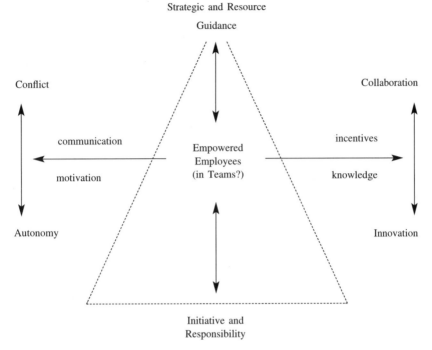

Strategic and Resource

Guidance

Conflict

Collaboration

communication

incentives

Empowered
Employees
(in Teams?)

motivation

knowledge

Autonomy

Innovation

Initiative and
Responsibility

Fig. 3.   The Major Concerns In "Soft" Change Management.

and responsibility; internal conflict, associated with silo autonomy, will be increasingly replaced by inter-unit collaboration (bearing in mind that positive conflict may be a necessary attribute of collaboration and autonomy a necessary check to groupthink).

Bossidy (AlliedSignal) and Summe (PerkinElmer) are explicit in emphasizing people selection over strategy (cf. Conference Board, 2000). Individual initiative and responsibility is fundamentally the problem of compensation and motivation (cf. Dessler, 1999; Morrison & Phelps, 1999). Failure to carry out what is known about improving performance, for example, has been characterized as a paradox (Cohen, 1998). In the change management literature, the problem is captured as resistance to change. A reading of this literature suggests that there are "No Easy Roads to Employee Involvement" (Peck, 1998). Peck (reporting research in the U.K. by Parker, Wall & Jackson, of the University of Sheffield) draws the interesting finding that getting employees to adopt a sense of ownership requires that empowered, self-managed teams must receive the autonomy "to learn and practice strategic behaviors." Dessler (1999, p. 58) offers that in "today's team-based, empowered, and technology-dependent organizations" motivation involves mission communication, organizational justice guarantees, a sense of community, employee development support, and "placing people first."

CONCLUSION

The limited purpose of this chapter has been to examine what is known about change management competencies as directed at improving collaborative work systems (both within and between organizations). Collaboration is apprehended as encompassing individual employee empowerment, inter-organizational networking, and teamwork (both within and across organizations). For this purpose, the desirability of collaboration (in some circumstances) is posited, so that attention can be focused on relevant change management competencies for obtaining greater collaboration. The chapter identifies and categorizes some key revealing cases of experience at companies with both successful and failed change approaches. Two fundamentally different models of change can be illustrated at Motorola (the steady investment approach) and General Electric (the burning platform approach). It is suggested that change management competencies will center on leadership, strategy and business renewal, process reengineering, organizational design (including both structure and culture), and empowerment. Attention is drawn to soft management skills, those directed at dealing with people. Soft management involves balancing of top-down strategic and resource guidance with individual initiative and responsibility on the one hand, and the balancing of conflict and autonomy into collaboration. Empowerment lies at the center of the problem where these two key balancing issues intersect.

REFERENCES

Abrahamson, E. (2000). Change without pain. *Harvard Business Review, 78*, 75–79.

Aguilar, F. S., & Bambri, A. (1986a). *Johnson & Johnson (A): Philosophy and culture*. Harvard Business School Case No. 9-384-053.

Aguilar, F. S., & Bambri, A. (1986b). *Johnson & Johnson (B): Hospital Services*. Harvard Business School Case No. 9-384-054.

Amabile, T. M. (1998). How to kill creativity. *Harvard Business Review, 76*, 76–87.

Anonymous. (1994). Change management fails to improve commitment or adaptability. *Industrial Relations Review & Report No. 567* (September), 3–4.

Applegate, L. M., & Cash, J. I. (1989, rev. 1991). *GE Canada: Designing a new organization*. Harvard Business School Case No. 9-189-138.

Argyris, C. (1998). Empowerment: The emperor's new clothes. *Harvard Business Review, 76,* 98–105.

Audia, P. G., Locke, E. A., & Smith, K. G. (2000). The paradox of success: An archival and a laboratory study of strategic persistence following radical environmental change. *Academy of Management Journal, 43,* 837–853.

Augustine, N. R. (1997). Reshaping an industry: Lockheed Martin's survival story. *Harvard Business Review, 75,* 83–94.

Baldwin, T. T., Danielson, C., & Wiggenhorn, W. (1997). The evolution of learning strategies in organizations: From employee development to business redefinition. *Academy of Management Executive, 11,* 47–58.

Bartlett, C. A., & Ghoshal, S. (1994). Changing the role of top management: Beyond strategy to purpose. *Harvard Business Review, 72,* 79–88.

Bartlett, C. A., & Ghoshal, S. (1995). Changing the role of top management: Beyond systems to people. *Harvard Business Review, 73,* 132–142.

Beam, H. H. (1998). Book review of Halal. *Academy of Management Executive, 12,* 87–88.

Beer, M., Eisenstat, R. A., & Spector, B. (1990). Why change programs don't produce change. *Harvard Business Review, 68,* 158–166.

Beer, M., & Nohria, N. (Eds) (2000). *Breaking the code of change.* Boston, MA: Harvard Business School Press.

Beer, M., & Nohria, N. (2000). Cracking the code of change. *Harvard Business Review, 78,* 133–141.

Boeker, W. (1997). Strategic change: The influence of managerial characteristics and organizational growth. *Academy of Management Journal, 40,* 152–170.

Borucki, C., & Barnett, C. K. (1990). Restructuring for self-renewal: Navistar International Corporation. *Academy of Management Executive, 4,* 36–49.

Brenneman, G. (1998). Right away and all at once: How we saved Continental [Airlines]. *Harvard Business Review, 76,* 162–179.

Byrne, H. S. (1988). They almost bought the farm: But Navistar and Varity are on the road to recovery. *Barron's, 68,* 6–7, 32–34.

Campbell, A., & Alexander, M. (1997). What's wrong with strategy? *Harvard Business Review, 75,* 42–51.

Carey, T. A. (1996). Book review of Handy (1996). *Academy of Management Executive, 10,* 75.

Chandler, A. D., Hagstrom, P., & Solvell, O. (Eds) (1998). *The dynamic firm: The role of technology, strategy, organization, and regions.* Oxford, U.K.: Oxford University Press.

Chilton, K. W. (1993). *The double-edged sword of administrative heritage: The case of Lincoln Electric.* St. Louis, MO: Washington University, Center for the Study of American Business (July).

Christensen, C. M. (1997). Making strategy: Learning by doing. *Harvard Business Review, 75,* 141–156.

Clemmer, J. (1996). "Change management" is an oxymoron. *Cost & Management, 70,* 6.

Cohen, H. B. (1998). The performance paradox. *Academy of Management Executive, 12,* 30–40.

Colby, D. (1996). The five great management myths. *Business Quarterly, 61,* 93–95 (Canada).

The Conference Board (2000). *Valuing people in the change process.* New York: Report No. 1265.

Cowley, M., & Domb, E. (1997). *Beyond strategic vision: Effective corporate action with Hoshin planning.* Boston, MA: Butterworth-Heinemann.

Coyne, K. P., Hall, S., & Clifford, P. G. (1997). Is your core competence a mirage? *McKinsey Quarterly* (1), 40–54.

D'Aveni, R. (1994). *Hyper-competition.* New York: Free Press.

Dessler, G. (1999). How to earn your employees' commitment. *Academy of Management Executive*, *13*, 58–67.

Drucker, P. F. (1999). *Management challenges for the 21st century.* New York: HarperBusiness.

Duck, J. D. (1993). Managing change: The art of balancing. *Harvard Business Review*, *71*, 109–118.

Duncan, W. J. (1989). Organizational culture: "Getting a fix" on an elusive concept. *Academy of Management Executive*, *3*, 229–236.

Evink, J. (1999). Book review of Flamholtz & Randle (1998). *Academy of Management Executive*, *13*, 114–115.

Farias, G., & Johnson, H. (Commentary). Worren, N., Ruddle, K., & Moore, K. (Response) (2000). Organizational development and change management: Setting the record straight; Response to Farias and Johnson's commentary. *Journal of Applied Behavioral Science*, *36*, 376–381. (See Worren et al., 1999.)

Fast, N. (1975, rev. 1983). *The Lincoln Electric Company.* Harvard Business School Case No. 9-376-028.

Flamholtz, E. G., & Randle, Y. (1998). *Changing the game: Organizational transformations of the first, second, and third kinds.* New York: Oxford University Press. See Evink (1999).

Forrester, R. (2000). Empowerment: Rejuvenating a potent idea. *Academy of Management Executive*, *14*, 67–80.

Fuffer, S. M. (Ed.) (1999). Global executive: Intel's Andrew Grove on competitiveness. *Academy of Management Executive*, *13*, 15–24.

Galagan, P. A. (1992). The truth about empowerment, according to D. Quinn Mills [Harvard Business School]. *Training & Development*, *46*, 31–32.

Galpin, T. J. (1996). *The human side of change: A practical guide to organization redesign.* San Francisco, CA: Jossey-Bass. See Karl (1996).

Garvin, D. A. (1993). Building a learning organization. *Harvard Business Review*, *71*, 78–91.

Gendron, M. (1998). Strategic planning: Why it's not just for senior managers anymore. *Harvard Management Update*.

Gersick, C. (1991). Revolutionary change theories: A multilevel exploration of the punctuated equilibrium paradigm. *Academy of Management Review*, *16*, 10–36.

Ghoshal, S., & Bartlett, C. A. (1995). Changing the role of top management: Beyond structure to processes. *Harvard Business Review*, *93*, 86–96.

Gilson, S. C., & Cott, J. (1994). *Navistar International.* Harvard Business School Case No. 9-295-030.

Goddard, J. (1997). The architecture of core competence. *Business Strategy Review*, *8*, 43–52.

Goffe, R., & Jones, G. (1996). What holds the modern company together? *Harvard Business Review*, *74*, 133–148.

Gogan, J. L., Zuboff, S., & Schuck, G. (1994a). *Motorola Corp.: The view from the CEO office.* Harvard Business School Case No. 9-494-140.

Gogan, J. L., Zuboff, S., Schuck, G., & Handel, M. J. (1994b). *Motorola: Institutionalizing corporate initiatives.* Harvard Business School Case No. 9-494-139.

Gordon, E. J. (1999). *Newell Company: Corporate strategy.* Harvard Business School Case No. 9-799-139.

Goss, T., Pascale, R., & Athos, A. (1993). The reinvention roller coaster: Risking the present for a powerful future. *Harvard Business Review*, *71*, 97–109.

Glynn, M. A., Barr, P. S., & Davin, M. T. (2000). Pluralism and the problem of variety. *Academy of Management Review*, *25*, 726–734.

Grover, V. (1999). From business reengineering to business process change management: A longitudinal study of trends and practices. *IEEE Transactions on Engineering Management*, *46*, 36–46.

Halal, W. E. (Ed.) (1998). *The infinite resource: Creating and leading the knowledge enterprise.* San Francisco, CA: Jossey-Bass. (See Beamm, 1998.)

Hamel, G. (2000a). *Leading the revolution.* Boston, MA: Harvard Business School Press.

Hamel, G. (2000). Reinvent your company. *Fortune, 141,* 98–118.

Hamel, G. (2000b). Waking up IBM: How a gang of unlikely rebels transformed Big Blue. *Harvard Business Review, 78,* 137–141.

Hamel, G. (2000). Why . . . it's better to question answers than answer questions. *Across the Board, 37,* 42–46.

Hamermesh, R. G., & Christiansen, E. T. (1980). *International Harvester (A).* Harvard Business School Case No. 9-381-052.

Hamilton, J. (1985). Levi Strauss wants to be a family affair again. *Business Week No. 2905 (Industrial/Technology Edition),* 28–29.

Handy, C. (1989). *The age of unreason.* Boston, MA: Harvard Business School Press.

Handy, C. (1994). *The age of paradox.* Boston, MA: Harvard Business School Press.

Handy, C. (1996). *Beyond certainty: The changing worlds of organizations.* Boston, MA: Harvard Business School Press. (See Carey, 1996.)

Hardy, C., & Leiba-O'Sullivan, S. (1998). The power behind empowerment: Implications for research and practice. *Human Relations, 51,* 451–483.

Harvard Management Update (2000). How to reengineer your unit.

Havelock, R. G., with Zlotolow, S. (1995) *The change agent's guide.* (2nd ed.). Englewood Cliffs, NJ: Educational Technology Publications (1973).

Heimbouch, H. (2000). Racing for growth: An interview with PerkinElmer's Greg Summe. *Harvard Business Review, 78,* 148–154.

Helyar, J. (1998). Solo flight: A Jack Welch disciple finds the GE mystique only takes you so far – "Gandhian resistance" greets Mr. Weber as he directs an Ohio hydraulics firm; got it. Next slide, please. *Wall Street Journal* (August 10), A1, A8.

Hendershot, A. (1996). How we brought teamwork to marketing [AlliedSignal Aerospace]. *Wall Street Journal* (August 26).

Herrenkohl, R. C., Judson, G. T., & Heffner, J. A. (1999). Defining and measuring employee empowerment. *Journal of Applied Behavioral Science, 35,* 373–389.

Higgins, J. M. (1995). Innovation: The core competence. *Planning Review, 23,* 32–35.

Higgins, J. M. (1996). Achieving the core competence – It's as easy as 1, 2, 3, . . ., 47, 48, 49. *Business Horizons, 39,* 27–32.

Hill, F. M., & Collins, L. K. (1999). Total quality management and business process re-engineering: A study of incremental and radical approaches to change management at BTNI [British Telecom Northern Ireland]. *Total Quality Management, 10,* 10–45.

Hill, L., & Wetlaufer, S. (1998). Leadership when there is no one to ask: An interview with Eni's Franco Bernabè. *Harvard Business Review, 76,* 81–94.

Howard. R. (1990). Values make the company: An interview with Robert Haas. *Harvard Business Review, 68,* 132–144.

Howard, R. (1992). The CEO as organizational architect: An interview with Xerox's Paul Allaire. *Harvard Business Review, 70,* 107–121.

Javidan, M. (1998). Core competence: What does it mean in practice? *Long Range Planning, 31,* 60–71.

Joyce, W. F. (1998). Book review of Miles (1997). *Academy of Management Review, 23,* 625–627.

Jung, D. I., & Avolio, B. J. (1999). Effects of leadership style and followers' cultural orientation on performance in group and individual task conditions. *Academy of Management Journal, 42,* 208–218.

Kanter, R. M. (1983). *The change masters: Innovations for productivity in the American corporation.* New York: Simon & Schuster.

Kanter, R. M. (1991). Championing change: An interview with Bell Atlantic's CEO Raymond Smith. *Harvard Business Review, 69*, 118–130.

Karl, K. A. (1996). Book review of Galpin (1996). *Academy of Management Executive, 10*, 68.

Katz, J. P. (1997). Book review of Tushman & O'Reilly (1997). *Academy of Management Executive, 11*, 125–126.

Katzenbach, J. R., & the RCL Team (1996). *Real change leaders: How you can create growth and high performance at your company.* New York: Times Business.

Kelly, E. P. (1998). Book review of J. Kurtzman (Ed.), *Thought leaders: Insights on the future of business* (San Francisco, CA: Jossey-Bass, 1998, 12 interviews). *Academy of Management Executive, 12*, 140–141.

Kilduff, M., & Dougherty, D. (2000). Change and development in a pluralistic world: The view from the classics. *Academy of Management Review, 25*, 777–782.

√ Kirkman, B. L., & Rosen, B. (1999). Beyond self-management: Antecedents and consequences of team empowerment. *Academy of Management Journal, 42*, 58–74.

Knight, C. E. (1992). Emerson Electric: Consistent profits, consistently. *Harvard Business Review, 70*, 57–70.

Koberg, C. S., Boss, R. W., Senjem, J. C., & Goodman, E. A. (1999). Antecedents and outcomes of empowerment. *Group & Organization Management, 24*, 71–91.

Kotter, J. P. (1995). Leading change: Why transformation efforts fail. *Harvard Business Review, 73*, 59–67.

Kotter, J. P. (1996). *Leading change.* Boston, MA: Harvard Business School Press.

Labianca, G., Gray, B., & Brass, D. J. (2000). A grounded model of organizational schema change during empowerment. *Organization Science, 11*, 235–257.

Leana, C. R., & Barry, B. (2000). Stability and change as simultaneous experiments in organizational life. *Academy of Management Review, 25*, 753–759.

Lewis, M. W. (2000). Exploring paradox: Toward a more comprehensive guide. *Academy of Management Review, 25*, 760–776.

Lord, V. (1990). An effective severance policy is essential to change management. *Bank Management, 66*, 21–22.

Loren, G. (1998). Organizing around intellect: An interview with James Brian Quinn. *Harvard Management Update.*

Lichtenstein, B. M. (1995). Evolution or transformation: A critique and alternative to punctuated equilibrium. *Academy of Management Best Papers Proceedings*, 291–295.

Lucas, J. R. (1998). *Balance of power: Authority or empowerment? How you can get the best of both in the "independent" organization.* New York: AMACOM.

Lyneham-Brown, D. (1997). Making change the culture – the National Initiative in Change Management [U.K.]. *Management Services, 41*, 38–41.

MacIssac, L. A. (1989). *Navistar: Managing change.* Harvard Business School Case No. 9-490-003.

Malone, T. W. (1997). Is 'empowerment' just a fad? Control, decision-making, and information technology. *Sloan Management Review, 38*, 23–35.

Malone, T. W., & Laubacher, R. J. (1998). The dawn of the e-lance economy. *Harvard Business Review, 77*, 145–152.

Maruca, R. F. (1999). Redesigning business: A conversation with Jay Walker. *Harvard Business Review, 77*, 19–21.

McKinley, W., & Scherer, A. G. (2000). Some unanticipated consequences of organizational restructuring. *Academy of Management Review, 25*, 735–752.

Micklethwait, J., & Wooldridge, A. (1996) *The witch doctors: Making sense of the management gurus*. New York: Times Books.

Miles, R. H. (1997). *Leading corporate transformation: A blueprint for business renewal*. San Francisco, CA: Jossey-Bass. (See Joyce, 1998.)

Morrison, E. W., & Milliken, F. J. (2000). Organizational silence: A barrier to change and development in a pluralistic world. *Academy of Management Review, 25*, 706–725.

Morrison, E. W., & Phelps, C. C. (1999). Taking charge at work: Extra-role efforts to initiate workplace change. *Academy of Management Journal, 42*, 403–419.

Nooteboom, B. (1989). Paradox, identity and change in management. *Human Systems Management, 8*, 291–300.

O'Connell, J. (1998). *Lincoln Electric: Venturing abroad*. Harvard Business School Case No. 9-398-095.

√ Pascale, R., Millemann, M., & Gioja, L. (1997). Changing the way we change. *Harvard Business Review, 75*, 126–139.

Pasternack, B. A., & Viscio, A. J. (1998). *The centerless corporation: A new model for transforming your organization for growth and prosperity*. New York: Simon & Schuster.

Pawar, B. S., & Eastman, K. K. (1997). The nature and implications of contextual influences on transformational leadership: A conceptual examination. *Academy of Management Review, 22*, 80–109.

Peck, S. R. (1998). No easy roads to employee involvement. *Academy of Management Executive, 12*, 83–84.

Piderit, S. K. (2000). Rethinking resistance and recognizing ambivalence: A multidimensional view of attitudes toward an organizational change. *Academy of Management Review, 25*, 783–794.

Porter, M. E. (1996a). Japanese companies rarely have strategies. *Harvard Business Review, 74*, 63.

Porter, M. E. (1996b). What is strategy? *Harvard Business Review, 74*, 61–78.

Prahalad, C. K., & Hamel, G. (1990). The core competence of the corporation. *Harvard Business Review, 68*, 79–91.

Price Waterhouse Change Integration Team (1995). *Better change: Best practices for transforming your organization*. Burr Ridge, IL: Irwin.

Price Waterhouse Change Integration Team (1996). *The paradox principles: How high-performance companies manage chaos, complexity, and contradiction to achieve superior results*. Chicago, IL: Irwin Professional. (See Vroman, 1996.)

Rajagopalan, N., & Spreitzer, G. M. (1997). Toward a theory of strategic change: A multi-lens perspective and integrative framework. *Academy of Management Review, 22*, 48–79.

Randolph, W. A. (2000). Re-thinking empowerment: Why is it so hard to achieve? *Organizational Dynamics, 29*, 94–107.

Reichers, A. E., Wanous, J. P., & Austin, J. T. (1997). Understanding and managing cynicism about organizational change. *Academy of Management Executive, 11*, 48–59.

Rheem, H. 1995. Technology: Core competence or diverse competencies? *Harvard Business Review, 73*, 11.

Romanelli, E., & Tushman, M. L. (1994). Organizational transformation as punctuated equilibrium: An empirical test. *Academy of Management Journal, 37*, 1141–1166.

Rose, R. L. (1996). Worst 10-year performer: Navistar International Corp. *Wall Street Journal* (February 29).

Rothstein, L. R. et al. (1995). The empowerment effort that came undone. *Harvard Business Review, 73*, 20–31.

Schaffer, R. H., & Thomson, H. A. (1992). Successful change programs begin with results. *Harvard Business Review, 70*, 80–89.

Schein, E. H. (1985, rev. 1992). *Organizational culture and leadership.* San Francisco, CA: Jossey-Bass.

Schein, E. H. (1999). *The corporate culture survival guide: Sense and nonsense about culture change.* San Francisco, CA: Jossey-Bass. See Spector (2000).

Schiller, Z. (1996). A model incentive plan gets caught in a vise: Lincoln Electric's remake forces a shift toward traditional pay. *Business Week* (January 22), 91–92.

Senge, P. (1990). *The fifth discipline.* New York: Doubleday.

Shapiro, E. (1997). Managing in the age of gurus. *Harvard Business Review, 75,* 142–148.

Sheff, D. (1996). Levi's changes everything: An inside account of the most dramatic change program in American business. *Fast Company No. 3,* 65–69, 72–74.

Siebert, K. W., Hall, D. T., & Kram, K. E. (1995). Strengthening the weak link in strategic executive development: Integrating individual development and global business strategy. *Human Resource Development, 34,* 549–567.

Smith, D. K. (1996). *Taking charge of change: 10 principles for managing people and performance.* Reading, MA: Addison-Wesley.

Spector, B. A. (2000). Book review of Schein (1999). *Academy of Management Executive, 14,* 156–157.

Stoddard, D. B., & Jarvenpaa, S. (1995). *Re-engineering* design *is radical; re-engineering* change *is not!* Harvard Business School Note No. 9-196-037 (July 18).

Stopper, W. G. (1998). Reengineering Levi Strauss & Co.: We met the enemy and it was us. *Human Resource Planning, 21,* 14–15.

Strebel, P. (1996). Why do employees resist change? *Harvard Business Review, 74,* 86–92.

Taylor, W. (1991). The logic of global business: An interview with ABB's Percy Barnevik. *Harvard Business Review, 69,* 90–105.

Thompson, K. R., Hochwarter, W. A., & Mathys, N. J. (1997). Stretch targets: What makes them effective? *Academy of Management Executive, 11,* 48–60.

Tichy, N. M., & Charan, R. (1989). Speed, simplicity, self-confidence: An interview with Jack Welch. *Harvard Business Review, 67,* 112–120.

Tichy, N. M., & Charan, R. (1995). The CEO as coach: An interview with AlliedSignal's Lawrence A. Bossidy. *Harvard Business Review, 73,* 69–78.

Turner, I. (1997). The myth of the core competence. *Manager Update, 8,* 1–12.

Tushman, M. L., & O'Reilly, C. A. (1997). *Winning through innovation.* Boston, MA: Harvard Business School Press. (See Katz, 1997.)

Uyterhoeven, H. E. R. (1996). *ABB Deutschland (A).* Harvard Business School Case No. 9-393-130.

Van de Ven, A., & Poole, M. S. (1995). Explaining development and change in organizations. *Academy of Management Review, 20,* 510–540.

Vroman, H. W. (1996). Book review of Price Waterhouse Change Integration Team (1996). *Academy of Management Executive, 10,* 71.

Wetlaufer, S. (1999a). Driving change: An interview with Ford Motor Company's Jacques Nasser. *Harvard Business Review, 77,* 77–88.

Wetlaufer, S. (1999b). Organizing for empowerment: An interview with AES's Roger Sant and Dennis Bakke. *Harvard Business Review, 77,* 110–123.

Wetlaufer, S. (2001). The business case against revolution: An interview with Nestlé's Peter Brabeck. *Harvard Business Review, 79,* 113–119.

Whitney, J. O. (1996). Strategic renewal for business units. *Harvard Business Review, 74,* 84–98.

Wiggenhorn, W. (1990). Motorola U: When training becomes an education. *Harvard Business Review, 68,* 71–83.

Williams, F. (1993). Navistar creates unique retiree health plans. *Pensions & Investment Age*, *21*(1), 47.

Wilmot, R. W. (1987). Change in management and the management of change. *Long Range Planning*, *20*, 23–28.

Worren, N., Ruddle, K., & Moore, K. (1999). From organizational development to change management: The emergence of a new profession. *Journal of Applied Behavioral Science*, *35*, 273–286. (See Farias et al., 2000.)

Zahra, S. A. (1999). Book review of Chandler et al. (1998). *Academy of Management Review*, *24*, 861–863.

ASSESSING ORGANIZATIONAL CONTEXT IN TEAM-BASED ORGANIZATIONS

Toni L. Doolen and Marla E. Hacker

ABSTRACT

Time to market, product quality, and product complexity are key organizational drivers. Many organizations have responded to these pressures by creating teams. While teams provide the right mix of personnel to respond to business and technical challenges faced by the organization, many organizations have failed to adjust their organizational processes, culture, and systems to create a context where teams can thrive. Identifying the key changes needed to support teams can be a daunting task. The ultimate goal of this research is the development of a tool that will allow organizational leaders to gain a better understanding of what organizational factors should be considered in designing an environment that will enable teams to perform at an optimal level. Previous research findings and semi-structured interviews of organizational leaders were used to develop a framework for studying these organizational processes, culture, and systems. A survey was developed to measure these different characteristics of the parent organization. Findings from the initial interviews and a pilot study utilizing the survey are summarized.

Team-Based Organizing, Volume 9, pages 67–90.
ISBN: 0-7623-0981-4

INTRODUCTION

Research to understand the complex set of interactions between a team and the parent organization is not new. The use of teams in the work environment is pervasive across a wide range of industries and for a wide variety of purposes. Team roles vary dramatically from one organization to another. Even within a given organization, many different types of teams are often used. There are many examples of companies that have successfully used teams to improve their capabilities and overall competitiveness. Case studies often highlight teams that have achieved breakthrough results. Anecdotal and research evidence can also be found for teams that have failed in their quest to improve organizational results. While contradictory findings might be puzzling, they are not entirely surprising. Teams do not exist within a vacuum; rather they are part of a larger system of organizational activity. It is critical to consider the role of this organizational activity that surrounds a team when evaluating the performance of a team.

A review of past research was completed to develop an initial set of constructs to define different aspects of organizational context. Following this review, a framework was developed to group constructs that were similar. In particular, this framework groups the constructs based on the origin of the factor. In this early stage of development, three team leaders were interviewed to verify the constructs developed and to help identify other organizational factors impacting team effectiveness. These interviews were used to further refine the constructs. The survey scales and items were then developed based on the existing body of knowledge in the areas of teams, management systems, and organizational design as well as the early input of these team leaders. This paper highlights the previous research used to develop the scales, summarizes the key findings from the team leader interviews, and summarizes the results of a pilot study used to check the reliability of the survey scales that were developed.

OPERATIONALIZING ORGANIZATIONAL CONTEXT

The larger organizational context that surrounds a team has been the focus of many recent reviews of the team effectiveness literature. These reviews call for researchers to focus on the role played by organizational context in determining work team effectiveness. In other words, rather than studying the team by looking inward, researchers have been called to broaden the knowledge surrounding intact teams in organizations by looking outside of the team. Guzzo and Shea (1992) summarize the need for this type of research in their comprehensive discussion of task performance in groups.

Improvements in group effectiveness can best be obtained by changing the circumstances in which groups work. Thus, organizational reward systems can be changed to recognize team accomplishments, group and organizational goals must be actively managed to ensure that group and organizational goals are aligned, technical and human resource support systems can be adapted to promote the welfare of work groups, and so on. A diagnosis of the contextual factors facilitating or inhibiting group effectiveness should precede implementing changes in order to identify the specific changes to be made to enhance effectiveness (p. 306).

In the team effectiveness literature, a number of models have been created to shed light on the nature of relationships between factors both internal and external to the team and a team's overall effectiveness. While these models capture the relationship between organizational context and team effectiveness, the specifics of the relationships differ from one model to the next. These models along with studies of intact work teams were used to create the organizational context framework and constructs developed for this research. Various research efforts have taken the approach of defining a critical set of organizational characteristics, systems, or processes to study the relationship between team performance and the larger organization. Hall and Beyerlein (2000) define nine organizational processes or support systems that impact team performance. The support systems defined by Hall and Beyerlein include traditional human resource management systems such as performance appraisal and training. This work also recognizes that organizational systems not traditionally associated with human resource management; such as processes for establishing performance metrics and information systems have the potential to impact team-level performance. Sundstrom (1999) also describes nine support systems that have the potential to impact team performance. The support systems described by Sundstrom include structures to support the definition of team roles, team leader roles, team staffing, team training, performance metrics, reward systems, information and communication systems, as well as the necessary physical facility for the team.

In looking beyond the characteristics and processes directly associated with the team towards organizational-level factors, there are numerous characteristics that have the potential to impact team performance. The purpose of survey development in this study is to provide feedback to organizational and team leaders on team member perceptions of the organizational factors that might impact team performance. To provide organizational and team leaders guidance in developing a supportive organizational context in which teams can be successful, it is important to provide leaders with both a reasonably small number of factors as well as to operationalize the factors in such a way that they are actionable.

In the original pilot survey, nine scales were developed to operationalize and to assess employee perceptions of organizational context. The characteristics associated with the management processes, organizational culture, and organizational systems were the focal point of this study. Management processes are the processes used by leaders in the organization in setting and meeting organizational objectives. The survey specifically addresses the management processes used to establish team goals, to create goal alignment, and to support the team through the allocation of resources. Organizational culture can be described as the set of values, beliefs, and behavioral norms that guide how teams in the organization get work done. The survey addresses the organizational norms associated with team integration, management support for teams and teamwork, and interactions between teams within the organization. Organizational systems are the human resource management processes and arrangements used by and supported in the overall organization. The survey evaluates the organizational systems used to provide performance feedback and recognition, training, and information to teams within the organization. This framework and the nine associated constructs are summarized in Fig. 1.

THE DEVELOPMENT OF AN ORGANIZATIONAL CONTEXT FRAMEWORK

In their study of teams of knowledge workers from various information systems departments, Janz, Colquitt, and Noe (1997) tested the role of goal quality on team performance. One aspect of the goal quality construct focused on whether or not team members understood their team goal. They found a correlation

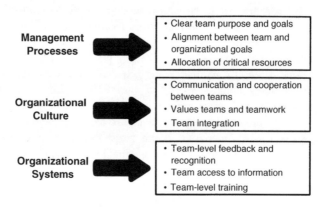

Fig. 1.   Organizational Context Framework and Constructs.

between high quality goals and effectiveness as measured by team performance (using measures of quality, efficiency, and timeliness), team commitment, and team satisfaction. In their study of project teams, Pinto, Pinto and Prescott (1993) tested a similar construct. They conclude that managers need to develop an over-riding set of goals to enhance levels of cross-functional cooperation. Higher levels of cross-functional cooperation will in turn improve the effectiveness of the team. Similarly, Hyatt and Ruddy (1997) found that alignment of a team's goals with the organization's stated goals is an important determinant of team success. They conclude that factors external to the team, i.e. organizational context, are as important in determining team effectiveness as factors internal to the team itself.

Vinokur-Kaplan's (1995) study of interdisciplinary treatment teams of mental health professionals was designed to test Hackman's (1987) normative model of team effectiveness. Within the normative model, the sufficiency of material resources is hypothesized to influence group effectiveness. In the Vinokur-Kaplan study, one of the variables evaluated and compared between teams was the existence of confidential meeting rooms and the necessary equipment for the team to hold a productive and confidential meeting. Vinokur-Kaplan (1995) found a statistically significant relationship between the allocation of material resources and collaboration and group interdependence. Hyatt and Ruddy (1997) found that ensuring that teams had access to the necessary material resources was critical to the overall success of the team.

These studies highlight the influential role of management processes on team effectiveness. Consistent with this supporting research, management processes that create clearly defined team goals, align team and organizational-level goals, and allocate critical resources to teams are captured within this research.

The ecological model of team effectiveness developed by Sundstrom, De Meuse and Futrell (1990) emphasizes patterns of relationships between teams and their environment. Within this model, organizational culture is identified as one of eight different organizational context factors. While there are many different aspects of organizational culture to consider, the three aspects of organizational culture chosen for this research are consistent with previous team-based research.

Campion, Papper and Medsker (1996) found significant correlation between communication and cooperation between teams of knowledge workers and all measures of team effectiveness. The authors postulate that communication and cooperation between teams is critical for professional jobs because these teams must routinely interact with other parts of the organization to complete their tasks. Van Aken and Kleiner (1997) also found that team-level relationships and interorganizational perspective correlated to various team performance measures. From these results, it appears that a supportive organizational culture that supports communication and cooperation between teams within the organization will produce more effective teams.

Campion et al. (1996) also found a significant and high correlation between management support for teams and manager and employee judgments of team effectiveness in their study of knowledge workers. Van Aken and Kleiner (1997) found that teams that were better connected with other parts of the organization had higher performance. Research findings such as these provide evidence that organizational culture impacts team effectiveness. Consistent with this supporting research, three aspects of organizational culture are captured within this research – support for communication and cooperation between teams, management support for teamwork, and integration of teams into the organization.

"The sociotechnical framework is a major intellectual perspective for understanding groups in organizations" (Goodman, Ravlin & Argote, 1986, p. 4). In their study of timber harvesting teams, Kolodny and Kiggundu (1980) developed a model of team effectiveness consistent with the sociotechnical framework. Because this model was built upon a framework that emphasizes the interaction between the technological and social characteristics of an organization, organizational context factors are included in the model in a couple different ways. One dimension incorporated in the model is organizational arrangements. Organizational arrangements are factors that are external to the work group but impact the work group task. In this model, organizational arrangements are a mediating factor in the creation of an effective group. Organizational arrangements are defined as the ways in which people and equipment are put together. This would include factors such as shift structures, reward systems, and information systems (Kolodny & Kiggundu, 1980, p. 628). In this study, the authors discuss, for example, a bonus system that was introduced to increase cooperation between team members and increase overall productivity within a work group. This bonus was paid out equally to all group members if certain productivity targets were met. Kolodny and Kiggundu found that this bonus system did have the impact of increasing both team cohesion and productivity for some of the teams within their study.

Organizational context is one of five groups of variables specified in the normative model of team effectiveness developed by Hackman (1987). Hackman (1991) defines organizational context as an environment that supports and reinforces the work of the team through the reward, education, and information systems. Organizational context along with group design and group synergy influences how well team members are able to apply their skills and knowledge to the team task (Goodman et al., 1986). Similar to the sociotechnical model, organizational context is hypothesized to influence factors internal to the team and subsequently impact the overall effectiveness of the team.

Both the sociotechnical and normative models of team effectiveness provide support for the organizational systems category of organizational context factors. Consistent with these models and supporting research, organizational systems that provide team-level feedback and recognition, training, and information are captured within this research.

TEAM LEADER ASSESSMENTS OF ORGANIZATIONAL CONTEXT

There are many different theoretical perspectives to use in understanding how individuals make sense of social organizations such as teams. One such perspective from the discipline of sociology is symbolic interactionism. From a symbolic interactionist perspective, meaning and reality are defined through the actions, interactions, and negotiations that occur between individuals within the social entity (O'Brien & Kollock, 1997). In other words, reality is socially constructed by and through the interactions and actions taken by members of the entity. Consequently, meaning and reality are derived from an individual's interpretation of interactions as well as their subsequent response based on this interpretation (Burrell & Morgan, 1979). Using this perspective, organizational context can be determined in part by the team leader's own interactions with members of the team, the team leader's own actions, as well as interactions between the team and the rest of the organization.

Within any social organization, interactions between members tend to become regularized over time (Charon, 1999). These organized patterns of interaction will subsequently exert influence on individuals within the organization. As a result, individuals will define organizational context based not only on interactions with other team members but also based on how these interactions compare or contrast with what they have come to expect. In other words, there is a circular and reciprocal relationship between new interactions and previously established patterns of interaction. As a result, it is necessary to look at both the interactions between team leaders and others in the organization as well as at the expectations based on previous interactions.

A second relevant aspect of the symbolic interactionist perspective is that members of a social entity will use a variety of cues to help interpret how these various actions and interactions fit together. All aspects of a formal organization are rich in symbolic meaning to the members of the organization. "Organizational structure, rules, policies, goals, missions, job descriptions, and standard operating procedures . . . act as primary points of reference for the way people think about and make sense of the contexts in which they work" (Morgan, 1997). In other words, people use a variety of social artifacts to guide them in making sense of the environment they are part of. As a result, these aspects of the organization will also play a role in how team leaders define the organizational context in which they and their teams operate.

Taken together, previous patterns of interactions, the current patterns of interactions between team members and the team leader along with various artifacts of the larger organization can be studied to develop an understanding of the organizational context that exists within an organization. The interviews completed focus on those interactions and organizational artifacts as seen from the perspective of the team leader.

Team Leader Interviews

Semi-structured interviews of three team leaders were used to further develop the organizational context framework developed based on previous research findings. The team leaders included in this phase of the study managed teams of four to ten team members. While the specific tasks of the teams varied, all three team leaders and their teams are responsible for managing complex, technical projects such as software development. An interview protocol was developed and used for each of the interviews (see Table 1). Consistent with a symbolic interactionist perspective, the focus of each question was to gain an understanding of a particular relationship between the team and the organization from the team leader's perspective. In addition to the items included in Table 1, follow-up questions were asked by the interviewer to seek clarity about the interactions and organizational cues that were used by the team leader to come to a particular conclusion. Interviews were 60–90 minutes in length.

Team leaders are identified as Leader 1, Leader 2, and Leader 3 throughout the remainder of this paper. Extracts from the data have been included within the text of this paper to maintain the richness of information and to provide a better frame of reference for the reader. Since the interviews were not recorded, excerpts are based on detailed notes taken by the interviewer at the time of the interview. Text contained in brackets within these excerpts is clarifying text added by the authors to provide implied content that is not clear without the entire dialog.

Discussion of Team Leader Interviews

From this set of interviews, three unifying themes were found. While the specifics of the issues described by the three team leaders included in this phase

Table 1. Interview Protocol.

Management Processes

MP1 How do teams know what they are supposed to be working on?

MP2 Do you know what your organization's vision is? How does this information get communicated?

MP3 Do you think that the goals of your team are the same as those of the organization?

MP4 How do you know how well your team is performing?

MP5 What resources does your team need? Do you have access to these resources?

Organizational Culture

OC1 Is the concept of teams supported by your organization? Why do you think this (or not)?

OC2 Does your manager support your team? In what ways do you see this?

OC3 Does your team communicate regularly with your manager?

OC4 Do you talk to other people in the company besides the people on your team?

OC5 Do you feel that your team competes with other teams in the organization? How does this impact your team?

Organizational Systems

OS1 Is your team recognized/rewarded for its performance? How is the team recognized/rewarded?

OS2 Has the team received any technical training in the last year?

OS3 Has the team received any skills training for the team (e.g. communication, organization, interpersonal, etc.) in the last year?

OS4 Does the team receive information from your manager? Is it accurate? Is it timely?

OS5 Does the team usually have access to the information you need?

of the research clearly differ, these common themes help characterize three components of organizational context that were seen as exerting significant influence on their teams. The first theme was developed from the team leaders' responses regarding the importance and challenge of providing team performance feedback. The second theme was developed from responses to questions centered on the management processes used within the organization to allocate resources. The third theme was developed from responses related to the need for organizational-level recognition of team accomplishments. Each of these themes is discussed in more detail below. Interview extracts are included for each of the three themes.

TEAM PERFORMANCE FEEDBACK

One of the roles common to all three leaders interviewed was to provide feedback to their team regarding their performance as a team. In other words, all three leaders were expected to interpret both direct and indirect information from other parts of the organization to gauge how well their team was performing. In all three cases, this particular responsibility was characterized as difficult in one manner or another. The lack of direct information from other organizational players or customers creates a situation where the team leader and perhaps even the team are unable to assess how others in the organization perceive their work.

For Leader 3, the lack of direct information on the team's performance made it difficult to provide much feedback to the team. Leader 3 responded by creating processes to provide individual level feedback to members of the team in an effort to compensate for the lack of direct information from the larger organization on the team's performance. For Leader 1 and Leader 2, project schedules or checkpoints were used as the primary team performance metrics used to gauge overall team performance. This information, however, was available only "after the fact," and as a result was used primarily as an indicator only when things were going poorly. In addition, because the information was available only after schedules and/or checkpoints were missed or incomplete, it was difficult for the team to respond in a proactive way based on this information.

Team leaders look to other sources, such as customers or project plans, to find out how well their team is performing. All three team leaders expressed some level of uncertainty in "knowing" how well their team was performing. "Users screaming," "gut feel," and knowing "how bad of shape you are in" are the phrases used by these leaders to describe how they are able to interpret how their team is performing.

Extracts

Leader 3: When we don't have users screaming at us. It is about the only way. We have a yearly performance review coming up for the team. For myself, this is the only way I know, unless I ask point blank on a specific thing, but I usually get a generic response. With the group that works for me, I use monthly one on ones. I ask for constructive feedback on my performance and about concerns and projects. It's an open door. So if I need rapport later on, it is already there.

Leader 2: For my project team, performance is tightly measured by program objectives when in the development stages. The project is not necessarily measured by meeting objectives though. We must deliver something that meets specific goals. With the timeline of tasks and meeting of goals you know how bad of shape you are in. We use timelines for each round or two to closely monitor where we will meet checkpoints. Quarterly reviews, though, are not set by time, but by other program teams and their objectives.

Leader 1: [In my organization] it is hard to tell – it is almost like a gut feel and how they perform against plan, but it is hard to come up with generic measures to gauge their productivity. The teams know how they are doing based on how the project is going verses the schedule and based on customer feedback, particularly after beta testing.

RESOURCE AVAILABILITY

A second interesting pattern of responses centered on the procurement of resources needed by the team. In all cases, the leaders saw resource acquisition as a role that they were responsible for. The team leaders mentioned different techniques for resource acquisition, but one common process used to acquire needed resources was negotiating with other organizational members. The resources discussed by the leaders included money, people, materials, information, and training. Team leaders in this study felt that is was important to "provide" the necessary resources for their team to be successful. For example, Leader 2 described a situation where team members were unable to get the resources they needed to meet their goals. Similarly, Leader 1 felt that the role of resource acquisition was particularly important when project goals or plans changed. The challenge faced by Leader 3 was somewhat different. Unlike Leader 1 and Leader 2 who deal with resource negotiations primarily in times of need or when changes have occurred, Leader 3 saw getting any resources (even low cost training documents) as a constant struggle.

The availability of resources, e.g. money, additional personnel, or time, is a key organizational factor as described by the three leaders. The leaders engage in interactions such as negotiations with other organizational members to make sure that these resources become available for their teams. These negotiations are themselves impacted by the context of the organization as defined by previous events, relationships, and by existing organizational processes or rules.

Extracts

Leader 2: Peer resources [other engineers], production resources [technicians], and materials are the main things the team needs. Sometimes they are in competition – they need to work against all the other things that are going on. They'll [the team member] be told, "O.K. we will schedule you, but there are other things to be done first." The interplay between projects is something they need [to understand]. This usually is the thing that drives projects within organization. We have to manage with the priority of the organization. Most of the time, engineers manage it themselves. If they are not successful, then they escalate it to me. Then I go across to the production manger, my peer, instead of supervisors [the engineer's peer].

Leader 1: Generally, needs are defined as the project gets defined so we identify people and dollars early. If the needs change during the course of the project, the project team will raise the issue for additional needs through project manager and sponsor and address it through a change in scope or schedule.

Leader 3: We have a bad history because [our predecessor] didn't approach getting resources correctly, and this is held over our heads even though it was three to four years ago. I am conservative in asking. It is still a fight, even when I look at things logically. It is a real struggle.

SUPPORT FOR TEAMS AND TEAMWORK

The third common theme revolves around the issue of recognizing and supporting team-level efforts and results. Leader 2 had many different examples of rewards that were used to recognize the team's performance. Leader 1 spoke of methods for rewarding teams for their achievements. The lack of team recognition at the organizational level, however, was a theme common to both Leaders 1 and 3. Both leaders felt that their teams were often slighted by the lack of organizational recognition for their accomplishments. They further stated that this had a negative impact on the their teams. Even though team leaders could themselves recognize the contributions of the team to the larger organization, the shared sentiment was that higher-level organizational recognition was also necessary and important to the team.

Extracts

Leader 1: There are sort of three forms of recognition. One form comes from inside the organization, for example giving verbal or written feedback about doing a good job. Major event celebrations, for example taking the group out to lunch, and recognition from customers at the end of the project are two other forms or recognition used. This may include written feedback expressing the customer's appreciation for the work done. The problem is that from higher up in the organization, [my team's] work doesn't get recognized like other work in the organization . . .

Leader 3: About two years ago, . . . the team received "employee of the quarter" award for our work. In the three years I have been here this is the only time we have been recognized . . . just once, [the leaders] need to mention thanks to everyone else for supporting these people. We have had to set up systems and bust our tails. Just taking the time to say what our purpose is, just to mention the three or four departments to give people a sense of how they fit into the big picture. They don't spend enough time on recognition.

TEAM LEADER INTERVIEWS SUMMARY

This analysis has explored three different organizational factors identified as being relevant to the team leaders interviewed. This discussion and the excerpts included in this analysis are only a subset of a much broader set of organizational systems, processes, and cultural issues that influence both team leaders and teams. The three areas discussed were common to the leaders interviewed. The similarity of the issues faced by these leaders seems notable. These findings suggest that these factors may be important to a broader set of team leaders.

Within most engineering and scientific disciplines, there is a strong desire to decompose complex problems or issues (such as trying to understand the reasons some teams succeed and other teams fail), so that factors can be studied in relative "isolation." In this analysis, an alternate approach to studying teams in context was used. By looking for patterns and common themes through open dialogs, rather than trying to isolate or measure specific factors, some of the organizational context factors encountered by team leaders were highlighted. While these findings may or may not be more broadly applicable, they do provide insight into some of the issues faced by leaders managing teams in organizations today and the factors that contribute toward the creation of a supportive organizational context.

In addition to the common themes discussed, the team leaders interviewed shared other examples that highlighted the importance of management processes, organizational culture, and organizational systems in creating a supportive organizational context for teams. The qualitative information from these team leader interviews, previous research findings, and models of team effectiveness were used to create the framework for evaluating organizational context. Within this framework, nine different organizational context constructs were developed.

PILOT SURVEY DEVELOPMENT

In the next phase of this research, a survey was developed to further study the relationship between team effectiveness and organizational context. The primary focus of this initial phase of survey development was to develop nine scales to assess each of the different organizational constructs. Where possible, the pilot survey items selected were based on previously published surveys that were created to evaluate similar constructs. A 6-point Likert-scale (strongly disagree, disagree, tend to disagree, tend to agree, agree, strongly agree) was used for all survey items.

A pilot study using the survey was conducted within one business unit of a Fortune 50 high-technology company. The company is a producer of computer products and computer peripherals. The business unit studied manufactures consumer supplies for these product markets. The business unit is divided into smaller units by functional area, e.g. supply chain, manufacturing, marketing, and research and development. Within each functional area, the use of teams is widespread throughout the organization. Most employees are members of a primary work team, but in some areas, employees are also members of one or more project teams composed of members from other functional areas.

The pilot version of the survey was tested using five engineering work groups. The pilot teams were similar to one another in size but less so in general responsibilities. The specific outputs and tasks of the teams did vary. For example, some teams were involved primarily in assessing final product quality; whereas, other teams were concerned with the development of manufacturing processes responsible for producing the product. Team members participating in the pilot study provided both verbal input and written comments on the survey to identify confusing or ambiguous survey items.

Surveys were distributed directly to team members during a team meeting by one of the two authors. A brief explanation of the survey as well as information on survey confidentiality was read prior to survey distribution. Additional copies of the survey were provided for team members who were unable to attend the meeting. These copies included an addressed, stamped envelope so the survey could be completed and returned directly to the researcher. All elements of informed consent were included in the written instructions accompanying the survey.

The mappings between the nine organizational context constructs and the pilot survey items are summarized in Appendix A. If an item was adapted from a published survey, the source of the item is also noted. The pilot survey included 37 items related to the nine organizational context constructs. Survey items were assigned a random number to determine the ordering of questions. In addition to the survey items, team members were asked to identify their role on the team (team member or team leader), organization, job title, and shift.

PILOT SURVEY RESULTS

The internal reliabilities were assessed using Cronbach's alpha for each construct (see Table 2). Reliability of a set of measures refers to the consistency of the measures. In the development of survey scales, the issue of internal consistency or reliability is of particular interest because it assesses the degree to which different survey items are consistent with one another. Reliability is the proportion of the variability in the responses to a survey that is the result of differences in respondents as opposed to differences due to the survey items in a particular scale.

A Cronbach's alpha greater than 0.7 is often the criteria used to evaluate whether or not a scale possesses an acceptable level of internal reliability. For newly developed scales, slightly lower reliabilities are often considered acceptable. Four of the scales met the 0.7 criteria, and four others were greater than 0.6. Only one scale did not demonstrate an acceptable level of reliability.

As a result of both written and verbal feedback provided from team members who participated in the pilot study as well as the survey scale reliability analysis, a number of opportunities for improving the survey were identified. Those items referring to higher-level managers in the company were confusing to participants. Follow-up discussion with participants revealed that different participants defined higher-level managers differently depending on their knowledge of the organization. As a result, items such as "High management in the company supports teams," were either modified or eliminated in follow-on surveys.

The number of survey items used for each construct was relatively small for the pilot survey. To increase the robustness of the final scales, additional survey items

Table 2.   Pilot Study Cronbach's Alpha for Each Organizational Context Factor.

Organizational Context Construct	$N = 38$ Reliability	Number of Items
Establishment of clear team purpose and goals	0.8498	5
Alignment between team and organizational goals	0.6564	2
Resource allocation	0.8106	4
Communication and cooperation between teams	0.1699	4
Values teams and teamwork	0.7566	4
Team integration	0.6914	4
Performance feedback	0.7241	6
Team access to information	0.6133	5
Team-level training	0.6300	3

were developed for all constructs except for performance feedback. The number of items for the each of the final scales ranged from five to seven.

The reliability of the survey items selected to assess the level of cooperation and communication between teams within the organization was extremely low. During a post-hoc review of these items, one finding was that questions referring to other parts of the company were ambiguous to participants. Due to the large size of the company studied, it was difficult for participants to respond consistently to questions asking about relationships between an individual team and other teams in the company. For the final survey items, phrases such as "other teams in the company" were replaced with "other teams in the organization." Three additional survey items were also added to this scale in an attempt to improve the reliability of the scale and to further clarify the construct. These additional items were:

- My team has good relationships with other teams in the organization.
- My team is encouraged to work with other teams to get our work done.
- Members of my team work with other people in the organization besides the people on this team.

A follow-on study utilizing the updated set of items was completed. In this phase of the research, the survey was administered to teams that were all part of the same business unit of a Fortune 50 high-tech company. The survey was administered to nine engineering teams all working in the manufacturing function of the organization. These teams each had responsibility for hardware and software systems associated with various types of automated manufacturing equipment on the production shop floor. The updated survey maintained the nine scales tested in the pilot phase of the research and consisted of 51 items. The internal reliabilities were assessed using Cronbach's Alpha and are summarized in Table 3. All scales demonstrated acceptable reliabilities of greater than 0.70. In addition, only 2 scales, communication and cooperation between teams, and team integration, had reliabilities less than 0.80. By eliminating the item, "There is little competition between this team and other teams in the organization," the reliability of the communication and cooperation scale is improved with a Cronbach's Alpha of 0.8136. No additional improvements to the team integration scale were identified as a result of this follow-on study.

POST-HOC ANALYSES OF PILOT SURVEY DATA

In addition to assessing the reliability of the scales, post-hoc analysis of team-level results was also completed for the five teams participating in the pilot survey. Significant differences were observed between teams and between

Table 3. Follow-On Study Cronbach's Alpha for Each Organizational Context Factor.

| Organizational Context Construct | $N = 85$ | |
	Reliability	Number of Items
Establishment of clear team purpose and goals	0.9005	7
Alignment between team and organizational goals	0.8770	5
Resource allocation	0.8043	5
Communication and cooperation between teams	0.7647	7
Values teams and teamwork	0.9118	5
Team integration	0.7509	5
Performance feedback	0.8280	6
Team access to information	0.8478	6
Team-level training	0.8780	5

the nine scale averages. The results of these analyses are summarized in Table 4. More detailed graphical summaries of these results for the five pilot study teams are included in Appendix B.

In the pilot study, a variety of teams were selected to test for instrument robustness. Differences in team task, team composition, and team structure were not controlled for in the selection of teams for the pilot study. While team members of all five pilot teams were engineers, the educational background as well as the specific responsibilities of the teams differed. One team, for example, was composed of industrial engineers, two teams were composed primarily of mechanical engineers, one team was composed of software engineers, and the fifth team was composed of engineers from a mix of engineering disciplines. Team tasks were as variable as team composition. One team, for example,

Table 4. Pilot Study Results by Organizational Context Construct for Each Team.

Construct	Team 1	Team 2	Team 3	Team 4	Team 5
Establishment of clear team purpose and goals	4.78	3.71	4.65	4.35	3.78
Alignment between team and organizational goals	4.88	4.43	4.31	4.53	3.63
Resource allocation	4.75	4.25	3.84	4.50	4.06
Communication and cooperation between teams	4.66	4.64	4.38	4.25	4.69
Values teams and teamwork	5.13	5.43	5.42	5.44	4.96
Team integration	4.91	4.07	4.84	4.62	4.44
Performance feedback	4.00	3.45	3.13	3.99	3.65
Team access to information	4.43	4.26	4.28	4.53	3.75
Team-level training	4.08	4.24	4.54	4.17	4.42

was responsible for developing a complex software applications to support manufacturing lines across the world; whereas another team was responsible for the logistics associated with moving manufacturing equipment from one location to another. The remaining three teams were responsible for either product or process support and development.

Because of these significant differences, similarities or differences in perceptions regarding organizational context cannot be linked to performance metrics or attributed to specific common factors. However, in an effort to validate the results obtained for those scales that were found to be reliable in the pilot study, follow-up discussions with team leaders were completed. The researchers met with each team leader individually. The intent of these discussions was to ascertain, from the team leader's perspective, whether or not the team assessment of the nine organizational context constructs seemed consistent with the strengths and challenges currently facing the team. The follow-up discussions consistently confirmed that those constructs rated lower by teams were reflective of either local or larger issues facing the organization. For example, all five teams rated performance feedback lower than nearly all other constructs. At the time the survey was administered, changes in the performance appraisal process and compensation guidelines had just been introduced in the company. The lower rating on items associated with performance feedback could have been impacted by the introduction of these changes. All managers commented during the discussion that they were not surprised to see this area emerge as one of the lowest in the survey.

Ratings of other organizational context constructs also seemed to be consistent, from the team leader's perspective, with team-specific issues. In the discussion with the leader of Team 2, for example, the team leader noted that the team had recently gone through a fairly significant change in their team mission as a result of changes in the business. While much effort had gone into working on clarifying the role of the team, the team leader confirmed that, as a whole, team members were struggling to understand their new role. This seemed to be reflected in the lower rating of the survey items related to the establishment of clear goals and purpose. In contrast to Team 2, Team 1 rated most survey items associated with management processes higher than the other teams studied in the pilot phase. The team leader of Team 1 felt this was consistent with the team's role in the organization. The team was nearing the end of a difficult, but successful product introduction. The role that the team played in the product introduction, along with the team's understanding of the role of the product introduction on the larger organization had been clearly communicated and well defined by the organization. The leader of Team 1 felt that this clarity in purpose was critical to the team's success. While not all findings from the pilot study were validated in these discussions, the discussions did provide some evidence of a linkage between team-level perceptions and the team leader assessment of organizational factors influencing the team at the time of the survey.

SUMMARY

The use of teams in organizations has become commonplace. The exact structure and nature of the task assigned to a team will vary from one organization to another and even from one team to another within the same organization. Irrespective of the structure or team task, the larger organization will influence the team in both direct and indirect ways. To understand the complex set of interactions between a team and the larger organizational context it resides in, it is necessary to define the relevant aspects of organizational context. This research has taken a step in this direction. In particular, previous research findings, existing models of team effectiveness, and semi-structured interviews with team leaders have been used to create a framework for studying organizational context. Within this framework, nine constructs have been developed to operationalize organizational context. A survey to measure these nine constructs was developed and preliminary testing of the survey was completed. While additional development and testing of the survey is required, this work is central toward developing a better understanding of the relationship between teams and the rich environment in which they reside.

REFERENCES

Burrell, G., & Morgan, G. (1979). *Sociological paradigms and organisational analysis.* London: Heinemann Educational Books, Ltd.

Campion, M. A., Medsker, G. J., & Higgs, A. C. (1993). Relations between work group characteristics and effectiveness: Implications for designing effective work groups. *Personnel Psychology, 46,* 823–850.

Campion, M. A., Papper, E. M., & Medsker, G. J. (1996). Relations between work team characteristics and effectiveness: A replication and extension. *Personnel Psychology, 49,* 429–452.

Charon, J. M. (1999). *The meaning of sociology* (6th ed.). New Jersey: Prentice Hall.

Goodman, P. S., Ravlin, E. C., & Argote, L. (1986). Current thinking about groups: Setting the stage for new ideas. In: P. S. Goodman (Ed.), *Designing Effective Work Groups* (pp. 1–33). San Francisco, CA: Jossey-Bass.

Guzzo, R. A. & Shea, G. P. (1992). Group performance and intergroup relations in organizations. In: M. D. Dunnette & L. M. Hough (Eds), *Handbook of Industrial and Organizational Psychology* (Vol. 3, pp. 269–313). Palo Alto, CA: Consulting Psychologists Press.

Hackman, J. R. (1987). The design of work groups. In: J. W. Lorsch (Ed.), *The Handbook of Organizational Behavior* (pp. 315–342). Englewood Cliffs, NJ: Prentice-Hall, Inc.

Hackman, J. R. (Ed.) (1991). *Groups that work (and those that don't): Creating conditions for effective teamwork*. San Francisco: Jossey-Bass.

Hall, C. A., & Beyerlein, M. M. (2000). Support systems for teams: A taxonomy. In: M. M. Beyerlein, D. A. Johnson, & S. T. Beyerlein (Eds), *Advances in Interdisciplinary Studies of Work Teams: Vol 5. Product Development Teams* (pp. 89–132). Stamford, CT: JAI Press.

Hyatt, D. E., & Ruddy, T. M. (1997). An examination of the relationship between work group characteristics and performance: Once more into the breech. *Personnel Psychology, 50*, 553–585.

Janz, B. D., Colquitt, J. A., & Noe, R. A. (1997). Knowledge worker team effectiveness: The role of autonomy, interdependence, team development, and contextual support variables. *Personnel Psychology, 50*(4), 877–904.

Kline, T. J. B., & MacLeod, M. (1997). Predicting organizational team performance. *Organizational Development Journal, 15*(4), 77–85.

Kolodny, H. F., & Kiggundu, M. N. (1980). Towards the development of a sociotechnical systems model in woodlands mechanical harvesting. *Human Relations, 33*(9), 623–645.

Morgan, G. (1997). *Images of organization* (2nd ed.). London: Sage Publications.

O'Brien, J., & Kollock, P. (1997) *The production of reality: Essays and readings on social interaction* (2nd ed.). London: Pine Forge Press.

Pinto, M. B., Pinto, J. K., & Prescott, J. E. (1993) Antecedents and consequences of project team cross-functional cooperation. *Management Science, 39*(10), 1281–1296.

Sundstrom, E. D. (1999). *Supporting work team effectiveness: Best management practices for fostering high performance*. San Francisco: Joseey-Bass.

Sundstrom, E. D., De Meuse, K. P., & Futrell, D. (1990). Work teams: Applications and effectiveness. *American Psychologist, 45*(2), 120–133.

Van Aken, E. M., & Kleiner, B. M. (1997). Determinants of effectiveness for cross-functional organizational design teams. *Quality Management Journal, 4*(2), 51–79.

Vinokur-Kaplan, D. (1995). Treatment teams that work (and those that don't): An application of Hackman's group effectiveness model to interdisciplinary teams in psychiatric hospitals. *Journal of Applied Behavioral Science, 31*(3) 303–327.

APPENDIX A

Organizational Context Survey Items from Pilot Survey

Survey Item	Adapted from	Construct
Management Processes		
The objectives this team must achieve to fulfill our purpose are clear.		Team Goals
My entire team understands this team's purpose.		Team Goals
There is a clear mission statement or charter for this team.		Team Goals
Team members know what they are supposed to be doing on this team.	Janz et al. (1997)	Team Goals
My team has a clear idea of what is expected from them.		Team Goals
The goals of my team are aligned with those of the organization.	Kline and MacLeod (1997)	Goal Alignment
My team knows what the organization's vision is.		Goal Alignment
My team has enough money to get our work done.		Resources
My team has enough people to get our work done.		Resources
My team has enough materials and supplies to get our work done.		Resources
My team gets what we need from the leaders of this organization.	Van Aken and Kleiner (1997)	Resources
Organizational Culture		
There is little competition between this team and other teams in the company.	Campion et al. (1993)	Comm/Cooperation
Members of my team frequently talk to other people in the company besides the people on this team.	Campion et al. (1993)	Comm/Cooperation
Teams in the company cooperate to get the work done.	Campion et al. (1993)	Comm/Cooperation
My team coordinates with other teams that might be impacted by our work.	Van Aken and Kleiner (1997)	Comm/Cooperation
My manager treats this team with respect.	Hyatt and Rudy (1997)	Teamwork
My team feels comfortable speaking with our manager about business issues.	Hyatt and Rudy (1997)	Teamwork
Higher management in the company supports teams.	Campion et al. (1993)	Teamwork
My manager supports this team.	Campion et al. (1993)	Teamwork
My team is an important part of the organization		Integration

Survey Item	Adapted from	Construct
Organizational Culture		
My team feels isolated from the rest of the organization		Integration
My team has its own identity.		Integration
My team is readily identifiable from the rest of the organization.	Kline and MacLeod (1997)	Integration
Organizational Systems		
My team knows how well we are performing.	Janz et al. (1997)	Feedback
My team receives frequent reports on our team performance.	Janz et al. (1997)	Feedback
My team receives honest feedback from our manager.	Hyatt and Rudy (1997)	Feedback
Many rewards from my job (e.g. pay, promotion, etc.) are determined in a large part by my contributions as a team member.	Campion et al. (1993)	Feedback
The reward system is set up to recognize team performance.	Kline and MacLeod (1997)	Feedback
My team receives recognition for our performance.	Hyatt and Rudy (1997)	Feedback
My team receives timely information from our manager.	Hyatt and Rudy (1997)	Information
My team needs a better way to get news from outside the team.	Janz et al. (1997)	Information
My team has access to the technical information we need to be successful.		Information
My team has access to the business information we need to be successful.		Information
My team receives critical information too late.	Janz et al. (1997)	Information
The organization provides adequate quality training for my team.		Training
The organization provides adequate team skills training for my team (e.g. communication, organization, interpersonal, etc.).	Campion et al. (1993)	Training
The organization provides adequate technical training for my team.	Campion et al. (1993)	Training

APPENDIX B

Pilot Study Survey Results Summaries

Summary of average team scores for pilot survey items assessing management processes.

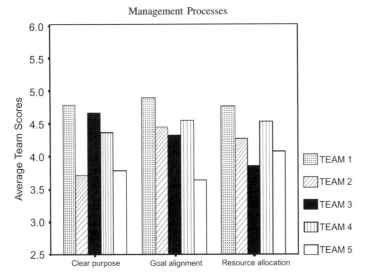

Summary of average team scores for pilot survey items assessing organizational culture.

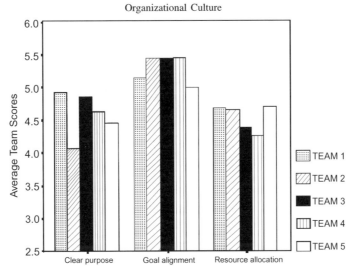

Summary of average team scores for pilot survey items assessing organizational systems.

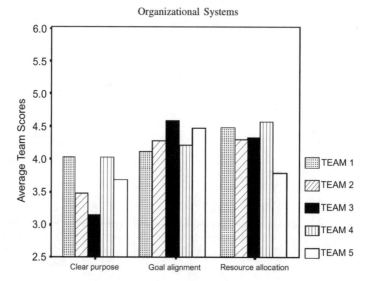

Organizational Systems

MANAGING A TEAM-BASED ORGANIZATION: A PROPOSED STRATEGIC MODEL

Frances Kennedy

ABSTRACT

This chapter proposes a model, or blueprint, for team-based organizing. The goal is to help provide an overview of how teams integrate within the organization to achieve the organization's strategic objective. It positions managers as a key component and discusses three different levels of decision control. Finally, it offers seven key attributes of a team-based organization.

INTRODUCTION

In today's organizations, managers are regularly faced with decisions that most of their predecessors as recently as the 1980s did not. These decisions revolve around encouraging and nurturing workers to engage collaboratively in order to gain competitive advantage. In another age, managers planned, directed and delegated to get the job done. Now, managers must still plan. However, rather than directing and delegating, they are told that they must empower, encourage and support. But where is the rulebook for this type of manager?

This chapter proposes a model, or blueprint, for team-based organizing. The goal is to help provide an overview of how teams integrate within the organization to achieve the organization's strategic objectives. Most importantly, it

Team-Based Organizing, Volume 9, pages 91–111.
© 2003 Published by Elsevier Science Ltd.
ISBN: 0-7623-0981-4

positions managers as a key component and clearly defines their roles in this structure – a frequently neglected link.

A major strength of this model is that it is the product of a collaborative endeavor by representatives of six major international companies. As corporate sponsors of the Center for the Study of Work Teams at the University of North Texas, these representatives worked with researchers on a virtual team for a period of three years. The mission of the team was to develop a model that was dynamic enough to apply to different industries. A common belief among the team's members was that, though differences in size, market, product and customers were significant, there were basic 'truths' about teaming in the organizations that were pervasive. And it was just these commonalities that would provide the blueprint they needed to manage their organizations to succeed. The model presented in this chapter is the result of the company representatives' collective efforts to develop a working model for their own company's use.

This chapter will first elaborate on the different levels of decision control and the types of questions and issues that managers must address daily. It will then discuss elements of the proposed model and how they relate to these questions and decisions. Specific attention is paid to various areas of decision control and strategic alignment. Finally, the chapter will conclude with a seven-point summary illustrating how the model can be used to inform manager decisions.

DECISION CONTROL

Taking a broad view of team-based organizing, we can see three levels of decision making that must integrate to make a successful whole: team members, team managers and senior managers. Each of these levels of decision makers regularly make decisions that will either support strategic goals or that will result in hampering progress towards those goals. Each level is faced with different questions, because each has a different responsibility to the organization. Table 1 outlines these levels, rolls, and focus and provides examples of questions facing these decision-makers.

Team Members

Team members' responsibilities include evaluating processes, performing root cause analyses, weighing alternative solutions and recommending a course of action or improvement. These tasks require (among other things) information, resources, and contacts with other members of the organization. Weighing

Table 1. Decision Levels in the Team-Based Organization.

Decision Level	Organizational Role	Focus	Questions
Team Member	• Improve Processes • Source Problems • Recommend Solutions	Task or Project/Process Level	• What is our team's purpose? • Which process/problem will we work on to improve or solve? • What is the root cause of the problem? • How do we decide what information we need to proceed? • Which of these is the 'best' solution? • Have any other teams tackled this problem? Or tried this solution?
Team Manager	• Coaching • Identify resource needs • Provide resources • Evaluate team outcomes • Align team goals with organizational goals	Team Level	• Is the team making progress? Or do they seem to be stuck on one step? • Do they need training in conflict management or communication? • Do the meetings seem to run smoothly? • Are the measures of performance appropriate for this team's goals? • Does the team need any more information from elsewhere in the organization? • Does the recommendation they have made make sense? Do I want to endorse it?
Senior Manager	• Identify competencies • Evaluate team system • Allocate resources • Align goals with strategic vision	Organizational Level	• How successful have the teams been in reaching their goals? • Has the money that I have invested thus far paid off? • Do I want to continue down this path and continue to provide resources? • Do I want to copy this structure at another facility? • Is it better to invest in another initiative instead of teaming?

alternatives requires some method of quantitative comparison of impact on the organization. Team members focus at the project and task level.

Team Managers

Team managers (sometimes called coaches or facilitators) are the managers to whom the team turns for support, guidance and resources. Usually, the team managers are charged with monitoring team progress and 'greasing the wheel' by facilitating resources and information. These managers are faced with deciding whether the team is making adequate progress and, if not, what to do about it. When the team makes a recommendation for a process change or project solution, the team manager must weigh the recommendation before deciding whether to proceed.

A major issue confronting managers is that they cannot actually sit in on meetings and 'make' the team succeed. What he or she can do is to provide the resources needed by the team to tackle their job. The team manager must vigilantly use observation and inquiry to answer questions like these that help to determine the needs of the team.

Senior Managers

Establishing a strategy, setting objectives and selecting human resource development as a core competence are the purview of senior managers. They communicate goals and strategy to the rest of the company through budgets and objectives. They decide to invest funds into establishing a team-based organization. At some point, however, they must evaluate whether these initial decisions resulted in leading the organization closer to its goals. Team-based systems require ongoing investment in support, such as training, rewards and facilities. Responsible managers want to 'see' the difference in organizational performance prior to allocating more resources to the system. Common questions for upper management include: It is the job of upper management to evaluate the success/failure of teams as a human resource initiative. Doing this requires an overall assessment of financial and behavioral impact on the organization to demonstrate the wisdom of the investment.

MODEL OVERVIEW

The model presented in Fig. 1 has much in common with many organizational designs.[1] It begins with company strategy (goal), includes an initiative (how), a measure of performance (outcome) and feedback loops to readdress strategic

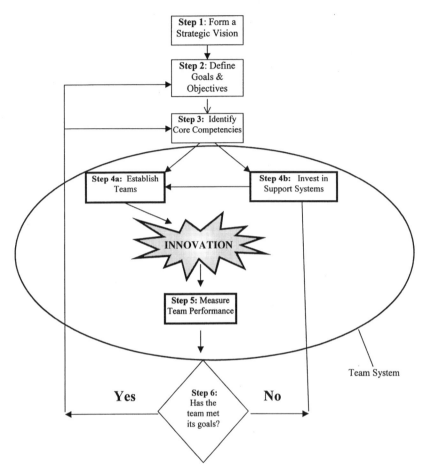

Fig. 1. A Team-Based Organization: A Descriptive Model.

and operational issues. It differs, however, on an essential point: the focus is not wholly on the teams, but also highlights the essential role managers must play in a successful TBO.

Step 1: Form Strategic Vision

Global competition and rapidly advancing technology are driving organizations to discover new ways to gain advantage. As quickly as one company masters a new technology, another company is just as quickly emulating that change. The need for flexibility and speed in satisfying and exceeding customer expectations is essential in drafting organizational strategy. The first step of the Team-Based Organization (TBO) Model is to form a strategic vision, setting the course for the organization.

Step 2: Define Goals and Objectives

Strategic vision is given shape and form through goals and objectives. Long range planning, such as five and ten year product and profit plans, communicates strategic vision to the organizational community. These plans set priorities and provide structure to daily decision-making.

Step 3: Identify Core Competencies

The third step in the TBO Model is to craft a strategy that will enable the organization to achieve the goals and objectives articulated in the strategy. Crafting a strategy involves analyzing the industry, market, and competitors and identifying core competencies (Kaplan & Norton, 1996). "Core competencies are the collective learning of the organization, especially how to coordinate diverse production skills and integrate multiple streams of technologies" (Prahalad & Hamel, 1990, p. 82). Firms must learn to build into their organization the capacity to anticipate change and opportunities (Best, 1990). This requires a focus on organizational learning (Senge et al.,1994).

Organizational learning is about having the appropriate culture, structure and systems to encourage people to develop continually and share their knowledge with others. In the coming decade, companies will be judged on how well they identify and exploit their core competencies to their advantage (Prahalad & Hamel, 1990). The one competitive advantage that cannot be copied easily is people (Heracleous, 1995; Prahalad & Hamel, 1990; Senge et al., 1994; Stewart, 1997; Sveiby, 1997). By developing this resource, a company creates a unique advantage – a knowledge base.

Quinn et al. (1996) outline three critical characteristics of intellect. The first is the exponentiality of knowledge. Once knowledge is captured, communicated and internalized, the knowledge base becomes higher.

The second characteristic comes from the benefits of sharing. As knowledge is shared, it grows at a tremendous rate (Nonaka & Takeuchi, 1995). Communication theory states that a network's potential benefits grow exponentially as the nodes it can successfully interconnect expand numerically (Quinn et al., 1996).

The last characteristic is the opportunity for expansion. Unlike physical assets that decrease in value as used, human intellect increases in value with use (Prahalad & Hamel, 1990; Quinn et al., 1996; Senge et al., 1994).

The challenge for the modern corporation becomes managing this collective intellect resulting from knowledge capture and sharing. New technologies and organizational structures allow companies to design their systems around the intellectual flow rather than the traditional hierarchical control concepts. Managing intellectual flow refers to devising "systematic structures for developing, focusing, leveraging, and measuring . . . intellectual capabilities" (Quinn et al., 1996, p. 25). Concerning new organization forms, Quinn proposes that the main function of the organization in today's hypercompetitive environment is to develop and deploy intellect effectively (Quinn et al., 1996).

Many organizations are turning to team structures as one way to share, capture and deploy the intellect and knowledge needed for competitive advantage. Work teams are becoming an increasingly important factor in management transformations. This interest in groups is reflected in a 1993 survey of Fortune 1000 companies, which revealed that the use of employee participation teams has increased from 70% in 1978 to 91% in 1993 (Lawler et al., 1998). Lawler et al.'s most recent update of this survey illustrates that the use of employment involvement practices[2] has since leveled off at this high level. This clearly shows a majority of corporations using teams to manage their daily decisions.

Step 4a: Establish Teams

An increasing number of companies are involving teams in their business transformations. Companies often initiate multiple change initiatives in their organizations. Companies normally employ several initiatives simultaneously to gain advantage. Just-In-Time (JIT), Lean Manufacturing, and Electronic Data Transfer (EDT) are just a few examples of popular initiatives. They represent major changes in processes that involve both people and technology. A growing number of companies are using teams as a socio-technique to integrate the rapid changes in the environment (Lawler et al., 1998).

A meta-analysis of 131 studies of organizational change conducted by Macy and Izumi (1993) found that initiatives with the largest effects upon financial measures of the organization were those that included the use of teams. Step 3 in the TBO Model represents the selection of human resource development as a key core competence of the organization, while Step 4a identifies teaming as the selected method of developing human resource potential.

According to Guzzo and Dickson, "a work group or team is an identifiable, interdependent group of individuals who are embedded in a larger social system"

(1996, 308–309). Similar definitions have been developed, such as those by Katzenbach and Smith (1994) and Mohrman (1995). Common to all definitions is that the team is a group of individuals interdependent in both task and goals and they exist within a larger system.

Thoughtful consideration must be given when establishing teams. Several types of teams have emerged in organizations. Appropriately matching team purpose with team type is a crucial step in team design. The type of team is usually dependent upon the type of task. Several different typologies have been used to categorize teams (Katzenbach & Smith, 1994; Mohrman et al., 1995; Sundstrom et al., 1990). One compelling theory is Cohen and Bailey's four types of teams: work, parallel, project and management. What distinguishes Cohen and Bailey's (1997) typology from the others is the division of improvement teams into parallel and project teams. This distinction is useful, since parallel teams are normally on-going with permanent membership and project teams have a limited life. Participating teams will need to be classified consistently across companies using the Cohen and Bailey typology. Each of these categories is described in Table 2.

Once management within a team-based organization has decided upon its strategy and identified knowledge as a core competency and its development as imperative, they establish a blend of these four team types to achieve the goals of the organization. Teams use their unique combination of skills to solve problems, improve processes and make faster, more effective decisions.

Step 4b: Invest in Support Systems

An organization that wants their teams to develop into high performance teams (Katzenbach & Smith, 1994) must also recognize the need to develop environmental support, providing the resources and direction they need to achieve their goals. A decision to invest in a team-based organization should involve more than putting seven or so people in a room and telling them to get started (Katzenbach & Smith, 1994; Mohrman et al., 1995). Consideration should be given to team membership and training in team skills. The team should have a clear understanding of their mission and how their performance contributes to organizational objectives.

In addition to these basic factors, teams need access to information about processes and resources. They need performance measures and appropriate rewards to guide and motivate their behavior. Most of all, they need managerial support for their decisions and recommendations. These factors are called support systems (Hall, 1998; Hall & Beyerlein, 2000; Sundstrom, 1999), climate (Burningham & West, 1995) or context factors (Stevens & Campion, 1994).

Table 2. Types of Teams.

Work Teams	Work units responsible for producing goods or providing services. Membership is usually on-going and typically from the same function. Work cycles are continuous and repetitive. Traditionally, supervisors guide these teams. However, more recently, companies are engaging in self-organizing practices that extend to these teams. Examples of this type of team include production lines, audit teams, maintenance teams, distribution teams and customer satisfaction teams.
Parallel Teams	Cross-functional teams used for problem-solving and improvement activities. Membership is on-going and draws from different functions or departments whose work processes overlap. These are called 'parallel' because they co-exist with the members' home department responsibilities. People from different work units are pulled together to perform functions that the regular organization is not well equipped to perform. The teams' objective is to analyze a process and make recommendations to management. Examples of parallel teams include scrap reduction teams, inventory accuracy teams and vendor certification teams.
Project Teams	Cross-functional and used for problem-solving. They differ from parallel teams in that they are brought together with a specific goal and, once achieved, they disband and return to their functional group. They are time-limited and usually have a mandate of innovation. Their output is highly unpredictable and members normally require a high level of individual expertise. Examples of project teams include new product development teams, project implementation teams and task forces.
Management Teams	Teams that coordinate and provide direction for an organization or unit. Usually responsible for overall performance, it is composed of managing members from different functions with decision-making authority. These teams may occur at the executive level, as well as the division or subunit level.

Though referred to differently, descriptions of these factors are similar across the literature. Scott and Tiessen (1999) emphasize the importance of strong, effective support systems in developing effective teams. Integration of work processes and resources is necessary to develop high performing teams. These support systems are discussed in more detail later in this chapter.

Step 5: Measuring Team Performance

One of the most common reasons that teams are introduced into the organization is to facilitate change – to improve processes and solve problems more quickly than traditional environments. It is expected that the teams will recommend changes and solutions that will increase efficiencies, reduce cost, or increase market share and will do so very quickly. The assumption is that these operational changes will flow into real savings on the bottom line.

These changes or improvements are the result of *innovation* – "the act or process of innovating" or "something newly introduced; new method, custom, device, etc." (Webster, 1971). According to Katzenbach and Smith (1996) the intent behind team-based organizations is to produce new and better ways to meet customer demands and to do so more quickly and effectively than the competition by sharing ideas and knowledge in a supportive environment. In this TBO model, innovation refers to not only the leap improvements, but incremental improvements as well.

Critical to all plans is evaluation and adjustment. Evaluating performance implies some measurement of outcome. But how are these innovative changes measured and evaluated? The literature suggests that team results are observable in three dimensions: behavioral, attitudinal and performance effectiveness – all of which have an observable affect on operations. Behavioral measures include absenteeism, turnover and safety. Attitudinal outcomes include employee satisfaction, commitment and trust in management. Performance effectiveness assesses quantity and quality of outputs (e.g. efficiency, productivity, response times, quality and innovation) (Cohen & Bailey, 1997).

Financial measures of performance have rarely have been used to measure outcomes. Studies of management teams have used measures of firm performance such as return on assets, return on equity, and sales growth (Cohen & Bailey, 1997). These may be appropriate measures for management outcomes. However, there are many other factors that affect performance such as the economy, industry factors, and other management initiatives that make it difficult to use these measures as a dependable indicator of team performance. Furthermore, these overall performance measures are not appropriate for other types of teams. For example, return on assets would be inappropriate for a customer service team, since they have little control of assets.

Step 6: Has the team met its goals and objectives?

Team outcomes must in some way be measured to determine whether the team is still on track with company strategy. The final element in the model questions whether the team has met its goals and objectives. Having an appropriate measurement system in place is imperative when evaluating this question.

If the team has met its goals, then a feedback loop cycles back to the strategy and core competency elements. If the team has not achieved the desired results, an alternate feedback loop returns to the support system element. This is a very important deviation from many models. This step forces management to question whether there is sufficient support in place for the teams to perform. The following questions are examples of those that management may pose to determine whether the level of support is adequate or lacking:

- Are the necessary technical skills available within the team membership?
- Has the team's mission been clearly communicated? Do they have a charter?
- Have all the team members had team skill training, such as how to run meetings, resolve conflict, identify problems, and group decision-making?
- Do they have access to all the process information they need for their task?
- Do the performance measurements that are in place actually measure the expected outcome of this project/process?
- Is there a reward structure in place to motivate performance? Is there a conflict between the performance measures and the reward structure?
- Has the supervisor for this team been properly trained as a team facilitator?

By readdressing the area of support systems, managers can identify weaknesses or conflicting systems that may inhibit team performance. Once identified, management can then make decisions to strengthen their support in these areas and provide better resources for the teams to achieve their goals.

THE 'BLACK BOX' OF THE TBO MODEL

The previous section described all the elements in the TBO strategic model. This section provides a more detailed review of the core factors and the relationships among these elements and examines them more closely to gain a better understanding of their interrelationships. The highlighted elements in Fig. 1 are the focus of this discussion. This is the *black box*, if you will, of the organizational world.

Management determines that teams will form and then waits to assess the results. Understanding what happens between formation and outcome is critical to understanding how to manage teams for success. These core elements are support systems, teaming processes, potency and performance. Fig. 2 illustrates each element in more detail.

Support Systems

The previous discussion addressing the descriptive model introduced the basic premise: investment in support systems leads to increased ability of the team to

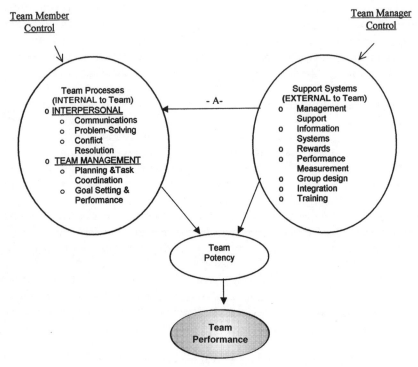

Fig. 2. Organizational Performance Model. (Adapted from Guzzo, 1993.)

achieve its goals. For example, an increase in team training leads to better problem solving and decision-making abilities and that increase in ability enables the team to perform at a higher level. Another example is that an appropriate and well-communicated set of performance measures promotes team-level goal setting and task management, enabling the team to perform well.

There are factors that influence how the team performs its task and over which management exercises some measure of control. Hall (1998) examined nine team support systems from the team members' perspective to determine which systems were considered more important. The nine systems described in his study are group design, defining performance, information systems, direct supervisor support, executive management support, training systems, performance appraisal system, rewards, and integration. Each system is described in more detail below.

Group Design

Group design involves aligning team mission with the skills and ability of specific teams. It also includes selecting appropriate team members and size (Hall, 1998). Several studies have found that group design, composition, and task alignment are related to team effectiveness (Campion et al., 1993; Gladstein, 1984; Wageman, 1997). Some studies refer to this system as a team characteristic rather than an environmental or support system. This is included here as a support system, because management decisions and planning can directly impact this factor, particularly at startup.

Information Systems

Information systems refer to the accessibility of information by the team. Information may entail collecting, organizing and storing process information (e.g. scrap rates, production quotas), resource or cost information (e.g. material prices, machine overhead) or customer feedback (e.g. satisfaction indices, returns). Support for this factor as a predictor of effectiveness has been found in several studies (Cohen et al., 1996; Hackman & Walton, 1986; Lawler et al., 1986).

Management Support

Hall (1998) distinguishes two types of management support – executive and supervisory. The role of the supervisor is one of facilitation and requires leadership and coaching skills. Facilitation includes providing necessary resources and, in many cases, acting as liaison with other parts of the organization. Executive managerial support involves communicating priorities to the teams and providing support (capital, facilities, resources) and encouragement (open to new ideas, acting on recommendations). Most studies do not distinguish between direct supervisor support and executive management support, but refer to managerial support as one factor (Burningham & West, 1995; Campion et al., 1993; Wageman, 1997). Studies using the more general term 'management support' usually align with this definition. This factor has been found to relate to team performance (Burningham & West, 1995, Campion et al., 1993).

Training Systems

Training systems develop the performance abilities of teams. They build skills (e.g. interpersonal, leadership, facilitation, decision-making, consensus building) that enable individuals to work as a team. Training has been examined in several studies and found to be a significant factor influencing performance (Campion et al., 1993; Cohen et al., 1996; Lawler, 1986).

Performance Measurement System

Performance appraisal systems assess the growth of the team and ability development. It also includes regular feedback to the team on their performance using understandable, well-defined metrics. Scott and Tiessen (1999) investigated the incidence and importance of performance measurement and found it positively associated with team performance. Burningham and West's (1995) results suggest that appraisal and monitoring group processes are of primary importance in predicting group innovation.

Performance measurement aligns team goals with those of the organization and ensures that they are clearly communicated to the team. Shea and Guzzo (1987) found indications that proper alignment of team and organizational goals is a predictor of team effectiveness. Kaplan and Norton (1996) clearly demonstrate that goal clarity and measures encouraging teamwork and are key to the success of teams.

Rewards

Rewards reinforce desirable goals and priorities and influence both individual and group behaviors. Rewards also include reinforcement and recognition programs. To be most effective, they need to align with organizational strategies. Several studies have found that reward systems affect team performance (Cohen et al., 1996; Hackman & Walton, 1986; Scott & Tiessen, 1999).

Integration

The role of integration systems is to provide a mechanism for teams to communicate with other teams and parts of the organization. Integration systems link operating units vertically and horizontally in an effort to share information and leverage knowledge developed by other teams.

Team Processes

The descriptive model in Fig. 1 shows that companies establish teams to meet their goals and support systems have an influence on these teams. The factors internal to teams reflected in the modified model in Fig. 2 are the teams' internal processes. This section discusses these internal processes.

The literature suggests that internal processes of the team may be guided by individual team member skills, abilities, task design, and motivation. Skills and abilities are influenced through experience and training, while task and environmental factors are determined by the social system within which teams are embedded. This section on team abilities focuses on those competencies necessary for smooth, effective team processes. Better internal processes drive better performance (Mohrman et al., 1995). Research by Stevens and Campion has culminated in a skill classification scheme that appears relevant to the study of team performance.

Stevens and Campion have developed and tested two categories of knowledge, skills, and abilities (KSA) required for successful teamwork: Interpersonal KSAs and Self-Mangement KSAs (Stevens & Campion, 1994, 1999). These two categories can be further broken down into five subcategories and are the basis of this discussion.

Interpersonal KSAs

The three categories of Interpersonal KSAs include conflict resolution, collaborative problem solving and communication KSAs. Conflict can have both a positive and a negative effect on group behavior. Stevens and Campion suggest that some level of conflict is inevitable in teams and actually required to reach optimal performance. They argue, "Without conflict, there may be no way to sense the need for change or draw attention to problem areas . . . constructive conflict allows teams to identify problems, develop solutions and work through tradeoffs without alienating members" (Stevens & Campion, 1994, p.507). However, when conflict is not reasonably managed, it can escalate to the point where it becomes a barrier to performance (Levine & Moreland, 1990). Conflict Resolution KSA characteristics recognized by Stevens and Campion focus on recognizing the sources of conflict employing appropriate resolution strategies.

The second subcategory of interpersonal skills is collaborative problem solving. In some circumstances, too much participation can complicate the decision processes and create tension, resulting in inefficiency and a poor decision. Participation may yield solution acceptance and ownership while the availability of information increases.

The last subcategory of interpersonal KSAs is communication. The characteristics in this category highlight casual, open communication, listening skills, nonverbal messages and talk. Small talk and casual greetings enhance personal relationships and encourage a relaxed atmosphere. One benefit of working in teams is the knowledge sharing that takes place. Interpersonal skills enable teams to optimize their opportunity to share and create solutions.

Self-Management KSAs

Teams vary with respect to their autonomy. Some team structures allow more self-management than others. Most teams function at some level of self-management. Stevens and Campion (1994) address two subcategories of self-management skills that facilitate successful task management. The first of these is goal setting and performance management, which focus on establishing goals and monitoring progress. Regular feedback is an essential element of any performance measurement system and allows for adjustment in strategy and planning (Kaplan & Norton, 1996; Robinson & Robinson, 1995). The second subcategory of self-management KSAs is planning and task coordination. Once goals and measures are established, activities need to be synchronized in a fashion that considers workload balance and task interdependencies.

In summary, teams need to be adept in these skills to smoothly develop and improve their internal processes. An improved internal process yields improved performance.

Team Potency

Figure 2 displays a construct labeled 'potency.' Potency ". . . is the collective belief in a group that it can be effective . . ." (Guzzo et al., 1993, p. 87). Generally, team members evaluate the probability that they will succeed by looking to the knowledge, skills and abilities of the team members and to the support provided by the organization. If the team perceives that they have sufficient ability and support, their confidence that they can achieve their goal (potency) increases. Whereas, team confidence decreases if they find their skills or management support lacking.

There is strong indication that team effectiveness is influenced by team potency (Shea & Guzzo, 1987; Campion et al., 1993; Guzzo et al., 1993). Guzzo et al. offer a conceptual framework that suggests that factors both internal to the team (e.g. abilities, experience, skills, knowledge, size, etc.) and external to the team (resources, goals, rewards, leadership, etc.) affect potency which, in turn, leads to effectiveness as illustrated in Fig. 2. Guzzo's model is modified to include the effect of support systems on team processes (Link A).

Campion et al. (1993) grouped nineteen characteristics into five broad categories: job design, interdependence, composition, context and process. They collected data on productivity, employee satisfaction and manager judgments from both team and management data. They found that potency (as a characteristic within the process category) was the only one of the nineteen factors that was significantly related in all six analyses.

Team Outcomes

Team outcomes occur at individual, group, business unit and organizational levels. Three dimensions of performance are commonly used in studies of teams. The two most common are behavioral and attitudinal with a focus on individual outcomes (absenteeism, turnover, employee satisfaction). Business unit and organizational level measures are harder to derive. Some studies have used broad financial measures like ROI (return on investment). Unfortunately, multiple management initiatives and market issues confound these measures (Cohen et al., 1996).

A third dimension of team performance is performance effectiveness measures. These measures assess the quantity and quality of outputs such as response times, quality, innovation and customer satisfaction (Cohen & Bailey, 1997). Cohen et al. (1996) also used employee attitudes (job satisfaction, organization commitment), performance effectiveness (controlling costs, productivity and quality) and employee behavior (absenteeism) as effectiveness measures.

Table 3 summarizes information provided in a review of studies from 1990 to 1995 by Cohen and Bailey. This table illustrates the dominance of the use of perceptions as outcome measures and the lack of objective financial outcome measures. Studies of top management teams are the only ones that used financial measures of performance. Generally, these measures were mostly measures of firm performance, such as ROA (return on assets). The rest of the objective measures are operational measures.

The literature is lacking in the use of accounting measures to monitor effectiveness at the group level. McGrath (1986) said that groups should be measured in context and at the group level. Project teams rarely use objective measures due to the longitudinal nature of their outputs (Cohen & Bailey, 1997). Dunphy and Bryant (1996) argue that there have been too few quantitative studies thus far, and those that are quantitative tend to concentrate on attitudinal and behavioral output measures. There is a call for new quantitative measures

Table 3. Summary of Outcome Measures.

Team Type	No. of Studies	Effectiveness: Objective Outcomes	Effectiveness: Perceptions of Outcomes	Behavioral	Attitudinal
Parallel	4	3	4	2	3
Project	13	0	12	0	3
Management	13	10	2	3	1
Work	24	9	18	10	16
Percentage	*100%*	*41%*	*67%*	*28%*	*41%*
TOTAL	54	22	36	15	23

Note: This table is a consolidation of detailed tables provided in Cohen & Bailey, 1997.

of team performance that may be compared to and aligned with organizational goals.

Alignment of team and organization goals has been found to be a major contributor to the success of team-based organizations (Shea & Guzzo, 1987). Organizational goals are guided by financial targets, so team goals should have a similar orientation. Indeed, management teams are unique in that their performance goals are largely based on financial metrics (Cohen and Bailey, 1997). It would be beneficial for future research to also use accounting-based measures to evaluate team performance for other types of teams enabling easier assessment of team alignment with the organization.

How it All Works Together

Guzzo et al. (1993) proposed a model of team performance that suggests that team perception of the adequacy of support systems (external to the team) and teaming processes (internal to the team) influence team potency, which in turn, influences team performance. Figure 2 incorporates Guzzo's model into the key elements of the TBO Model in Fig. 1, providing more detail behind each of the elements.

This illustration shows support systems as factors external to the team over which managers have influence to develop as available resources to support team needs. Support systems influence the manner and competence with which teams work together for a common goal by giving them skills, information and resources. They also influence the team's perception of team potency, which is the team's collective belief that they can accomplish their goals.

Skilled teaming processes enable teams to use their resources and skills to make informed, effective decisions. Having smooth and effective processes in place influences team potency and performance.

CONCLUSION

This chapter outlines a model of team-based organizations collaboratively developed with multiple companies' representatives. Similar to most organizational models, it begins with strategic vision and ends with an outcome assessment with feedback loops for adjustment. It is unique, however, in several areas. The critical points are summarized in seven fundamental attributes.

Seven Key Attributes of the TBO Model

Key No. 1   Recognizing and developing human resource as a core competence leads to competitive advantage.

Key No. 2   Simultaneous and continued investment in support systems is essential to teams' success because it both provides vital resources and skills and increases teams' perceptions of management support.

Key No. 3   Managers cannot affect change except through their influence on the environment surrounding the team.

Key No. 4   Team perception of their skills and level of organizational support is pivotal in motivating teaming behaviors and success.

Key No. 5   The product of teamworking is both leap and incremental innovation.

Key No. 6   Use outcome measures directly related to team goals and over which the team exercises control.

Key No. 7   When team performance falls short, first readdress support systems to ensure that the team has all the necessary resources it needs to succeed.

NOTES

1. This model was developed in partnership with corporate sponsors of the Center for the Study of Work Teams (CSWT) at the University of North Texas. Company representatives volunteered to work together on a team dedicated to measuring team effectiveness. This two-year effort resulted in the strategic model described in this section.

2. Teaming is one tool of several employee involvement practices that also includes knowledge management and quality circles.

REFERENCES

Best, M. H. (1990). *The New Competition*. Cambridge. MA: Harvard University Press.

Burningham, C., & West, M. (1995). Individual, climate, and group interaction processes as predictors of work team innovation. *Small Group Research, 26*(1), 106–117.

Campion, M., Medsker, G., & Higgs, C. (1993). Relations between work group characteristics & effectiveness: Implications for designing effective work groups. *Personnel Psychology 46*, 823–850.

Cohen, S., & Bailey, D. (1997). What makes teams work: Group effectiveness research from the shop floor to the executive suite. *Journal of Management, 23*(3), 239–290.

Cohen, S., Ledford, G., & Spreitzer, G. M. (1996). A predictive model of self-managing work team effectiveness. *Human Relations, 49*(5), 643–676.

Dunphy, D., & Bryant, B. (1996). Teams: Panaceas or prescriptions for improved performance? *Human Relations, 49*(5), 677–699.

Gladstein, D. (1984). Groups in context: A model of task group effectiveness. *Administative Science Quarterly, 29*, 499–517.

Guzzo, R., & Dickson, M. (1996). Teams in organizations: Recent research on performance and effectiveness. *Annual Review of Psychology, 47*, 307–338.

Guzzo, R., Yost P., Campbell, R., & Shea, G. (1993). Potency in groups: Articulating a construct. *British Journal of Social Psychology, 32*, 87–106.

Hackman, J. R., & Walton, R. E. (1986). Leading groups in organizations. In: P. S. Goodman (Ed.), *Designing Effective Work Groups* (pp. 72–119). San Francisco: Jossey-Bass.

Hall, C. (1998). Organizational support for team-based organizations: Employee collaboration through organizational structures. Ph.D. dissertation, University of North Texas, Denton.

Hall, C., & Beyerlein, M. (2001) Support system for teams: A taxonomy. In: M. Beyerlein, D. Johnson & S. Beyerlein (Eds), *Product Development Teams*. Greenwich, CT: JAI Press.

Heracleous, I. (1995). Spinning a brand new cultural web. *Personnel Management, 1*(22), 24–27.

Kaplan, R. S., & Norton, D. P. (1996). *The Balanced Scorecard*. Boston: Harvard Business School Press.

Katzenbach, J., & Smith, D. (1993). *The Wisdom of Teams* (1st ed.). Boston: Harvard Business School Press.

Lawler, E. E. (1986). *High-Involvement Management*. San Francisco: Jossey-Bass.

Lawler, E. E., Mohrman, S., & Ledford, G. (1998). *Employee Involvement and Total QualityManagement Practices and Results in Fortune 1000 Companies*. San Francisco: Jossey-Bass.

Lawler, E. E., Mohrman, S., & Benson, G. (2001). *Organizing for High Performance*. San Francisco: Jossey-Bass.

Levine, J. M., & Moreland, R. L. (1990). Progress in small group research. *Annual Review of Psychology, 41*, 585–634.

Macy, B. A., & Izumi, H. (1993). Organizational change, design, and work innovation: a meta-analysis of 131 North American field studies: 1961–1991. In: W. Pasmore & R. Woodman (Eds), *Research in Organizational Change and Development* (Vol. 7, pp. 235–313). Greenwich, CT: JAI Press.

McGrath, J. E. (1986). Studying groups at work: Ten critical needs. In: P. S. Goodman (Ed.), *Designing Effective Work Groups* (pp. 362–391). San Francisco: Jossey-Bass.

Mohrman, S., Cohen, S., & Mohrman, A. (1995). *Designing Team-Based Organizations* (1st ed.). San Francisco: Jossey-Bass.

Nonaka, I., & Takeuchi, H. (1995). *The Knowledge-Creating Company*. New York: Oxford University Press.

Quinn, J. B., Anderson, P., & Finkelstein, S. (1996). Leveraging Intellect. *Academy of Management Executive, 10*(3), 7–27.

Prahalad, C. K., & Hamel, G. (1990). The core competence of the corporation. *Harvard Business Review* (May-June), 79–91.

Robinson, D. G., & Robinson, J. C. (1995). *Performance Consulting: Moving Beyond Training*. San Francisco: Berrett-Koehler.

Scott, T. W., & Tiessen, P. (1999). Performance measurement and managerial teams. *Accounting, Organizations and Society, 24*, 263–285.

Senge, P., Kleiner, A., Roberts, C., Ross, R. B., & Smith, B. J. (1994). *The Fifth Discipline Fieldbook*. New York: Bantam Doubleday Dell Publishing Group, Inc.

Shea, G. P., & Guzzo, R. A. (1987). Group effectiveness: What really matters? *Sloan Management Review, 29*(3), 25–31.

Stewart, T. A. (1997). *Intellectual Capital*. New York: Bantam Doubleday Dell Publishing Group, Inc.

Stevens, M. J., & Campion, M. A. (1994). The knowledge, skill, and ability requirements for teamwork: Implications for human resource management. *Journal of Management, 20*(2), 503–530.

Stevens, M. J., & Campion, M. A. (1999). Staffing work teams: Development and validation of a selection test for teamwork settings. *Journal of Management, 25*(2), 207–228.

Sundstrom, E. (1999). *Supporting Work Team Effectiveness* (1st ed.). San Francisco: Jossey-Bass.

Sundstrom, E., Meuse, K. P. D., & Futrell, D. (1990). Work teams. *American Psychologist, 45*(2), 120–133.

Sveiby, K. E. (1997). *The New Organizational Wealth.* (1st ed.). San Francisco: Berrett-Koehler Publishers.

Wageman, R. (1997). Critical success factors for creating superb self-managing teams. *Organizational Dynamics, 26*(1), 49–61.

THE IMPORTANCE OF TEAM TASK ANALYSIS FOR TEAM HUMAN RESOURCE MANAGEMENT

Steven J. Lorenzet, Erik R. Eddy and
Gerald D. Klein

ABSTRACT

Recent reports suggest that the use of teams in organizations is increasing (Guzzo & Shea, 1992). In fact, many organizations are moving towards team-based approaches, where teams become the centerpiece of organizational structure. As a result of this emphasis on teamwork, it is becoming increasingly important for organizations to become skilled at identifying the task and skill requirements, as well as the cognitive demands of teams and team members. Effective identification of necessary team characteristics can inform several human resource management challenges for teams, including, team design, team training, rewards for team performance, team member selection, and the diagnosis and promotion of team effectiveness.

This paper suggests that one way to increase our understanding of teams is through the use of team task analysis (TTA). TTA is a process of analyzing and describing the tasks of teams and the jobs of team members and can be used to identify the knowledge, skills, and abilities (KSAs), and attitude requirements relevant to team performance. Despite the obvious importance of TTA, reviews of the literature (Baker, Salas & Cannon-Bowers, 1998;

Team-Based Organizing, Volume 9, pages 113–145.
ISBN: 0-7623-0981-4

Levine, Penner, Brannick, Coovert & Llobert, 1988) have found very little systematic work on the topic. Further, an examination of traditional job analysis sources (e.g. Gael, 1983; Gael, 1988; Harvey, 1992) revealed twelve pages devoted to TTA (Dieterly, 1988).

Based on the apparent lack of attention given to TTA, one purpose of this paper is to update previous work on TTA, by reviewing and integrating the existing literature. Another purpose of this paper is to offer researchers a foundation for additional theoretical work. Finally, we hope to contribute towards a framework, and/or tool, to aid practitioners in the delivery of human resource management services to teams.

In our review, we provide a comparison of individual task analysis vs. TTA and provide key points of departure between the two concepts. Additionally, a summary of TTA is provided as well as warnings to practitioners and researchers based on previous research and theorizing regarding the aggregation of data (e.g. Bowers, Baker & Salas, 1994; Brenner, Sheehan, Arthur & Bennett, 1998; Kenny & LaVoie, 1985; Klein, Dansereau & Hall, 1994; Rousseau, 1985). In particular, our warnings focus on the potential dangers associated with aggregating individual level information (e.g. individual job analysis data) to higher (e.g. team) levels.

Next, methods that have been used to collect TTA information are reviewed and classified. Then, the type of information gathered, such as, team competencies/skills (e.g. Cannon-Bowers, Tannenbaum, Salas & Volpe, 1995; Stevens & Campion, 1994), job characteristics (e.g. Campion, Medsker & Higgs, 1993; Campion, Papper & Medsker, 1996), and cognitive information (e.g. Brenner et al., 1998; Klein, 1993) are reviewed and categorized. Additionally, comparisons of individual cognitive task analysis (i.e. the mental processes needed to accomplish an individual task) and cognitive TTA (i.e. the integrative team mental processes needed to accomplish a team task) are provided.

We conclude with a presentation of criteria for evaluating TTA methodologies and a series of suggestions to guide both practitioners and researchers regarding future work in TTA. Our emphasis is on explaining the value of TTA and what it means to the reader, regardless of his/her occupation (e.g. practitioner or researcher).

INTRODUCTION

Teams are the building blocks of many organizational structures and have been the focus of attention for many researchers (e.g. Baker & Salas, 1996; Salas, Cannon-Bowers, Payne & Smith-Jentsch, 1998; Stout, Cannon-Bowers, Morgan

& Salas, 1989). A team can often accomplish more than what its members could achieve when working by themselves (Hackman, 1992; Maier, 1967). Combination of different talents, and the synergy created by teamwork, can overcome many challenges encountered in organizational life, including those associated with production, planning and problem solving. Recent reports suggest that the use of teams in organizations is increasing (Guzzo & Shea, 1992). In fact, many organizations are moving towards a team-based structure (Mohrman, Cohen & Mohrman, 1995; Wright & Noe, 1996), where teams become the centerpiece of organizational structure. As the use of teams continues to expand, it becomes increasingly important to identify the tasks, skill requirements, and cognitive demands of teams and team members. By identifying these characteristics, we can better design teams and team training, develop more appropriate rewards for team performance, and better diagnose and promote team effectiveness.

One way to increase our understanding of teams is through the use of "team task analysis" (TTA). TTA is a process of analyzing and describing the jobs of team members. This analysis may also result in the identification of relevant knowledge, skills, abilities, and attitudes for the team, which can be used to develop job descriptions, job specifications, and other useful systems.

Considering the prevalence of teams, and the fact that there are so many types of teams (e.g. cross-functional, executive, military), it is surprising that such little attention has been paid to the development of appropriate TTA methodologies. Reviews of the literature on TTA have found very little systematic work examining TTA. For example, Levine, Penner, Brannick, Coovert, and Llobert's (1988) review found no instances of a well-tested methodology for analyzing what teams do and how they do it. Ten years later, a review by Baker, Salas and Cannon-Bowers (1998) revealed one technical report (Levine et al., 1988) and five journal articles (Baker & Salas, 1996; Bowers, Baker & Salas, 1994; Bowers, Morgan, Salas & Prince, 1993; Campion, Medsker & Higgs, 1993; Campion, Papper & Medsker, 1996) devoted to TTA. Dieterly (1988) noted that traditional job analysis sources (e.g. Gael, 1983; Gael, 1988) have devoted a total of only twelve pages to TTA. It seems as though TTA has been forgotten in the extant literature.

The Importance of Task Analysis

The importance of individual level task analysis (sometimes referred to as job analysis) is well established. Task analysis is a method for identifying individual tasks, skill requirements, and cognitive demands. A great deal of work has examined the methods, purposes, and uses of individual level job analysis. Two particular areas of focus are *sources* of job data and *methods* of collecting job data.

Possible sources of information (as noted by Harvey, 1992) include job incumbents, supervisors, or trained job analysts. Gathering information from any one source can lead to bias in the resulting task analysis. This led Thompson and Thompson (1982) to advise that the safest strategy is one that gathers information from as many available sources as possible. This recommendation is also valid for TTA and was recommended by Brenner, Sheehan, Arthur and Bennett (1998) who suggested there does not appear to be one best TTA source and that team task analysts should not rely solely on one source of information.

Methods of collecting data for an individual level job analysis vary from having analysts observe the job, to asking subject-matter-experts (SMEs) to describe the job, to videotaping task performance, to having analysts perform the job as a participant-observer. When SMEs are involved, data collection typically consists of interviews, questionnaires, diaries, or a combination of these methods.

The importance of task analysis is clear. Task analysis is the foundation for many human resource management (HRM) practices. Practically all HRM activities (e.g. recruitment, selection, training, performance appraisal, compensation) can be traced back to information obtained from a job analysis. Thus, the validity and legal defensibility of all HRM decisions, to some degree, depend on the accuracy (i.e. reliability and validity) of the job analysis they are based on. Given the above, it is not surprising that Cascio (1987) has referred to job analysis as the "blueprint" for all HRM functions.

Individual versus Team Task Analysis

A substantial amount of empirical research has focused on ways of improving task analysis. However, this research, and the development of new and innovative methods for collecting job data, has focused on the individual level. This may prove to be a problem for organizations that use teams, since it is questionable whether individual task analysis methods generalize to the team level (e.g. Baker, Salas & Prince, 1991). With the increased use of teams in organizations, the generalizability of individual job analysis methods is something that HRM professionals will need to address.

Generally speaking, job analysis is a tool for analyzing and describing jobs, which results in the identification of relevant knowledge, skills, and abilities (KSAs) that are used to develop job descriptions and job specifications. Harvey (1992) added to this definition by stating that job analysis is "the collection of data describing: (a) observable job behaviors performed by workers, including both what is accomplished as well as what technologies are employed to accomplish the end result; and (b) verifiable characteristics of the job environment with which workers interact, including physical, mechanical, social, and informational elements" (p. 74). The goals of job analysis should be: (a) the description of observables; (b) the description of the job, not the individual holding the job; and (c) data that are verifiable and replicable (Harvey, 1992).

TTA differs from traditional task analysis in several ways. First, while traditional task analysis focuses solely on the individual, TTA focuses on the team and the interactions among team members. TTA is not only an analysis of a team's tasks, but is also a comprehensive assessment of a team's teamwork requirements (i.e. KSAs and attitude requirements) (Baker et al., 1998). Similar to job analysis, it is essentially the "blueprint" of all "team" HRM functions. However, TTA must go beyond traditional KSAs and consider factors like coordination, attitudes, team competencies, and differences between teamwork and taskwork (Morgan, Glickman, Woodward, Blaiwes & Salas, 1986). Morgan et al. (1986) have explained that taskwork consists of behaviors that are performed by individual team members, and are crucial to the execution of individual team member functions. Unfortunately Morgan et al. (1986) did not outline any specific team member tasks that were characteristic of these functions, which still remains an area that requires additional research. However, Morgan et al. (1986) did delineate a specific series of team behaviors that were organized into six dimensions of teamwork (i.e. team spirit, coordination, cooperation, adaptability, effective communication, and effective acceptance of suggestions or criticisms).

Team Task Analysis

The lack of empirically validated TTA methods has not precluded researchers and practitioners from analyzing and examining teams and the tasks they perform. In fact, the wealth of articles, books, technical reports, and other works is evidence that teams are a very popular topic of research. However, the primary strategies for TTA have come from the individual level (e.g. Prince & Salas, 1993). The frequent use of individual job analysis methods at the team level has occurred despite warnings from scholars about the dangers of generalizing individual level phenomena to the team level (e.g. Brenner et al., 1998; Kenny & LaVoie, 1985; Rousseau, 1985; Klein, Dansereau & Hall, 1994). It appears the primary reason for the reliance on individual methods is the lack of operational methods specifically designed for conducting TTA.

From a methodological/research standpoint several authors (Kenny & LaVoie, 1985; Rousseau, 1985; Klein et al., 1994) have expressed concerns about the wealth of valuable information that may be missed when higher level (e.g. team) phenomena are measured by simply aggregating individual level measures. Specific applications of hierarchical forms of analysis have come from numerous subdisciplines of human resource management, including groups and teams (Kidwell, Mossholder & Bennett, 1997; Yammarino & Markham, 1992). The primary concern of such hierarchical analyses is analyzing the data collected at the appropriate level (e.g. individual or team). The major concern addressed by research examining this issue is the potentially erroneous findings that may result from individual analyses aggregated to the team level. Simply stated, using a tool designed to measure individual level KSAs and applying it to team KSAs, is in essence using the tool for a purpose it was not intended, and may result in incorrect analyses and conclusions.

From a practitioner standpoint, concerns also exist regarding team information that may be missed by individual level job analysis methods. The major criticism of applying individual job analysis methods to teams is that critical teamwork behaviors like interdependence, coordination, and cooperation are simply not measured (Bowers et al., 1994). Additionally, it may be the case that important team attitudes like team cohesion and team efficacy may also be missed. Baker et al. (1998) suggested TTA can be thought of as a comprehensive assessment of a team's teamwork requirements (i.e. knowledge, skill, ability, and attitude requirements), that form the foundation for such important functions as team design, team performance, and team training. They further stated that TTA is essentially the building block for all team HRM functions. Given the Baker et al. (1998) definition and the obvious importance of TTA for team HRM functions, it becomes clear that aggregating individual job analysis methods as a substitute for TTA may place limitations on the effectiveness of organizational teams.

One exception to the dearth of team-focused methodology is the framework presented by Levine et al., 1988. In Levine et al.'s (1988) methodology, referred to as the MAP system, sets of descriptors, sources, methods of data collection, and methods of analysis/synthesis for job analysis at the individual level were modified to fit a team context. Despite the existence of this system, little empirical research has tested the validity of the model. With the exception of the MAP system and the work mentioned in Baker et al.'s (1998) review (e.g. Baker & Salas, 1996; Campion et al., 1993; Campion et al., 1996) very little empirical investigation has been performed on the topic of TTA. As a result, very little direct, systematic attention has been paid to the identification of teamwork KSAs, attitudes, competencies, and tasks.

The lack of attention paid to TTA and important team level phenomena has created several limitations. Team task and skill data are needed to effectively perform "team" HRM functions. Examples include designing team structures, developing team training, selecting team members, measuring team performance, rewarding team performance, building team competencies, developing career ladders for team members, creating career systems that develop team competencies, and diagnosing team effectiveness. Without reliable and valid methods for performing TTA, it is difficult to execute these critical "team" HRM functions. One may have to resort to using individual job analysis methods and attempting to generalize them to the team level. For the reasons previously mentioned (e.g. Baker et al., 1998; Bowers et al., 1994; Brenner et al., 1998; Kenny & LaVoie, 1985; Klein et al., 1994; Rousseau, 1985), it is difficult to have a great deal of confidence in the reliability and validity of such methods.

Therefore, a firm understanding of current task analytic methods and potential uses for TTA is essential to the growth and advancement of HRM. Without methods for TTA, researchers and practitioners may be basing HRM decisions on data that are inappropriate for the questions that they are asking. Research and development is needed to establish appropriate TTA methodologies for various team requirements. Several research questions seem relevant to TTA. For example, should TTA focus on team tasks, team competencies, team cognitive demands, or some combination of these? Should individual level issues be addressed (e.g. the teamwork/taskwork distinction)? Should other factors like obstacles to team success, importance of tasks (e.g. importance for team success), and level of competence (e.g. how strong is the team in a given area) be examined? In a particular organizational location what balance of technical KSAs and team KSAs should be sought? These are just some of the questions facing researchers interested in TTA. Research devoted to answering these and other questions, should help to advance "team" HRM policies and practices.

In summary, just based on the volume of print space devoted to teams it is clear that teams are both an important and interesting organizational topic of study. However, the lack of empirically tested and validated TTA methods suggests there may be methodological concerns as well as practical concerns (i.e. organizational effectiveness and legal defensibility) associated with aggregating individual task analysis methods and using them as a proxy for TTA. The limited theoretically guided, systematic work on TTA has not precluded HRM professionals and researchers from analyzing what teams do and developing team tools, but as Baker et al. (1998) noted, it would be more desirable to employ a comprehensive and valid system designed specifically for conducting TTA. Therefore, it is the goal of this paper to review the existing relevant work on TTA, to highlight the need for additional work examining TTA, and to provide guidance for future TTA efforts.

TEAM TASK ANALYSIS INFORMATION

Although an obvious current weakness of TTA is the lack of adequately designed methods, our review found a number of studies that promoted various methods for analyzing team tasks. After further examination, it appears useful to distinguish between methods used to gather information (e.g. questionnaires, interviews) and the types of information that are gathered (e.g. competencies/skills, job characteristics). Although most of the methods are borrowed from the literature on individual task analysis, it is important to have a clear understanding of the methods used to gather information and the type of information gathered during TTA.

Methods Used to Gather TTA Information

Four common methods used to conduct TTA include: (1) questionnaires; (2) interviews; (3) controlled observation; and (4) critical incidents. The use of questionnaires is quite common (e.g. Bowers et al., 1993; Campion et al., 1993; Campion et al., 1996). Typical assessments made by questionnaires include criticality of error, difficulty, time spent, difficulty of learning, and importance for training (e.g. Baker & Salas, 1996; Baker et al., 1991; Bowers et al., 1994; Levine, 1983; Sanchez & Levine, 1989). Questionnaires can also be used to investigate cognitive processes that underlie overt/observable performance. However, Klein (1993) has noted that one of the weaknesses of questionnaires is that they are prone to generate general or idealized information regarding performance.

Interviews are commonly characterized by asking SMEs to describe the activities they perform on the job. Interviews are typically conducted in either structured or open-ended format. The structured approach has the advantage of reducing random and systematic error, but may miss important information not built into the interview. The open-ended approach suffers from lack of structure, but has the advantage of gaining additional information that may have been missed in a structured approach. Another potential weakness of the interview approach, similar to questionnaires, is the potential for obtaining general or idealized performance information (Klein, 1993).

Controlled observation methods include having experts think out loud while performing the task, asking experts to provide a retrospective account after completing the task, or limiting the information given to experts and observing how they react to the deficiency. This method allows for data collection by observation and computer, and provides the opportunity for critical aspects of the task to be controlled and manipulated. However, Klein (1993) has noted that controlled observation may be unable to uncover new factors related to effective performance, since researchers have prepared scenarios in advance.

Another method used to identify critical team behaviors is the critical incidents approach (e.g. Morgan et al., 1986; Prince & Salas, 1993). Flanagan (1954) defined critical incidents as: (1) a description of the setting in which a behavior has occurred; (2) a description of the behavior itself (effective or ineffective); and (3) a description of the positive or negative consequences that resulted from the behavior. Previous work has used critical incidents to assist in the development of team performance criteria (Morgan et al., 1986). However, critical incidents can only be used for extant teams, making the method unlikely to be useful for designing new equipment, teams, or jobs.

Type of Information Gathered through TTA

Another important consideration in TTA, beyond the methods used, is the type of information gathered. Typical classifications in individual level task analysis include cross-job-relative, within-job-relative, and qualitative (Harvey, 1992). These distinctions may also be possible for TTA, but our review revealed another classification we believe is more appropriate. Based on our review, we have grouped information that can be gathered through TTA into three categories: (1) a team competencies/skills approach; (2) a job characteristics approach; and (3) a cognitive approach (see Table 1 for a summary of the various approaches).

Team Competencies/Skills

Cannon-Bowers, Tannenbaum, Salas and Volpe (1995) suggested that constructs like team performance and team training can be understood only in the context in which they occur. Based on this paradigm, Cannon-Bowers et al. (1995) proposed a model where organizational and situational characteristics have an impact on aspects of team performance and team functioning. In order to provide theoretically based prescriptions for selecting and designing training strategies, it is important to understand the relationships among team competencies, training requirements, and training strategies. Cannon-Bowers et al. (1995) made a distinction between individual competencies and team competencies. Team competency is defined as team knowledge, skills, and attitudes. Knowledge is defined as the principles and concepts underlying the team's effective task performance. Skills are the necessary team behaviors to perform a task effectively. Appropriate attitudes (about self and other team members) are those that foster effective team performance. This is essentially a derivation of the

Table 1.   Summary of Types of Information Gathered.

Category	Researchers	Recommended Information to Gather
Team Competencies/ Skills	Cannon-Bowers Tannenbaum, Salas and Volpe (1995)	• Context-driven competencies • Team-contingent competencies • Task-contingent competencies • Transportable competencies

	Stevens and Campion (1994)	• Interpersonal KSAs
		  • Conflict resolution
		  • Collaborative problem solving
		  • Communication
		• Self-Management KSAs
		  • Goal setting and performance management
		  • Planning and task coordination

Job Characteristics	Campion, Medsker and Higgs (1993) Campion, Papper and Medsker (1996)	• Job design • Interdependence • Composition • Context • Process
Cognitive Demands	Baker, Cannon-Bowers and Salas (1998)	• Cognitive skills • Task interaction and sequencing requirements • Knowledge and cognitive skills and abilities

	Blickensderfer, Cannon-Bowers, Salas and Baker (2000)	• Team knowledge requirements
		  • Pre-task knowledge
		  • Dynamic performance understanding

	Brenner, Sheehan, Arthur and Bennett (1998); Klein (1993)	• Psychological processes • Critical decisions and cognitive processes • Knowledge organization • Interrelationship between job concepts • Knowledge structures and mental processes

KSA approach from individual training proposed by Goldstein (1986). The difference being that skill contains both psychomotor and cognitive competencies. Further, skills in the Cannon-Bowers et al. (1995) approach combines Goldstein's (1986) skills and abilities. Additionally, based on the work of Dick and Carey (1990), attitudes are also included as necessary competencies since it has been shown that job-related attitudes can have an impact on performance.

Cannon-Bowers et al. (1995) next proposed different kinds/categories of team competencies and integrated them based on their relation to the team (specific vs. generic) and their relation to the task (specific vs. generic). Examples of team specific competencies are knowledge of teammates characteristics and attitudes that are outcomes of experiences with a particular team, such as team cohesion and a sense of collective efficacy. Team generic competencies, applicable to any team include communication, interpersonal and leadership skills and an individual's propensity to work in a team. Competencies pertinent to specific tasks include knowledge of the specific role responsibilities in the team, while general interpersonal, problem solving and planning skills are examples of task generic competencies. Thus, four specific competencies for effective team performance were proposed: (1) context-driven; (2) team-contingent; (3) task-contingent; and (4) transportable.

Context-driven team competencies are driven by the task and the team involved, and may be referred to as team-specific and task-specific. Teams with a membership that is relatively stable, and that perform a minimal amount of tasks, are likely to require context-driven competencies. Examples of such teams (provided by Cannon-Bowers et al., 1995) include combat teams and sports teams.

Team-contingent team competencies are those that are specific to a team, but not to a particular task. Teams whose members are consistent and work together on a variety of tasks tend to require team-contingent competencies. Examples of such teams (provided by Cannon-Bowers et al., 1995) include self-managed teams, management teams, and quality circles.

Task-contingent team competencies may be referred to as team-generic and task-specific. Teams that perform a specific task, but may not always perform it with the same group of team members, are likely to require task-contingent competencies. Examples of teams (provided by Cannon-Bowers et al., 1995) that require task-contingent competencies are medical teams, aircrews, and firefighting teams.

When team members work on a variety of tasks with a variety of different teams, transportable team competencies are required. These team competencies may be referred to as team-generic and task-generic. Teams that require transportable team competencies (provided by Cannon-Bowers et al., 1995) include task forces and project teams. For many organizations today facing rapid and significant change there is ample justification for providing employees with competencies that are transportable, and are applicable to any team and any task. In fact, there is some evidence to suggest that such a trend is emerging (Moravec & Tucker, 1992; Hammer & Champy, 1993; Bridges, 1994; Siegel, 1997; Dessler, 2000). Organizations require individual and team flexibility and the willingness of both to take their cues not only from job descriptions, team task descriptions, original team charters, and the instructions of supervisors but from the actual work that needs doing at the moment, and to change as that changes. With change, work associates, team members and tasks can vary and transportable competencies would seem most useful under these circumstances.

Stevens and Campion (1994) reviewed the literature on groups to determine the KSA requirements for teamwork. Their review focused on: (1) KSAs rather than personality traits; (2) team rather than technical KSAs; and (3) the individual rather than the team level of analysis. Based on their review, Stevens and Campion (1994) derived fourteen specific KSAs, which they categorized under five general requirements for teamwork (see Appendix A).

The five KSA requirements for teamwork were further categorized as either interpersonal or self-management KSAs. Interpersonal included conflict resolution, collaborative problem solving, and communication. Self-management included goal setting and performance management and planning and task coordination. Stevens and Campion (1994) listed several implications of teamwork KSAs for the design of HRM systems. Among their implications is that teamwork KSAs may be important for task analysis. Specifically, they suggest that task analysis procedures should include measures of teamwork KSAs if the teamwork trend continues (which it likely will). Finally, they propose that the teamwork KSAs identified in their review may provide a good starting point for future research and practice in task analysis.

Job Characteristics

Campion and his colleagues (e.g. Campion et al., 1993; Campion et al., 1996) have employed a job characteristics approach for examining the relation between team characteristics and effective teamwork. Based on an extensive literature review, Campion et al. (1993) identified nineteen job characteristics, which were then mapped onto five themes (see Table 2 for a summary). The five themes were job design, interdependence, composition, context, and process. Findings suggest that the five job themes were related to several effectiveness criteria (i.e. productivity, satisfaction, and manager judgements) for eighty intact work groups. Productivity, employee satisfaction, and manager judgements were all rated by both employees and managers, thus reducing the threat of single source bias.

Job design and interdependence characteristics showed relationships with several of the effectiveness criteria. Composition characteristics were also strong predictors, showing relationships with all three effectiveness criteria. Context characteristics showed relationships with satisfaction and manager judgements and process characteristics related mainly to productivity and manager judgements.

Table 2. Job Characteristics from Campion et al. (1993).

Theme	Characteristic	Definition
Job Design	Self-Management	Autonomy in the workplace.
	Participation	Degree to which all members participate in making decisions.
	Task Variety	Chance to perform a number of group tasks.
	Task Significance	Belief that team's work has significant consequences for customers and/or the organization.
	Task Identity	Degree to which the team completes a whole and separate piece of work.
Interdependence	Task interdependence	Degree to which group members interact and depend on one another to accomplish tasks.
	Goal Interdependence	Degree to which individual members' goals are linked to the team's goals.
	Interdependent Feedback and Rewards	Outcome interdependence.
Composition	Heterogeneity	Diversity in terms of abilities and experiences.
	Flexibility	Degree to which members can perform each other's jobs.
	Relative Size	Number of team members compared to actual number needed for the task.
	Preference for Group Work	Degree to which team members prefer to work in teams.
Context	Training	Interventions designed to increase team functioning.
	Managerial Support	Management's endorsement of the team and its goals.
	Communication/Cooperation Between Groups	Supervising boundaries and integrating the group with the rest of the organization.
Process	Potency	Team's belief that it can be effective.
	Social Support	Helping behaviors and positive social interaction among team members.
	Workload Sharing	Sharing work/task responsibilities.
	Communication/Cooperation Within Groups	Integrating the efforts of individual team members.

In a second study, Campion et al. (1996) sought to replicate the findings from Campion et al. (1993). The sample in the Campion et al. (1996) study differed from the previous sample in three ways. First, the 1993 study examined non-exempt administrative workers, whereas the 1996 study examined exempt professional workers (i.e. knowledge workers). Second, different effectiveness criteria were used, partly due to the different features of the different jobs. Similar to the 1993 study, opinion surveys and manager judgements were used in the 1996 study. However, due to the complexity and diversity of jobs, productivity measures could not be used. Four additional criteria not included in the 1993 study were also added to the follow-up. Senior and peer manager judgements provided an outside perspective on teams' effectiveness. To obtain an assessment of individual level performance, performance appraisal records of team members and managers were utilized. To examine temporal stability of the observed relationships, current judgements were collected along with follow-up judgements three months later. Additionally, to capture employees' perspectives, judgements of team effectiveness were obtained from employees. Finally, work units in the study, varied as to whether team members viewed their unit as a single team. For example, some employees worked on additional secondary teams, some team members were temporary, and some employees worked primarily with subgroups of co-workers, or individually as opposed to with their complete work unit.

Results of the Campion et al. (1996) study support the previous relationships found between work team characteristics and team effectiveness (Campion et al., 1993). Both job design and interdependence characteristics showed relationships with the majority of the effectiveness criteria. Composition characteristics demonstrated a minimal number of relationships with effectiveness. Contrary to the previous study, teams perceived as too small, or just the right size, were perceived as more effective. Finally, process and context characteristics both demonstrated several relationships with effectiveness.

The results of Campion et al. (1993) and Campion et al. (1996) suggest approaching TTA from a job characteristic perspective may be a valuable technique. Specifically, the work done by Campion and his colleagues has revealed several job characteristics for teams that are related to team effectiveness. These characteristics may be a possible starting point for TTA.

Integrating team competencies/skills and job characteristics. The previous section examined two kinds of information that can be gathered through TTA that would provide the basis for carrying out numerous human resource functions, including team member selection and training. Though the discussion above highlighted the differences in each of the approaches there are similarities in this work that are important to note. This section will examine further and compare the work in the team competencies/skills and the job characteristics approaches, before a third type of information that can be gathered through TTA is considered, cognitive task and cognitive team task analysis.

Certainly, an important issue as teams become more prevalent is determining the competencies required in teams and in team members. The authors cited in the previous section are explicitly or indirectly concerned with these competencies. The literature having a bearing on this issue is extensive and complex, in part because different labels are used to describe the same skills and similar labels are used for different skills (Cannon-Bowers et al., 1995). Though the major intent of Cannon-Bowers et al. (1995) is to provide theoretically based prescriptions for selecting and designing training strategies this work initially draws on an extensive body of conceptual and empirical work to identify the knowledge and skill competencies, and attitudes related to effective team performance. Team competencies are the explicit focus of Stevens and Campion (1994), authors of the other major work cited in the team competencies/skills category, though they are concerned with knowledge, skills and abilities and not with attitudes. Important to researchers and to practitioners is that each set of authors, in developing their lists of key team competencies, draw on previous work in different fields. Cannon-Bowers et al. (1995) draw primarily on human factors and military research. Stevens and Campion derive their KSAs from conceptual and empirical work primarily in social psychology, organizational behavior, sociotechnical systems and industrial engineering. Areas of agreement between the two that are discovered to exist, then, would suggest team competencies of potentially widespread value.

The work of Campion et al. (1993) and Campion et al. (1996) differs from the team competencies/skills approach because it considers some nineteen job or work team characteristics, including job design elements or variables, task elements or variables, setting or contextual variables and team processes. However, it does consider team member characteristics and qualities explicitly – team member affinity for teamwork, and potency (a collective sense of efficacy) – and the desirability of teams possessing other competencies, characteristics and qualities are implied by many of the work team characteristics. For example, the characteristic, Social Support, involves "helping behaviors and positive social interaction among team members," and Flexibility is "the degree to which members can perform each other's jobs" (Campion et al., 1993).

The work team characteristics proposed by Campion et al. (1993) and Campion et al. (1996), the teamwork KSAs of Stevens and Campion (1994), and teamwork skill dimensions from Cannon-Bowers et al. (1995) are compared in Table 3. The primary interest here is identifying areas of agreement between the three author sets, and areas of agreement between proponents of the job or work characteristics information and each of the proponents of the team competencies/skills information. An extensive review of overlap between authors in the team competencies/skills domain (i.e. Cannon-Bowers et al., 1995; Stevens & Campion, 1994) is reviewed in detail in Appendix B.

Table 3 indicates agreement among all authors concerning the importance of certain team competencies, including

- the ability to create or to clarify role expectations for individual team members, synchronize team member activities and solve problems;
- the ability to create shared, accepted team goals and individual member goals that support team goals;
- the ability to monitor, evaluate and provide feedback on team and individual team member performance;
- mutually respectful, cooperative, supportive and accurate communications among team members; and
- the proper sharing and balancing of workload in the team.

In other instances there is agreement among two sets of authors. The job or work characteristics approach (Campion et al., 1993; Campion et al., 1996) and Stevens and Campion (1994) both hold that team effectiveness involves, additionally, the ability to act autonomously and to reach decisions, for example, in such areas as establishing team goals, synchronizing team member interaction, and evaluating individual and team performance. Both sets of authors also identify as important, the second set implicitly, managerial support for team autonomy, and, in addition, the ability to create widespread participation in decision making. The job or work characteristics approach and Cannon-Bowers et al. (1995) view as desirable the ability of team members to perform a variety of teams tasks and each other's jobs, and team member awareness of the consequences of team performance on the other parts of the organization.

Cognitive Demands

A more recent development in task analysis is cognitive task analysis (CTA) (Baker, Cannon-Bowers & Salas, 1998; Brenner et al., 1998; Blickensderfer, Cannon-Bowers, Salas & Baker, 2000). CTA seeks to delineate the mental processes and skills needed to perform a task at high levels of proficiency (Ryder, Redding & Beckshi, 1987). Generally speaking, the function of CTA is to define the actual decision requirements of the task (Klein, 1993). Additionally, Klein's (1993) definition could be built on to include what an individual is thinking as they make decisions. Brenner et al. (1998) suggested

Table 3. A Comparison of Team Competencies/Skills with Work Team Characteristics.

Work Team Characteristics[1] (Campion, Medsker & Higgs, 1993; Campion, Papper & Medsker, 1996)	Teamwork KSAs[2] (Stevens & Campion, 1994)	Teamwork Skill Dimensions[3] (Cannon-Bowers, Tannenbaum, Salas & Volpe, 1995)
Job Design		
Self-Management (autonomy)	D. Goal Setting and Performance Mgt. KSAs (11, 12) E. Planning and Task Coordination KSAs (13, 14)[4]	
Participation	B. Collaborative Problem Solving KSAs (4,5) D. Goal Setting and Performance Mgt. KSAs (11,12) E. Planning and Task Coordination KSAs (13)	
Task Variety		Shared Situational Awareness
Task Significance		Shared Situational Awareness
Task Identify		Shared Situational Awareness
Interdependence		
Task Interdependence	B. Collaborative Problem Solving KSAs (4) E. Planning and Task Coordination KSAs (13,14)	Adaptability Shared Situational Awareness Interpersonal Relations Coordination
Goal Interdependence	D. Goal Setting and Performance Mgt. KSAs (11,12) E. Planning and Task Coordination KSAs (13,14)	Shared Situational Awareness Coordination
Interdependent Feedback and Rewards	D. Goal Setting and Performance Mgt. KSAs (12) E. Planning and Task Coordination KSAs (14)	Performance Monitoring and Feedback
Composition		
Heterogeneity		
Flexibility		Adaptability Shared Situational Awareness
Optimal Size		

Table 3. Continued.

Work Team Characteristics[1] (Campion, Medsker & Higgs, 1993; Campion, Papper & Medsker, 1996)	Teamwork KSAs[2] (Stevens & Campion, 1994)	Teamwork Skill Dimensions[3] (Cannon-Bowers, Tannenbaum, Salas & Volpe, 1995)
Composition		
Preference for Group Work		
Context		
Adequate Training	Authors assume that all KSAs, if not present, will be developed through training	
Managerial Support	Both the Goal Setting and Performance Mgt. KSAs (11,12) and the Planning and Task Coordination KSAs (13,14) assume the presence of managerial support	
Help with Communication and Cooperation Between the Teams		Shared Situational Awareness Communication
Process		
Potency		
Social Support	A. Conflict Resolution KSAs (1–3) C. Communication KSAs (6–10)	Leadership/Team Management Interpersonal Relations
Workload Sharing	E. Planning and Task Coordination KSAs (14)	Leadership/Team Management
Good Communication and Cooperation Within Teams	C. Communication KSAs (6) E. Planning and Task Coordination KSAs (13,14)	Adaptability Shared Situational Awareness Leadership/Team Management Interpersonal Relations Coordination Communication

[1] Definitions of each job/work team characteristic are in Table 2.
[2] Appendix A defines each of the fourteen teamwork KSAs from Stevens and Campion (1994). The listings above show general KSA categories and, in parentheses, specific KSAs.
[3] Appendix B contains full definitions of each teamwork skill dimension, from Cannon-Bowers et al. (1995).
[4] KSAs 13 and 14 indicate that *teams* have the ability to make certain important decisions and to initiate certain actions.

that regardless of the method used CTA should consist of the following five steps. First, task analysis should be used to map out the task. Second, critical decision points should be identified. Third, decision points should be clustered and linked. Fourth, decision points should be prioritized. Finally, decisions as to the strategies used, cues signaling the decision points, and the inferences made regarding cues and decision points, should be diagnosed and characterized.

Klein (1993) has noted several key differences between task analysis and CTA. CTA is focused on the underlying psychological processes responsible for behavior, where task analysis concentrates on observable behavior and ignores information dealing with overall organization of knowledge. Additionally, CTA examines critical decisions and cognitive processes that distinguish experts from novices (Roth, Woods & Pople, 1992). CTA is also intended to identify changes in knowledge structures as an individual progresses from a novice to an expert.

More recently, Klein (2000) has further noted that behavioral accounts of team performance provide information like which team member is responsible for which subtasks, how responsibility for the subtask shifts through performance cycles, and observation of how well a team is following procedures. However, a behavioral account of team performance only provides information regarding the steps a team follows and misses vital information relevant to the way the team is thinking. Klein (2000) suggests examples of such information missed by a behavioral account of team performance include how the team interprets a given situation, how team decision-making occurs, how role confusion among and between different members occurs, and how the team self-monitors to make adaptations and revisions when necessary.

Cognitive team task analysis (CTTA) requires analysis of the cognitive skills used by a team, the corresponding task interaction and sequencing requirements, and the knowledge and cognitive skills and abilities that underlie task performance (Baker et al., 1998). The principal reason to conduct a CTTA is to improve team cognitive performance (Klein, 2000). CTTA can be used as the basis for several HRM decisions and functions. In particular, development of training content, job redesign, construction of performance measures, and development of selection procedures (Baker et al., 1998; Salas, Dickinson, Converse & Tannenbaum, 1992).

Blickensderfer et al. (2000) have suggested one of the major requirements of CTTA is to identify, define, and describe team knowledge. This team knowledge (i.e. shared problem models) is believed to be directly related to team performance (Cannon-Bowers, Salas & Converse, 1993). Blickensderfer et al. (2000) also added that team knowledge has the potential to affect teamwork at two levels. First, when communication channels are limited, team knowledge assists in anticipating other team members' behavioral and informational requirements. Second, team knowledge allows team members to operate from a similar frame-of-reference.

A conceptual framework for team knowledge. Based on the work of Stout, Cannon-Bowers and Salas (1996, 1997), Blickensderfer et al. (2000) presented a conceptual framework for depicting team knowledge as composed of two major elements: (1) pre-task team knowledge; and (2) dynamic team knowledge. Pre-task team knowledge was defined as knowledge existing prior to task activities and dynamic team knowledge was defined as an understanding that develops during performance.

Pre-task team knowledge exists in long-term memory and is brought to the team by its individual members. A team whose members come to the task with a great degree of compatible knowledge and mental models is considered to have a high level of pre-task team knowledge.

Dynamic team knowledge (dynamic task understanding) is the degree to which teammates develop compatible assessments of cues and patterns in the situation. This type of knowledge evolves as the team is performing its task(s). Dynamic understanding is a combination of pre-performance knowledge, with specific characteristics of the situation.

Blickensderfer et al. (2000) summarized by explaining that team knowledge provides the foundation for certain team skills. Teams with team knowledge are better able to manage their interdependencies and coordinate their effort. Thus, it is imperative that CTTA be able to identify team knowledge requirements necessary to accomplish a team task. These requirements include both pre-task team knowledge and dynamic performance understanding.

Cognitive team task analysis versus cognitive task analysis. Baker et al. (1998) have suggested that CTTA must include analyses of the interaction and sequencing requirements of cognitive team tasks, as well as analyze the individual cognitive task requirements of each member. The analysis of coordination, which is intrinsic in teamwork, is unique to CTTA and is what separates it from CTA (Baker et al., 1998). Additionally, certain knowledge may need to be shared among team members while other knowledge may not. These shared mental models (i.e. shared problem models) (Cannon-Bowers et al., 1993) were discussed previously. Team performance appears to be facilitated and maintained by shared problem models, so it is critical that CTTA be able to identify and classify these shared knowledge structures.

A taxonomy for cognitive team task analysis. Past research has done very little to identify which specific CTTA methods are beneficial for capturing team members' knowledge about their team and its tasks (Blickensderfer et al., 2000). Current CTTA methods that have received some attention include guided observation, simulations, interviews, and critical incidents (Klein, 2000). Similar to task analysis, most approaches to analyzing cognitive task requirements have been conducted at the individual level. Recently, research on teams has focused on the development of taxonomies of team KSAs and attitudes (Cannon-Bowers et al., 1995; Stevens & Campion, 1994). Other research efforts have attempted to identify important job characteristics (Campion et al., 1993; Campion et al., 1996). Comparatively, considerably less research exists on taxonomies for cognitive task requirements. Baker et al. (1998) note one possible exception to this is the Occupational Information Network (O*NET). The O*NET is a Department of Labor initiative designed to be a comprehensive database system for collecting, organizing, describing, and disseminating data on job characteristics and worker attitudes and is intended to replace the outdated Dictionary of ccupational Titles.

By combining information from the O*NET and existing taxonomies of team KSAs (Cannon-Bowers et al., 1995; Stevens & Campion, 1994), Baker et al. (1998) have developed a preliminary taxonomy (e.g. analyzes teamwork data, updates shared mental models of teamwork) for CTTA. The taxonomy is intended to serve as a foundation for performing CTTA as it provides relevant information regarding critical cognitive tasks and team knowledge, skill, and attitude requirements. Because Baker et al.'s (1998) taxonomy is derived primarily from a literature review and is yet to be tested, it should only be considered a preliminary taxonomy. Regardless of this fact, the taxonomy serves as a potentially positive first step to developing psychometrically sound and valuable CTTA methods.

Summarizing the Current State of Team Task Analysis

TTA has been approached from several perspectives. Different methods have been used to conduct analyses and different types of data have been gathered. Examples of TTA methods used include questionnaires, interviews, controlled observation, and critical incidents. Examples of types of data gathered include, team competencies/skills, job characteristics, and cognitive requirements. The majority of these approaches have been derived from previous work done on individual level task analysis. However, several researchers (e.g. Baker et al., 1998; Brenner et al., 1998) have questioned the appropriateness of generalizing individual task analysis techniques to the team level. Clearly, there is additional work that needs to be done on TTA.

NEXT STEPS IN TEAM TASK ANALYSIS

Although several methods have been used to gather TTA information (e.g. critical incidents, questionnaires) and several types of TTA information have been gathered (e.g. competencies/skills, job characteristics, cognitive), little is known about the validity or practical applicability of TTA. HRM practices designed to enhance team effectiveness could be improved by research that examines the validity and practicality of various TTA methodologies. Several important issues should guide TTA research and development efforts.

Criteria for Evaluating Team Task Analysis Methodologies

To refine team task analysis methods and establish confidence in their validity and utility, criteria need to be established for evaluating their effectiveness. Future work should establish a comprehensive list of criteria, but any list should include at least the four criteria described below:

Theoretically Grounded

Any TTA approach should be based on a theoretical understanding of team performance. There are numerous theories that can help guide the development and identification of appropriate approaches and specific tools. Conceptual developments in team KSAs (Cannon-Bowers et al., 1995), cognitive processing (Klein, 1993), shared mental models (Cannon-Bowers et al., 1993), and job characteristics (Campion et al., 1993; Campion et al., 1996) can serve as starting points for establishing scientifically grounded TTA methodologies. Numerous "popular" team assessment and diagnostic tools currently exist in the commercial market, most of which are unfortunately atheoretical in nature.

Purpose Guided

As noted earlier, no TTA approach can serve all purposes. For example, TTA can be used to guide the development of team training scenarios, identify team member requirements for selection purposes, or establish team design or structural requirements. Different data will be needed to accomplish each purpose. Thus, different methods are called for as well. Many of the TTA developers to date have not been clear about the intended use of the approach. Any effective approach should have a clearly, explicitly established purpose(s) so that users know how to use it, and its effectiveness can be evaluated against its intended use.

Empirically Tested

For us to be confident that a TTA approach works, even if it was theoretically grounded and purpose-guided during development, it must be empirically tested and validated. This means conducting research that demonstrates that the measures and approaches being used yield reliable and valid data. Two key issues are whether the approach yields stable results (e.g. across data collectors, over time), and whether the approach produces construct valid results (i.e. it measures what it should measure based on its theoretical foundation and purpose). One way of doing this is to demonstrate that the results demonstrate theoretically predicted covariation (and lack of covariation where predicted) with other constructs. To date, few methods have received thorough empirical testing, particularly those in popular use.

A second component of empirical testing is testing against its intended purpose. If the purpose is to yield data that guides better selection decisions, did this happen? If the purpose is to develop better team training scenarios, did this happen?

User Accepted

TTA is intended to be a practical, applied tool. Therefore, any method with an applied purpose must meet the criterion of user acceptance. This means that users find the method meaningful and usable and they understand how to use the approach. Perhaps equally important is that decision-makers (a different type of user) find the results understandable and believe that it can help guide decision-making. Users that believe the approach is useful are more likely to have confidence in TTA outcomes. Thus, they will be more likely to take actions based on those outcomes. In order for TTA to be a useful tool for HRM decisions, it will have to gain the acceptance of those using it.

Research Needs

Several research needs exist in TTA. There are many questions that we, as well as other researchers (e.g. Baker et al., 1998; Baker et al., 1998), have raised. Research designed to answer these questions is sorely needed. The following sections identify potential, future TTA research needs.

Examine Untested Taxonomies and Methodologies

Several taxonomies have been proposed for describing teamwork (Baker et al., 1998; Campion et al., 1993; Campion et al., 1996; Cannon-Bowers et al., 1995;

Levine et al., 1988; Stevens & Campion, 1994). Despite their existence, these taxonomies have yet to be adequately tested. The exceptions are Campion et al. (1993) and Campion et al. (1996) and even these authors acknowledged that future research is necessary. Most of the above taxonomies or methods would meet one or more of our effectiveness criteria, but few if any, could currently meet all four. Hence, the need for further research linking methods to purpose, empirically testing/validating, and determining user acceptance/ usability. It may also be possible for future work to attempt to integrate the taxonomies into a larger overarching taxonomy. The framework for such investigations already exists, and should be further explored.

Link Methods to Purpose

Our review has revealed several methods for conducting TTA, as well as several types of information that can be gathered. Future research should examine whether specific methods are better suited for gathering specific types of information. For example, Cannon-Bowers et al. (1995) have suggested collecting team competencies/skills information for use in TTA. Research should explore the types of TTA methods that best lend themselves to gathering team competencies/skills data. It may be the case that questionnaires, controlled observation, or some other method is the most suitable. Similar questions could be asked for other types of information gathering (e.g. job characteristics, cognitive demands). Results of such studies would allow future team task analysts to be able to choose appropriate methods based on the type of data they wish to collect.

Develop Tools

All tools currently used in TTA have their origins in individual task analysis. New TTA tools need to be developed. Several important factors should be considered in the development of these tools. We have already recommended an integration of types of methods with types of information gathered. We also suggest that the purpose of the TTA should be integrated with the methods and types of information gathered. Specifically, the methods and types of information gathered should reflect the specific "team" HRM functions the TTA is intended for (e.g. training, selection, compensation). Using TTA tools that were specifically designed for given "team" HRM decisions can enhance the reliability and validity of those decisions. Once these tools are developed, they should be subjected to appropriate testing and validation.

Potential computer applications should also be considered. For example, it may be possible to use a computer to administer TTA and analyze the information collected. It is conceivable methods could be developed (e.g. surveys) and computerized. One of the advantages of this approach would be to simplify administration and analysis of TTA.

Other possible computer applications also exist. It may be possible to develop a computer-based guide for selecting the most appropriate methods and types of information based on a given "team" HRM need. The value of such decision model approaches has been well established in previous research on leadership and decision making (e.g. Vroom & Jago, 1988). This computer system might suggest the use of a combination of methods to gather appropriate information.

There is also the possibility of mono-method bias if TTA methods rely on a single method to gather TTA information, thus making the method itself an irrelevancy that cannot be separated (Cook & Campbell, 1979). In other words, TTA methodologies that rely on a single method to collect TTA information will generate results that cannot be generalized beyond the individual method used. Tools that approach TTA from multiple methods (e.g. questionnaire and critical incidents) may reduce the threat of obtaining TTA findings that are method bound.

SUMMARY

Task analysis is an important tool for HRM. An extensive amount of previous work (e.g. Harvey, 1992; McCormick, 1976) has examined individual level task analysis. Despite the increased use of teams in organizations (Guzzo & Shea, 1992; Hackman, 1992), very little work on task analysis has focused on the team level. A recent summary by Baker et al. (1998) revealed that a common strategy for analyzing what teams do has been to borrow individual techniques from task analysis. For example, Morgan et al. (1986) and Prince and Salas (1993) used critical incidents, Stout, Prince, Baker, Bergondy, and Salas (1992) used task importance scales, and Bowers et al. (1993), Campion et al. (1993) and Campion et al. (1996) used questionnaires. The concern with these approaches is that team phenomena are different from individual phenomena (Brenner et al., 1998; Bowers et al., 1994; Kenny & LaVoie, 1985; Klein et al., 1994; Rousseau, 1985) and thus, these techniques may not generalize to the team level. Clearly, additional research examining TTA needs to be done.

The goal of this paper was to review the existing TTA literature, to highlight the need for additional research and practical efforts focused on TTA, and to provide methodological as well as practical guidance for future TTA efforts. It is our hope that our review has provided possible directions and guidance for future team task analysts. Clearly, we have raised several interesting questions. For some of these questions we have attempted to provide answers and guidance. Still other issues raised will require additional research in order for answers to be obtained. We are optimistic that the research needs identified in this review as well as the criteria suggested for evaluating TTA methodologies will be utilized by researchers and practitioners in future TTA efforts.

REFERENCES

Baker, D. P., Cannon-Bowers, J. A., & Salas, E. (1998). A taxonomy for cognitive team task analysis. Unpublished manuscript.

Baker, D. P., & Salas, E. (1996). Analyzing team performance: In the eye of the beholder? *Military Psychology, 8*, 235–245.

Baker, D. P., Salas, E., & Cannon-Bowers, J. (1998). Team task analysis: Lost but hopefully not forgotten. *The Industrial-Organizational Psychologist, 35*, 79–83.

Baker, D. P., Salas, E., & Prince, C. (1991). *Team task importance: Implications for conducting team task analysis.* Paper presented at the sixth annual meeting of the Society for Industrial and Organizational Psychology, St. Louis, MO.

Blickensderfer, E., Cannon-Bowers, J. A., Salas, E., & Baker, D. P. (2000). Analyzing knowledge requirements in team tasks. In: J. M. Schraagen, S. Chipman & V. Shalin (Eds), *Cognitive Task Analysis.* Mahwah, NJ: Lawrence Earlbaum Associates.

Bowers, C. A., Baker, D. P., & Salas, E. (1994). The importance of teamwork in the cockpit: The utility of job/task analysis indices for training design. *Military Psychology, 4*, 205–214.

Bowers, C. A., Morgan, B. B., Salas, E., & Prince, C. (1993). Assessment of coordination demand for aircrew coordination training. *Military Psychology, 5*, 95–112.

Brenner, T., Sheehan, K., Arthur, W., & Bennett, W. (1998). Behavioral and cognitive task analysis integration for assessing individual and team work activities. *Proceedings of the Annual Meeting of the International Military Testing Association.*

Bridges, W. (1994). The end of the job. *Fortune*, (September 19), 64.

Campion, M. A., Medsker, G. J., & Higgs, A. C. (1993). Relations between work group characteristics and effectiveness: Implications for designing effective work groups. *Personnel Psychology, 49*, 823–850.

Campion, M. A., Papper, E. M., & Medsker, G. J. (1996). Relations between work team characteristics and effectiveness: A replication and extension. *Personnel Psychology, 49*, 429–452.

Cannon-Bowers, J. A., Salas, E., & Converse, S. A. (1993). Shared mental models in expert team decision making. In: N. J. Castellan, Jr. (Ed.), *Current Issues in Individual and Group Decision Making* (pp. 221–246). Hillsdale, NJ: Lawrence Earlbaum.

Cannon-Bowers, J. A., Tannenbaum, S. I., Salas, E., & Volpe, C. E. (1995). Defining team competencies and establishing team training requirements. In: R. Guzzo & E. Salas (Eds), *Team Effectiveness and Decision Making in Organizations* (pp. 149–203). San Francisco: Jossey-Bass.

Cascio, W. (1987). *Applied psychology in personnel management.* Englewood Cliffs, NJ: Prentice-Hall.

Cook, T. D., & Campbell, D. T. (1979). *Quasi-experimentation: Design and analysis issues for field settings.* Boston: Houghton Mifflin.

Dessler, G. (2000). *Human Resource Management* (8th ed.). Upper Saddle River, NJ: Prentice Hall.

Dick, W., & Carey, L. (1990). *The systematic design of instruction* (3rd ed.). Glenview, IL: Scott, Foresman.

Dieterly, D. L. (1988). Team performance requirements. In: S. Gael (Ed.), *The Job Analysis Handbook for Business, Industry, and Government* (pp. 766–777). New York: Wiley.

Flanagan, J. C. (1954). The critical incidents technique. *Psychological Bulletin, 51,* 327–358.

Gael, S. (1983). *Job analysis: A guide to assessing work activities.* San Francisco: Jossey-Bass.

Gael, S. (1988). *The job analysis handbook for business, industry, and government.* New York: Wiley.

Goldstein, I. L. (1986). *Training in organizations: Needs assessment, development and evaluation* (2nd ed.). Monterey, CA: Brooks/Cole.

Guzzo, R. A., & Shea, G. P. (1992). Group performance and intergroup relations in organizations. In: M. D. Dunnette & L. M. Hough (Eds), *Handbook of Industrial & Organizational Psychology* (2nd ed., Vol. 3, pp. 269–313). Palo Alto, CA: Consulting Psychologists Press, Inc.

Hackman, J. R. (1992). Group influences on individuals in organizations. In: M. D. Dunnette & L. M. Hough (Eds), *Handbook of Industrial & Organizational Psychology* (2nd ed., Vol. 3, pp. 199–267). Palo Alto, CA: Consulting Psychologists Press, Inc.

Hammer, M., & Champy, J. (1993). *Reengineering the corporation: A manifesto for business revolution.* New York: Harper Business.

Harvey, R. J. (1992). Job analysis. In: M. D. Dunnette & L. M. Hough (Eds), *Handbook of Industrial & Organizational Psychology* (2nd ed., Vol. 2, pp. 71–163). Palo Alto, CA: Consulting Psychologists Press, Inc.

Kenny, D. A., & LaVoie, L. (1985). Separating individual and group effects. *Journal of Personality and Social Psychology, 48,* 339–348.

Kidwell, R. E., Jr., Mossholder, K. W., & Bennett, N. (1997). Cohesiveness and organizational citizenship behavior: A multilevel analysis using work groups and individuals. *Journal of Management, 23,* 775–793.

Klein, G. A. (2000). Cognitive task analysis of teams. In: J. M. Schraagen, S. Chipman & V. Shalin (Eds), *Cognitive Task Analysis* (pp. 417–429). Mahwah, NJ: Lawrence Earlbaum Associates.

Klein, G. A. (1993). *Naturalistic decision making: Implications for design.* Crew System Ergonomics Information Analysis Center.

Klein, K. J., Dansereau, F., & Hall, R. J. (1994). Levels issues in theory development, data, collection, and analysis. *Academy of Management, 31,* 9–41.

Levine, E. L. (1983). *Everything you always wanted to know about job analysis.* Tampa, Fl: Mariner.

Levine, E. L., Penner, L. A., Brannick, M. T., Coovert, M. D., & Llobert, J. M. (1988). *Analysis of job/task analysis methodologies for team training design* (Tech. Rep. No. DAAL03-86-D-0001). Orlando, FL: Naval Training Systems Center.

Maier, N. R. F. (1967). The need for an integrative function. *Psychological Review, 4,* 239–249.

McCormick, E. J. (1976). Job and task analysis. In: M. D. Dunnette (Ed.), *Handbook of Industrial and Organizational Psychology* (pp. 651–696). Chicago: Rand McNally.

Milan, M., & Tucker, R. (1992). Job descriptions for the 21st century. *Personnel Journal* (June), 37–44.

Mohrman, S., Cohen, S., & Mohrman, A. (1995). *Designing team-based organizations: New forms for knowledge work.* San Francisco: Jossey Bass.

Moravec, M., & Tucker, R. (1992). Job descriptions for the 21st century. *Personnel Journal, 71*(6), 37–44.

Morgan, B. B., Glickman, A. S., Woodward, E. A., Blaiwes, A. S., & Salas, E. (1986). *Measurement of team behaviors in a Navy environment* (Tech. Report No. NTSC TR-86-014). Orlando, Fl: Naval Training Systems Center.

Prince, C., & Salas, E. (1993). Training and research for teamwork in the military aircrew. In: E. L. Weiner, B. G. Kanki & R. L. Helmreich (Eds), *Cockpit Resource Management* (pp. 337–366). Orlando, FL: Academic Press.

Roth, E. M., Woods, D. D., & Pople, H. E. (1992). Cognitive simulation as a toll for cognitive task analysis. *Ergonomics, 35*(10), 1163–1198.

Rousseau, D. (1985). Issues of level in organizational research: Multi-level and cross-level perspectives. *Research in Organizational Behavior, 7*, 1–37.

Ryder, J. M., Redding, R. E., & Beckshi, P. F. (1987). Training developments for complex cognitive tasks. *Proceedings of the Human Factors Society 31st Annual Meeting* (pp. 1261–1265). Santa Monica, CA: Human Factors Society.

Salas, E., Cannon-Bowers, J. A., Payne, S. C., & Smith-Jentsch, K. A. (1998). Teams and teamwork in the military. In: C. Cronin (Ed.), *Military Psychology: An Introduction* (pp. 71–88). Needham Heights, MA: Simon & Schuster.

Salas, E., Dickinson, T. L., Converse, S. A., & Tannenbaum, S. I. (1992). Toward an understanding of team performance and training. In: R. W. Swezey & E. Salas (Eds), *Teams: Their Training and Performance* (pp. 3–29). Norwood, NJ: Ablex.

Sanchez, J. I., & Levine, E. L. (1989). Determining important tasks within jobs: A policy-capturing approach. *Journal of Applied Psychology, 74*(2), 336–342.

Siegel, G. B. (1997). Job analysis in the TQM environment. *Public Personnel Management, 25*(4), 485–494.

Stevens, M. J., & Campion, M. A. (1994). The knowledge, skill, and ability requirements for teamwork: Implications for human resource management. *Journal of Management, 20*(2), 503–530.

Stout, R. J., Cannon-Bowers, J., Morgan, B. B., & Salas, E. (1989). The development of a scale to assess the teamwork needs of training situations. *Proceedings of the Human Factors Society 33rd Annual Meeting*, 1268–1272. Orlando, FL.

Stout, R. J., Cannon-Bowers, J. A., & Salas, E. (1996). The role of shared mental models in developing team situational awareness: Implications for training. *Training Research Journal, 2*, 85–116.

Stout, R., Prince, C., Baker, D. P., Bergondy, M. L., & Salas, E. (1992). Aircrew coordination: What does it take? *Proceedings of the Thirteenth Psychology in the Department of Defense Symposium*, 133–137.

Thompson, D. E., & Thompson, T. A. (1982). Court standards for job analysis in test validation. *Personnel Psychology, 35*, 865–874.

Vroom, V. H., & Jago, A. G. (1988). *The new leadership: Managing participation in organizations.* Englewood Cliffs, NJ: Prentice Hall.

Wright, P. M., & Noe, R. A. (1996). *Management of organizations.* Boston: Irwin McGraw-Hill.

Yammarino, F. J., & Markham, S. E. (1992). On the application of within and between analysis: Are absence and affect really group-based phenomena? *Journal of Applied Psychology, 77*, 168–176.

APPENDIX A

Knowledge, Skill, and Ability (KSA) Requirements for Teamwork

I. INTERPERSONAL KSAs

A. Conflict Resolution KSAs
1. The KSA to recognize and encourage desirable, but discourage undesirable, team conflict.
2. The KSA to recognize the type and source of conflict confronting the team and to implement an appropriate conflict resolution strategy.
3. The KSA to employ an integrative (win-win) negotiation strategy rather than the traditional distributive (win-lose) strategy.

B. Collaborative Problem Solving KSAs
4. The KSA to identify situations requiring participative group problem solving and to utilize the proper degree and type of participation.
5. The KSA to recognize the obstacles to collaborative group problem solving and implement appropriate corrective actions.

C. Communication KSAs
6. The KSA to understand communication networks, and to utilize decentralized networks to enhance communication where possible.
7. The KSA to communicate openly and supportively, that is, to send messages which are: (1) behavior- or event-oriented; (2) congruent; (3) validating; (4) conjunctive; and (5) owned.
8. The KSA to listen nonevaluatively and to appropriately use active listening techniques.
9. The KSA to maximize consonance between nonverbal and verbal messages, and to recognize and interpret the nonverbal messages of others.
10. The KSA to engage in ritual greetings and small talk, and a recognition of their importance.

II. SELF-MANAGEMENT KSAs

D. Goal Setting and Performance Management KSAs
11. The KSA to help establish specific, challenging, and accepted team goals.
12. The KSA to monitor, evaluate, and provide feedback on both overall team performance and individual team member performance.

E. Planning and Task Coordination KSAs
13. The KSA to coordinate and synchronize activities, information, and task interdependencies between team members.
14. The KSA to help establish task and role expectations of individual team members, and to ensure proper balancing of workload in the team.

From Stevens and Campion, 1994, p. 505.

APPENDIX B

Comparison of Cannon-Bowers et al. (1995) and Stevens and Campion (1994)

Team-Relevant Knowledge and Teamwork Skill Dimensions (Cannon-Bowers, Tannenbaum, Salas and Volpe, 1995)	Teamwork KSAs[1] (Stevens and Campion, 1994)
Knowledge Competencies for Teams	
Accurate shared mental models – e.g., team knowledge of	E. Planning and Task Coordination KSAs (13,14)
• Roles of teams members	E. Planning and Task Coordination KSAs (13,14)
• Relationships among team members	
• Temporal patterns of team performance	C. Communication KSAs (6)
• Appropriate communication channels and pattern of information flows	E. Planning and Task Coordination KSAs (13,14)
Knowledge of teamwork skills required for successful performance	All KSAs
Knowledge of overall team goals, objectives and missions	D. Goal Setting and Performance Mgt. KSAs (11)
Knowledge of the boundary spanning roles individual members play and the team's relationship to the larger organization	
Knowledge of team member's roles and responsibilities	E. Planning and Task Coordination KSAs (13,14)
Cue-strategy association	
Teamwork Skills	
Adaptability The process by which a team is able to to use information gathered from the task environment to adjust strategies through the use of compensatory behavior and reallocation of intrateam resources	A. Conflict Resolution KSAs (2) B. Collaborative Problem Solving KSAs (4) D. Goal Setting and Performance Mgt. KSAs (12) E. Planning and Task Coordination KSAs (13,14)

APPENDIX B Continued.

Team-Relevant Knowledge and Teamwork Skill Dimensions (Cannon-Bowers, Tannenbaum, Salas and Volpe, 1995)	Teamwork KSAs[1] (Stevens and Campion, 1994)
Shared Situational Awareness The process by which team members develop compatible models of the team's internal and external environment, includes skill in arriving at a common understanding of the situation and applying appropriate task strategies	A. Conflict Resolution KSAs (2,3) B. Collaborative Problem Solving KSAs (4,5) D. Goal Setting and Performance Mgt. KSAs (11,12)
Performance Monitoring and Feedback The ability of team members to give, seek, and receive task-clarifying feedback; includes the ability to accurately monitor the performance of teammates, provide constructive feedback regarding errors, and offer advice for improving performance	D. Goal Setting and Performance Mgt. KSAs (12)
Leadership/Team Management The ability to direct and coordinate the activities of other team members, assess team performance, assign tasks, motivate team members, plan and organize, and establish a positive atmosphere	C. Communication KSAs (6-10) D. Goal Setting and Performance Mgt. KSAs (11,12) E. Planning and Task Coordination KSAs (13,14)
Interpersonal Relations The ability to optimize the quality of team members' interactions through resolution of dissent, utilization of cooperative behaviors, or use of motivational reinforcing statements	A. Conflict Resolution KSAs (1-3) B. Collaborative Problem Solving KSAs (4,5) C. Communication KSAs (7-9) D. Goal Setting and Performance Mgt. KSAs (12)
Coordination The process by which team resources, activities, and responses are organized to ensure that tasks are integrated, synchronized, and completed within established temporal constraints.	E. Planning and Task Coordination KSAs (13,14)

APPENDIX B Continued.

Team-Relevant Knowledge and Teamwork Skill Dimensions (Cannon-Bowers, Tannenbaum, Salas and Volpe, 1995)	Teamwork KSAs[1] (Stevens and Campion, 1994)
Communication The process by which information is clearly and accurately exchanged between two or more team members in the prescribed manner and with proper terminology; the ability to clarify or acknowledge the receipt of information	C. Communication KSAs (6-9) D. Goal Setting and Performance Mgt. KSAs (12) E. Planning and Task Coordination KSAs (13,14)
Decision Making The ability to gather and integrate information, use sound judgment, identify alternatives, select the best solution, and evaluate the consequences (in team context, emphasizes skill in pooling information and resources in support of a response choice)	B. Collaborative Problem Solving KSAs (4,5) D. Goal Setting and Performance Mgt. KSAs (11,12) E. Planning and Task Coordination KSAs (13,14)

[1] Appendix A defines each of the fourteen teamwork KSAs identified in Stevens and Campion (1994).
The listing above shows general KSA categories and, in parentheses, specific KSAs.

Appendix B offers a more detailed comparison of the work of Cannon-Bowers, et al. (1995) and Stevens and Campion (1994), both advocates of the team competencies/skills approach to TTA. In Appendix B the knowledge competencies for teams (six) from Cannon-Bowers, et al. (1995) are listed along with their list of eight critical teamwork skills from Table 3, with each skill defined. The KSAs of Stevens and Campion, of course, include knowledge requirements believed to be important in teams. As can be seen there is, across authors, considerable and general agreement in the knowledge and skill competencies thought to be associated with effective team performance. A significant difference between Cannon-Bowers, et al., and Stevens and Campion is that the former hold that team member attitudes, such as a collective orientation (i.e., affinity for teamwork), and collective efficacy are important and associated with team success. These attitudinal requirements are not shown in Appendix

B. Stevens and Campion discount personality factors and attitudes as strong predictors of workplace behavior (1994, p. 504). Another significant difference, of course, is that Cannon-Bowers et al. (1995) hold that the required competencies for team members varies and depends on particular aspects of the work situation.

GROUP PERSONALITY COMPOSITION AND WORK TEAM EFFECTIVENESS: KEY FACTOR IN STAFFING THE TEAM-BASED ORGANIZATION?

Terry Halfhill, Joseph W. Huff, Eric Sundstrom and Tjai M. Nielsen

ABSTRACT

This chapter analyzes the role of work team personality composition – or mix of individual personality traits – in team-based organizations. It offers a framework for analysis that identifies the key variables and relationships of importance to the TBO practitioner. Within that framework it reviews current, empirical evidence relevant to the links between individual personality and work team effectiveness. Finally, it identifies key, practical issues raised by work team personality composition for staffing in TBO, and proposes a series of best management practices.

INTRODUCTION

As today's businesses increasingly rely on Team-Based Organizations, or TBOs (Lawler, Mohrman & Ledford, 1998), managers focus on practical ways of supporting and promoting the effectiveness of work teams (Sundstrom, 1999). Among the features of work teams consistently related to their effectiveness is

Team-Based Organizing, Volume 9, pages 147–167.
ISBN: 0-7623-0981-4

group composition, or mix of members' individual characteristics. Empirical research has found work team effectiveness related to composition on individual members' values (Harrison, Price & Bell, 1998); demographic characteristics (Jackson, Brett, Sessa, Cooper, Julin & Peyronnin, 1991) and cognitive ability (Tziner & Eden, 1985). Recent studies also suggest a relationship with *work team personality composition,* or the mix of a group members' individual personality traits, such as conscientiousness, extraversion, or agreeableness (Sundstrom, McIntyre, Halfhill & Richards, 2000).

Unfortunately, current literature on Team-Based Organizations (TBO) offers little guidance to practitioners on dealing with questions of personality composition in work teams. This gap in guidance gains importance in light of evidence of a powerful relationship between personality and individual performance (Hough, 1992). Researchers have only begun to explore how individual personality traits interact at the team level (Barrick, Stewart, Neubert & Mount, 1998; Halfhill, Sundstrom, Lahner, Calderone & Nielsen, 2002). Emerging evidence confirms many managers' beliefs that certain personality compositions spell success for a team while others represent recipes for failure. The "big five" model (*agreeableness, conscientiousness, extraversion, openness, and neuroticism*) provides a framework for understanding individual personality traits (McCrae & Costa, 1987; Costa & McCrae, 1989). Needed now is a model of team personality composition.

This chapter explores the role of personality composition in work team effectiveness from the perspective of staffing the team-based organization. It has three major sections. The first presents a framework for analysis that identifies the key variables and relationships of importance to the TBO practitioner. The second section reviews current, empirical evidence relevant to the links between individual personality and work team effectiveness. The third and concluding section addresses the practical applications of current knowledge through best practices for staffing work teams.

WORK TEAM PERSONALITY COMPOSITION AND EFFECTIVENESS: A FRAMEWORK

Work teams consist of interdependent individuals who share responsibility for specific outcomes for their organizations, and their effectiveness includes both their performance and their collective viability as a work unit (Sundstrom, DeMeuse & Futrell, 1990). *Performance* refers to the extent to which a work team satisfies the expectations of its key counterparts – including customers, managers, staff, and regulators – concerning production efficiency, quality, and timeliness of its outputs of services and/or products (Sundstrom, 1999).

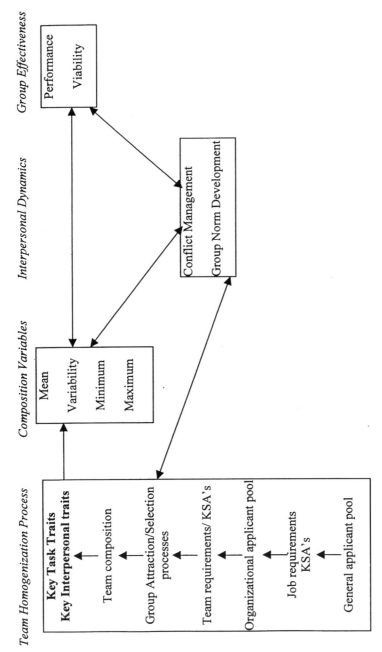

Fig. 1. Framework for Studying Group Personality Composition (GPC) and Group Effectiveness.

Viability refers to a team's continued capacity as a work unit, including its maintenance of technical capacity, cohesion, and continuity over time. Because a work team can potentially produce excellent performance in the short term, and through personality conflicts "burn out" and lose capacity to perform in the long term (e.g. Hackman, 1990), it is important to consider both performance and viability.

Shown in Fig. 1, a framework for analyzing work team personality composition focuses on a series of four group-level factors in effectiveness: key traits, composition variables, interpersonal dynamics, and group norms. Each of the four factors involves issues that face a work team as a whole. This framework recognizes the importance of focusing on the group as the performing unit, and avoids assuming that what is true at the individual level automatically applies at the group level.

Key Personality Traits

Key personality traits for work team effectiveness depend on the team's role as a work unit and its counterparts defined by its mission and position in the organization's work flow. To the extent that a team's role calls for *task focus*, or timely coordination and production of output for a customer with demanding expectations of quality, a key personality trait may be conscientiousness. To the extent that a work team deals directly with external counterparts, such as customers, in interactions that require interpersonal sensitivity and empathy, a key trait may be individual agreeableness.

Composition Variables

The two most important composition variables in relation to group members' personalities concern the collective level and diversity on its key traits. *Collective level* refers to the group's average standing on a trait, considering all members. For example, a group might have a high level of conscientiousness, above the 90th percentile in the adult workforce, or a medium level near the median. In contrast, *diversity* refers to the variability among members on a key trait.

Two additional composition variables include the groups' *minimum* and *maximum* scores, which receive less attention in this chapter in the interest of space. Psychologists are usually interested in job relevant traits, particularly increased levels of the traits. As a result, group maximum scores are typically range restricted and provide little variance. Although group minimum scores often correlate with group effectiveness, they are highly correlated with variance, as the minimum scores are often responsible for an increase in variance (e.g. as the minimum score departs from the mean there is a corresponding increase in group variance).

Homogenization Process. Both theory and research indicate that many organizations are range-restricted for personality variables (Schneider, 1984; Eigel & Khunert, 1996; Judge & Cable, 1997). It isn't a stretch to assume that the teams within them may represent a similar level of range restriction. This dynamic staffing process at the team level is similar to what Schneider (1984) termed the "ASA" process (Attraction/Selection/Attrition) at the organizational level. That is, similar types of individuals are attracted/recruited, selected, and dismissed/retained by work teams. Dissimilar individuals who are selected may eventually leave. At the team level this will result in restriction of range in group mean scores and thus reduce correlations between mean group personality scores and group performance. Thus, the minimum and variance scores may provide more between-group variance than the mean score, resulting in less restricted correlations with group performance.

Why might teams demonstrate homogeneous personalities? For one, the major duties that are accomplished by the team may require minimal levels of specific KSAOs (Knowledge, Skill, Ability and Other attributes) necessary for optimal performance. One category of these KSAOs is the personality of team members (Cohen & Bailey, 1997). For instance, few would argue that the typical personality profiles of salespeople might differ from police officers. Salespeople might function best with certain level of extroversion, while also having sufficient levels of agreeableness to be able to persuade as well as to form relationships with customers. Police officers may also need to exhibit extroversion and agree-ableness to some degree, yet levels of emotional stability may be more crucial, especially in stressful situations.

Figure 2 shows three diagrams that illustrate how employee personality variables may be constrained at both the organizational and group levels of analysis. The first panel describes the general population on the trait of openness to experience. If openness is assessed with 12-items scored on a five-point scale, scores can range between 12 and 60, and probably will be normally distributed.

The second panel demonstrates the sample of employee openness scores assuming that the organizational culture may embrace creativity and innovation at the organizational level. If organizational ASA processes set a lower limit on employee openness at, say, 36, the population median and mean, the range would be restricted to the top 50% of individuals in that population.

The third panel describes a further restricted range of employee openness values for research and development teams within the larger organization. The R&D teams might set strict team-level norms on openness, since it is a valued

Panel (a) Normal distribution of scores for the personality trait
"Openness to new experience."

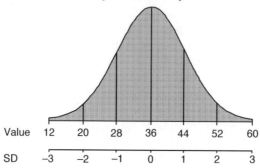

Panel (b) Hypothetical organizational distribution for the personality trait
"Openness to new experience."

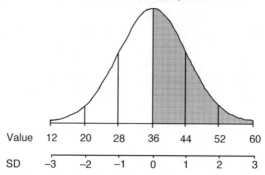

Panel (c) Hypothetical team distribution for the personality trait
"Openness to new experience."

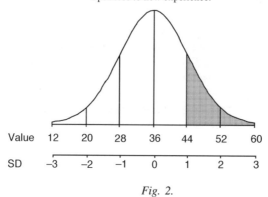

Fig. 2.

trait for team members to possess. The minimum might shift over time to 44, or about one standard deviation above the mean of the general population. At this point, only about 16% of the general population would have a sufficiently high level of openness to meet team norms, and be accepted members of the R&D teams. These examples assume that both organizational and team-level processes restrict the range of the personality trait. There are likely instances when this is the case at only one level of analysis (e.g. organizational or team-level only), or may not occur at either level.

Assuming that personality traits within teams are range restricted opens up a number of issues for studying the personality composition of teams. For example, we maintain that the purpose of psychological instruments is to discriminate between high and low scoring individuals (or groups of individuals), and that fine gradations at any point on the scale are not usually informative.

Consider an example involving U.S. Army Special Forces "A" teams. The selection process is extremely demanding and very few applicants are selected. Let's assume that "attention to detail," a facet of conscientiousness, is an essential trait for this job. The difference between a score of 48 and 58 (on our 12–60 point scale) might indicate that an individual would be late for one meeting out of 10, or forget to write one important detail from a briefing that will be disseminated to his teammates, even though he scores, roughly, 1.5 S.D. above the mean in the general population. Here, a practical difference exists in the absence of a statistical difference.

So, it is possible that *team members*, not the personality instrument, can make finite distinctions that personality measures cannot. A generic measure of conscientiousness can discriminate among individuals that score high or low within the general population, for example, between the scores of 25 and 40. However, in those organizations where nearly every member scores at the high end of the scale (39–60), there is insufficient scale variance to make meaningful distinctions. So, to the extent that these differences are perceptible and meaningful to other team members, these "low" scoring members can have tremendous effects on group process and effectiveness.

Table 1 quantitatively illustrates this example. A hypothetical organization's mean conscientious score is approximately 50 (on our 12 to 60 point scale) with a S.D. of 3, and we wish to compare two teams from the same organization. For the six members of Team 1, scores range from 39 to 58, which is a range of approximately +0.38 to +2.75 standard deviations above the mean of the general population. This yields a mean score of 49.83, equivalent to the organizational mean. This heterogeneity is likely perceptible among team members and may impact team processes and team effectiveness (c.f., LePine, Hollenbeck, Ilgen & Hedlund, 1997). Team 2 is likewise composed of six

Table 1.   Hypothetical Comparison of Team-Member Conscientiousness
Scores.

Team Member	Team Conscientiousness Profile Team 1	Team 2
1	39	45
2	43	46
3	50	48
4	53	50
5	56	52
6	58	58
Mean	*49.83*	*49.83*
Minimum	*39*	*45*
Maximum	*58*	*58*
Variance	*55.77*	*22.57*

members that all have high conscientiousness scores near the organizational
mean. Perhaps, more importantly, the conscientiousness scores of the members
of Team 2 are more homogenous than the scores of the members of Team 1.
This may result in restriction of range in group *mean* scores and thus reduce
the correlations between mean group personality scores and group performance.
The *minimum* or *variance* score may provide more between-group variance than
the mean score, resulting in less restricted correlations with group performance.

This compositional distinction may be important for group functioning, even
though the mean scores are not statistically different. In other words: (a) the
compositional issue is masked by the group's mean score; and (b) more finite
distinctions made by organizational members may be manifest in relationships
between group composition and group performance via the group's minimum
and variance scores. This does not invalidate the use of the mean as a good
source of information for team personality composition. In the case of range-
restricted samples, the mean must be considered with other information, such
as a measure of variability, to fully understand the implications of member
personality on team functioning.

Group Dynamics Related to Personality Composition

The key dynamics related to personality composition in groups relate to the
application of the key personality trait to the group's performance, all of which
have direct implications for the group's viability. These dynamics address two
issues that arise in any group from differences among members' personalities:
norm development and conflict management.

Group norm development. Norms – or beliefs, habits, and practices shared among the members of a group (Hackman, 1976) – gain their importance from the well-documented tendencies of group members to conform with norms, and of groups to enforce their norms when members begin to deviate. Developing norms in a group homogeneous on a key trait may occur with little effort or strain. For example, if all members of a group have the same task-related trait, conscientiousness, they have little reason to spend time discussing their approach to task-orientation. They could explicitly or implicitly adopt norms consistent with their collective personality trait – such as punctuality, attention to detail, double-checking quality features – and get to work.

In contrast, a group heterogeneous on a key trait faces a more complicated norm development process. First, the group may or may not recognize the heterogeneity among members. If diversity goes unrecognized – for example if the group's leader assumes that all share his or her style and dictates it as the norm – a group might have a norm that conflicts directly with some members' personalities. Failing to address them could lead to future problems and performance gaps. If so, the group has a hidden conflict management problem that can act like a time bomb.

In a heterogeneous group the members can identify, recognize, and openly discuss and evaluate relevant differences, and develop group norms that take those differences into account. If they succeed, heterogeneity brings a cost in the form of time and effort required to build consensus around norms concerning a personality difference among members. At the same time, consensus building can bring a benefit by boosting team cohesion and viability. The time and effort required for norm development can detract from short-term performance possible in homogeneous groups.

Members of a heterogeneous group might get into conflict over personality differences, either by identifying their differences explicitly or discovering them inadvertently while attempting to cooperate. If so, they then have to manage the conflicts that emerge. Groups that are homogeneous on key traits may not have to deal with this kind of conflict, and can focus their energies on task-related conflicts.

Group conflict management. To the extent that members of heterogeneous groups develop conflicts over personality differences related to key traits, they face an obstacle that homogeneous groups do not. At a minimum, conflict carries costs, either in the form of time and effort to manage them, or from interpersonal tension and individual stress from failing to manage them. In either case, the group has less energy and attention available to allocate to performance. Research shows that in some work teams, performance correlates negatively with inter-member conflict (Jehn, 1995).

Factoring in the dynamics of group norms and conflict we return to the team example presented previously (see Table 2). If we assume that both teams have norms that specify that conscientiousness is equally important and set a floor for conscientiousness at a value of 44, which is one standard deviation above the norm of general population, we can examine the two teams more closely. We note that team one has two team members that score below the team norm. Team two consists of members that all score above our hypothetical team norm for conscientiousness. Even though both teams have very conscientious members (all above the population mean), team one may be at a disadvantage in comparison with team two. Team one will need to deal with the two members who fail to meet the minimal normative criterion for conscientiousness. For instance, the two members may be ignored or treated poorly by other team members. They may also be given less important or interesting tasks. Some teams may actively attempt to reinforce the conscientiousness norm by informing the two members that their behavior is inappropriate. Finally, the team may attempt to develop the two members so that they can increase their conscientious-related behavior at work. Although these strategies vary, they do share one short-term commonality – loss of focus on the group task due to maintenance functions.

Tables 3 and 4 represent additional scenarios where the ramifications for team outcomes are less clear. The data presented in Table 3 demonstrate where team one has a lower overall mean score of conscientiousness, yet has less variability than team two. Thus, one team has a lower mean and lower variability while the second team has a higher mean, yet more variability. In this case it is

Table 2. Hypothetical Comparison of Team-Member Conscientiousness
Scores.

Team Member	Team Conscientiousness Profile	
	Team 1	Team 2
1	39	45
2	43	46
3	50	48
4	53	50
5	56	52
6	58	58
Norm	*44*	*44*
Mean	*49.83*	*49.83*
Minimum	*39*	*45*
Maximum	*58*	*58*
Variance	*55.77*	*22.57*

Table 3.   Comparison of Team-Member Conscientiousness Scores.

	Team Conscientiousness Profile	
Team Member	Team 1	Team 2
1	36	36
2	38	43
3	40	47
4	42	50
5	43	52
6	45	53
Norm	*36*	*36*
Mean	*40.67*	*46.83*
Minimum	*36*	*36*
Maximum	*45*	*53*
Variance	*11.07*	*41.37*

Table 4.   Alternative Comparison of Team-Member Conscientiousness
Scores.

	Team Conscientiousness Profile	
Team Member	Team 1	Team 2
1	39	45
2	43	46
3	50	48
4	53	50
5	56	52
6	58	58
Norm	*38*	*47*
Mean	*49.83*	*49.83*
Minimum	*39*	*45*
Maximum	*58*	*58*
Variance	*55.77*	*22.57*

unknown which team will function better. It may depend upon the norms set
by the teams. If we assume that both teams set the minimal value of 36, then
both teams consist of members who meet the minimal norms for
conscientiousness. In this case, will the difference in the means or degree of
variation matter for team performance or viability?

Finally, Table 4 presents a second more ambiguous situation. Here we
essentially replicate those data contained in Table 1, yet change the norms for
the two groups. Team one sets a norm for conscientiousness at 38 while team

two sets a norm for conscientiousness at 47. In this situation, the two means are both approximately 50, while both the variance and norms differ. In this case, team two, with the lower level of variance for conscientiousness has two members that do not meet the stringent team norm of 48. Will we find that team one, which has much more variation will be the team that performs better, is more cohesive, and is more viable for future interaction? If so, this may indicate the relative importance of compliance to team norms in comparison to simply high team scores or low variation in team member scores.

A myriad of possible combinations between team member personality score norms, mean, and variability could be presented. However, without further attention to this issue, the question is not answerable. In addition, by presenting the argument that teams, like organizations, can become relatively homogeneous around one or more core personality characteristics, a multitude of questions can be advanced.

LITERATURE REVIEW

To this point we have discussed theory and presented a framework outlining key features of group personality composition and effectiveness. We turn now to a review of available empirical studies that support the framework. Studies are grouped by their research setting, laboratory and field.

Laboratory Studies

Barry and Stewart (1997) conducted a laboratory study involving 61 graduate student groups of four and five members. Groups engaged in a problem-solving task over a period of several weeks. Group level personality variables included big five traits, and were operationalized as the proportion of group members scoring above a T score (standardized measures with a $M = 50$, $SD = 10$) of 55. This classification was nearly identical to choosing individuals in the top third of the distribution. Group performance consisted of average instructor ratings of the quality of group performance on three problem-solving tasks. None of the big five traits correlated significantly with group cohesion or group performance.

Similarly, Bond and Shiu (1997) conducted a longitudinal laboratory study with 17 teams over three trial periods. Students participated as groups in completing course requirements. Personality measures were correlated with two broad measures of team process, performance focus and shared exchange. Mean and variance scores were nonsignificant for measures of intellect, extraversion, emotional stability, and helpfulness. Brandstatter and Farthofer (1997) compared group levels of emotional stability, dominance, and extraversion with self and others ratings of social influence. Dominance and emotional stability were negatively related to social influence. Dirks (1999) focused on trust, but the level of trust within groups was manipulated via instructions (high and low) and was not considered in the review. However, this study did measure motivation and it correlated significantly with both group effectiveness and efficiency. Hendrick (1979) measured abstractness among undergraduate and graduate students, and split them into high and low abstract groups based on the results. Low abstract groups required nearly twice as long as high abstract groups to successfully complete the assigned task. Kabanoff and O'Brien (1979) composed groups based on ability relative to a creative verbal task. Groups with high ability leaders and members were more productive than groups with low ability members.

LePine et al. (1997) conducted a laboratory study involving 51 four-person student teams involved in a three-hour group decision-making session. Group personality composition was operationalized as the minimum score within the group. Group performance was operationalized as team decision accuracy (TDA). In the course of the experiment, participants made 33 decisions, and after each decision team members received feedback on the accuracy of each members' decision. TDA was the average decision accuracy over the 33 decisions. TDA was highest when both the leader and the staff were high on cognitive ability and conscientiousness. Strube et al. (1989) examined the influence of Type A behavior on group performance of a sinking ship exercise. They found that when Type A leaders were in conflict with a Type A member, groups arrived at poorer decisions. Williams and Sternberg (1988) measured empathy, extraversion, dominance, likeableness, and cooperativeness in groups that performed a creativity task. They found that mean levels of extraversion (talkativeness) and dominance correlated significantly with group product quality. Maximum talkativeness also correlated significantly with group product quality.

Bouchard (1972) compared the effect of motivation and training on the performance of brainstorming groups. Groups low in motivation consistently scored lower than groups higher in motivation. Similarly, Camacho and Paulus (1995) predicted that dispositional anxiousness (emotional stability) would negatively affect individuals while brainstorming as a member of a group, but not individually. Groups low in dispositional anxiousness outperformed groups high in dispositional anxiousness. Waung and Brice (1998) measured conscientiousness in brainstorming groups and found that group conscientiousness was related to the quality of ideas generated, but not to the quantity of ideas.

Field Studies of Work Team Effectiveness and
Group Personality Composition

Barrick et al. (1998) surveyed 51 assembly and fabrication teams from four organizations. They operationalized personality as the group mean, group variance, minimum, and maximum scores in the group for the big five traits. Social cohesion served as a process variable, and group effectiveness criterion included measures of team viability and supervisory ratings of team performance. Although many of the relationships were significant, agreeableness and extraversion were consistently related to group cohesion, and conscientiousness to group performance.

Burningham and West (1995) studied 13 teams from an oil company in Britain. They found that a group's level of task orientation was significantly related to group innovation. Similarly, Eigel and Khunert (1996) studied management problem-solving teams from a national retail chain store. They found that quality of interaction process (communication, trust, and openness) was related to productivity.

Halfhill, Sundstrom, and Nielsen (1999, 2001, 2002) conducted three field studies involving military teams. Study one consisted of 31 mechanized infantry teams located in the northeast U.S. Studies two and three consisted of 55 teams and 40 teams (respectively) from an air-refueling wing in the southeastern U.S. The studies operationalized personality as group average, minimum, maximum, and variance scores. Supervisor ratings of performance served as the group level criteria for the studies. In all of these studies the minimum score for conscientiousness was a more robust predictor than the mean, and variance for selected traits (conscientiousness and agreeableness) correlated negatively with group performance. Task interdependence moderated the relationships.

Hyatt and Ruddy (1997) studied 100 work groups of electronic equipment repair teams. Among other predictors used in the study were commitment to common goals, effective communication, cooperation, and trust. They were able to obtain data on six unique aspects of group performance. Results indicate that the predictors correlate with manager ratings and response time the best.

Mohammed et al. (2000) studied 25 student teams enrolled in a Hotel, Restaurant, and Institutional Management (HRIM) course at a northeastern university. Twice during the semester, each of these teams were responsible the planning, execution, and delivery of meals in a cafeteria-style dining facility. The second iteration for each team was separated by a five-week period, allowing for a repeated measures design. This design aspect also enabled the researchers to double their number of teams to 50 for a repeated measures multiple regression analysis (RMMR) upon completion of the study. Group personality composition was operationalized as the group mean score, and two types of performance, task and contextual, were measured in this study. Task performance was assessed by instructor ratings for each iteration of the meal delivery task. These scores were worth 13% and 20% of the teams' total grade. Peer ratings of volunteering, cooperating, taking initiative, and working enthusiastically served as a measure of contextual performance. Conscientiousness was unrelated to task performance, and agreeableness predicted contextual performance. Extraversion and emotional stability both predicted task performance.

Neuman, Wagner, and Christiansen (1999) studied 82 four-person teams in a large retailing organization with stores located across the U.S. The authors use the terms Team Personality Elevation (TPE) and Team Personality Diversity (TPD) to refer to the mean and variance operationalizations of agreeableness and conscientiousness. The final group effectiveness measure was a composite of two ratings of team performance. The first rating was based on the number of customer complaints the group received over a one-month period, and the second rating was based on the number of days the group completed work on time over a one-month period. Mean scores of agreeableness and conscientiousness were related to performance, variance of extraversion and emotional stability were related to team performance.

Neuman and Wright (1999) studied 79, four-person, human resource work teams from a large wholesale department store organization. These teams were structured to maximize interaction and interdependence. Each team member was responsible for a different phase of the work process, but shared the responsibilities of payroll and benefit tasks. A bonus, equivalent to 25% of employee's salary, could be earned on the basis of team performance. Teams had been together for three years at the time of data collection. In this study, agreeableness and conscientiousness were operationalized as group *minimum* score. Group effectiveness criterion included archival records of work completed and work accuracy, as well as supervisor ratings of group performance. Additionally, a peer rating measure of individual team member effectiveness was factored into two subscales, task performance (overall performance, problem solving, work procedures, and planning) and interpersonal skills (conflict resolution and team communication). Extraversion and emotional stability were not related to accuracy, work completed or interpersonal skills. Conscientiousness was related to task performance and accuracy, agreeableness was related to task performance, interpersonal skills, and work completed.

Neuman (2000) used an input-process-output model of team effectiveness to study 76 work teams from three manufacturing organizations. The teams had similar tasks, 39 assembled electronic components, 23 assembled and manufactured doors, and 14 assembled small appliances. In this study, agreeableness, conscientiousness, and extraversion were operationalized as group *minimum* score. Team process measures were rated by team members, and included task focus, team cohesion, and communications. Three group-level criterion measures included: (1) work complete – a percentage based on the number of days for one year that team task assignments were completed within scheduled time limits; (2) supervisor ratings of group performance; and (3) supervisor ratings of team viability. Group minimum agreeableness was related to cohesion, viability, and team performance. Group minimum conscientiousness was related to task focus, team performance, and work completed.

In summary, evidence from published field research shows a clear association of group personality composition with several indicators of work team effectiveness. Group average and group minimum scores on several traits – particularly "Big Five" personality traits of conscientiousness, agreeableness, and extraversion – correlated with measures of both group performance and viability.

BEST MANAGEMENT PRACTICES RELATED TO STAFFING THE TBO

Taken together, the evidence of a link between group personality composition and work team effectiveness represents a call to action for leaders of team-based organizations (TBOs). The research suggests that managing the personality composition of work teams through staffing practices can help optimize their performance and viability. Unfortunately much of the foundation remains to be built for staffing practices that focus on group personality composition. The savvy manager of a TBO will start building that foundation by introducing practices such as these:

(1) *Incorporate into staffing systems routine assessment of personality traits demonstrably related to individual employee performance.* Recent research relates the "Big Five personality traits to individual performance (Hough, 1992), providing a basis for using personality traits in selecting employees in some individual jobs. For other jobs current research provides a rationale for validation research to assess how well certain personality traits predict individual performance. Staffing managers who collect data on individual personality for purposes of validating individual measures may not use personality as a screen for hiring decisions until the validation work is done. However, the validation research generates a database that enables an assessment of the relationship of group personality composition and

effectiveness. Quick, low-cost measures of personality are now widely available. For example, Lewis Goldberg (2002) has developed reliable and valid scales to assess the "Big Five" personality traits, now in the public domain, with as few as 50 items each (http://ipip.ori.org/new_home.htm). Such personality scales can take less than five minutes to complete, and carry no costs for royalties.

(2) *Generate and maintain an individual-level database of employee profiles on work-related personality traits, individual performance measures, and other outcome variables.* An individual employee database allows assessment of relationships of individual's personality trait scores with specific, individual performance measures, and – eventually – composite performance indices. This process can create validity data necessary to begin to use personality traits as selection criteria for team members. Such a database enables job analytic data for individual personality traits for team-level outcomes. A related procedure, team task analysis, is outlined by Lorenzet (2002, this volume).

(3) *Routinely compute indices of team personality composition and team performance and viability outcomes, and build a team-level database on personality composition and effectiveness.* Multiple composition indices for each personality trait for each team (minimum, maximum, mean, and variance) can be related to team performance measures such as sales, production, quality, and cost over/under budget. Similar indices of team viability can also be measured and entered into the database: cohesion, viability, potency, and others. Team-level relationships of particular composition predictors and effectiveness serve to determine the general role of personality composition in team effectiveness within the context of the particular TBO. Analyses can identify various types of teams with specific duties and responsibilities. Later research may indicate generalities across team types or functions in what might be called *team-level validity generalization studies* for team personality composition.

(4) *Identify and track team-level composition indices that predict team effectiveness.* Before a TBO manager can argue persuasively for adding a team composition index to existing team staffing systems, the index has to pass the test of time-based linkage to team effectiveness within the organization. This in turn calls for selecting, tracking over time, and monitoring selected composition indices by managers. For example, a team-level database might reveal a correlation between team minimum conscientiousness and accuracy in logistics teams, providing an impetus to track team minimum conscientiousness over time. Like other key indicators, it would call for monitoring by management teams at appropriate levels in

the organization. A dependable performance link would call for further
action, including testing and evaluation of staffing practices based on
personality.

(5) *Develop and use measures of team norms potentially related to team
effectiveness within the organization, and incorporate them into the
team-level database.* A critical implication of a link between personality
composition and team effectiveness focuses on team norms as the
mechanism underlying the link. If teams develop norms reflecting
the predominant personality style in the group (for example as outlined in
Tables 2, 3 and 4), and if the norms drive performance or viability
outcomes, these norms become potential targets for concerted management
in a TBO. Team norms arguably represent a key focus of leadership in a
TBO anyway, so measuring and tracking critical team norms represents
a priority in a TBO. For example, in an organization with customer service
teams, managers might call for measuring and tracking team service norms.
If a service norm correlated with, for example, team minimum agreeableness scores, the correlation might explain the better performance among
teams with high minimum team agreeableness scores. Unfortunately, as far
as we know the TBO literature contains no well-developed measures of
team norms, nor established procedures for applying the measures, so the
TBO manager interested in measuring norms becomes the development
sponsor for measures of team norms. Such development may have a quick,
practical payoff: Knowing the normative level of a trait in conjunction with
each team member's actual level may help in understanding a mis-fit of
an individual team member in a team. Such knowledge might allow a TBO
manager to address the source of team conflict or process loss.

(6) *Involve team members in decisions about team staffing, solicit team
members' input about team personality composition, and keep notes for a
qualitative database on team composition and staffing.* Many TBOs today
give the members of existing teams a voice in selecting new members.
Not only does this practice make sense in view of the evidence linking
personality composition and effectiveness, it gives an opportunity to hear
from team members about the key issues related to personality composition
for particular types of teams. For a savvy TBO manager, conversations
with teams about personality composition represent a valuable source of
qualitative data.

(7) *Use team-level data on personality composition to guide team re-
composition, coaching, and training.* Even when TBO staffing practices
incorporate the valid use of personality measures to compose teams, the
TBO manager will still have to deal with personality mis-fits among team

members. Among the potential solutions are team re-composition practices that allow team members to easily change teams. Procedures with non-punitive, non-judgmental processes for open flow of members among teams can facilitate an ASA (attraction-selection-attrition) process that helps the organization. Because team re-composition can be both disruptive and expensive, another solution involves coaching and training team members to deal with personality-based conflicts. Data on personality composition can point to teams likely to experience conflict and have trouble developing the norms needed for effective functioning. While TBO managers build the basis for personality composition as a staffing factor, the necessary measurements can serve as diagnostic flags for team coaching and training.

CONCLUSION

In conclusion, our analysis of the extant literature suggests that team-level indices of personality composition may predict team effectiveness in the TBO. Research evidence points to a team-level link between certain, easily measured traits such as conscientiousness and agreeableness with team performance. As TBO managers lay the foundation for valid use of personality in composing teams, databases on team personality composition can point the way for practices involving measurement and tracking of team norms and coaching and training to deal with personality-based conflicts within teams.

REFERENCES

Barry, B., & Stewart, G. L. (1997). Composition, process, and performance in self-managed groups: The role of personality. *Journal of Applied Psychology, 82,* 62–78.

Barrick, M. R., Stewart, G. L., Neubert, J. M., & Mount, M. K. (1998). Relating member ability and personality to work-team processes and team effectiveness. *Journal of Applied Psychology, 83,* 377–391.

Bond, M. H., & Shiu, W. Y. (1997). The relationship between a group's personality resources and the two dimensions of its group processes. *Small Group Research, 28,* 194–217.

Bouchard, T. J. (1972). Training, motivation, and personality as determinants of the effectiveness of brainstorming groups and individuals. *Journal of Applied Psychology, 56,* 324–331.

Brandstatter, H, & Farthofer, A. (1997). Personality in social influence across tasks and groups. *Small Group Research, 28,* 146–163.

Burningham, C. & West, M. A. (1995). Individual, climate, and group interaction processes as predictors of work team innovation. *Small Group Research, 26,* 106–117.

Camacho, L. M., & Paulus, P. B. (1995). The role of social anxiousness in group brainstorming. *Journal of Personality and Social Psychology, 68,* 1071–1080.

Cohen, S. G., & Bailey, D. (1997). What makes teams work: Group effectiveness research from the shop floor to the executive suite. *Journal of Management, 23,* 239–290.

Costa, P. T., Jr., & McCrae, R. R. (1988). Personality in adulthood: A six-year longitudinal study of self-reports and spouse ratings on the NEO personality inventory. *Journal of Personality and Social Psychology, 54,* 853–863.

Costa, P. T., Jr., & McCrae, R. R. (1989). *The NEO-PI/NEO-FFI manual supplement.* Odessa, FL: Psychological Assessment Resources.

Dirks, K. T. (1999). The effects of interpersonal trust on work group performance. *Journal of Applied Psychology, 84,* 445–455.

Eigel, K. M., & Kuhnert, K. W. (1996). Personality diversity and its relationship to managerial team productivity. In: M. Ruderman, M. Hughes-James & S. E. Jackson (Eds), *Selected Research on Work Team Diversity.* Greensboro, NC: Center for Creative Leadership.

Hackman, J. R. (1976). Group influences on individuals. In: M. D. Dunnette (Ed.), *Handbook of Industrial and Organizational Psychology.* Chicago, IL.: Rand-McNally.

Hackman, J. R. (1990). *Groups that work (and those that don't): Creating conditions for effective teamwork.* San Francisco: Jossey-Bass.

Halfhill, T., Weilbaecher, A. D., & Sundstrom, E. (1999). Personality Predictors of Performance in Military Teams: Agreeableness and Conscientiousness. Paper presented at the 14th Annual Meeting, Society for Industrial and Organizational Psychology, Atlanta, GA.

Halfhill, T. R., Sundstrom, E., Lahner, J., Calderone, W., & Nielsen, T. M. (2002). *Group Personality Composition and Group Effectiveness: A Meta-Analysis.* In: T. Nielsen & T. Halfhill (Co-Chairs), Team Effectiveness: Recent Innovations in Group Composition Research. Symposium presented at the 17th annual Society for Industrial and Organizational Psychology; Toronto, Canada (April 12–14).

Halfhill, T. R., Sundstrom, E. & Nielsen, T. (2001). Military work team personality composition, norms, and effectiveness. Paper presented at the 16th annual meeting of the Society for Industrial/Organizational Psychology, San Diego, CA (April 27–29).

Harrison, D. A., Price, K. H., & Bell, M. P. (1998). Beyond relational demography: Time and the effects of surface and deep level diversity on work group cohesion. *Academy of Management Journal, 41*(1), 96–107.

Hendrick, H. W. (1979). Differences in group problem-solving behavior and effectiveness as a function of abstractedness. *Journal of Applied Psychology, 64,* 518–525.

Hough, L. M. (1992). The "Big-Five" personality variables – Construct confusion: Description vs. prediction. *Human Performance, 5,* 139–155.

Hyatt, D. E., & Ruddy, T. M. (1997). An examination of the relationships between work group characteristics and performance: Once more into the breech. *Personnel Psychology, 50,* 553–585.

Jackson, S. E., Brett, J. F., Sessa, V. I., Cooper, D. M., Julin, J. A., & Peyronnin, K. (1991). Some differences make a difference: Individual dissimilarity and group heterogeneity as correlates of recruitment, promotions, and turnover. *Journal of Applied Psychology, 76,* 675–689.

Jehn, K. A. (1995). A multimethod examination of the benefits and detriments of intragroup conflict. *Administrative Science Quarterly, 40,* 256–282.

Judge, T. A., & Cable, D. M. (1997). Applicant personality, organizational culture, and organization attraction. *Personnel Psychology, 50,* 359–394.

Kabanoff, B., & O'Brien, G. E. (1979). Cooperation structure and the relationship of leader and member ability to group performance. *Journal of Applied Psychology, 64,* 526–532.

Lawler, E. E., Mohrman, S. A., & Ledford, G. E. (1998). *Strategies for high performance organizations: Employee involvement, TQM, and re-engineering programs in Fortune 1,000 corporations.* San Francisco: Jossey-Bass.

LePine, J. A., Hollenbeck, J. R., Ilgen, D. A., & Hedlund, J. (1997). Effects of individual differences on the performance of hierarchical decision-making teams: Much more than g. *Journal of Applied Psychology, 82*(5), 803–811.

Lorenzet, S. (2002). The importance of team task analysis for team human resource management. In: M. Beyerlein, D. Johnson & S. Beyerlein (Eds), *Team-Based Organizing*. London: Elsevier Publishing (this volume).

McCrae, R. R., & Costa, P. T., Jr. (1987). Validation of the five-factor model of personality across instruments and observers. *Journal of Personality and Social Psychology, 52*, 81–90.

Mohammed, S., Mathieu, J. E., & Bartlett, B. (2000). Individual differences, team effectiveness, and contextual performance: Considering the influence of teamwork and taskwork composition variables. In: S. Mohammed (Chair), *The effect of team composition on team process and performance: What's the mix? What's the measurement? What's the message?* A symposium presented to the Fifteenth Annual Meeting of the Society for Industrial/Organizational Psychology, New Orleans, LA.

Neuman, G. A., & Wright, J. (1999). Team effectiveness: Beyond skills and cognitive ability. *Journal of Applied Psychology, 84*, 376–389.

Neuman, G. A., Wagner, S. H., & Christiansen, N. D. (1999). The relationship between work-team personality composition and the job performance of teams. *Group & Organization Management, 24*, 28–45.

Neuman, G. A. (2000). An IPO model of team effectiveness. Northern Illinois University. Unpublished Manuscript.

Schneider, B. (1987). The people make the place. *Personnel Psychology, 40*, 437–454.

Strube, M. J., Keller, R. N., Oxenberg, J., & Lapidot, D. (1989). Actual and perceived group performance as a function of group composition: The moderating role of the Type A and B behavior patterns. *Journal of Applied Social Psychology, 19*, 140–158.

Sundstrom, E. (1999). Challenges of supporting work team effectiveness. In: E. Sundstrom & Associates (Eds), *Supporting Work Team Effectiveness: Best Management Practices for Fostering High Performance* (pp. 3–23). San Franciso: Jossey-Bass.

Sundstrom, E., DeMeuse, K. P., & Futrell, D. (1990). Work teams: Applications and effectiveness. *American Psychologist, 45*, 120–133.

Sundstrom, E., McIntyre, M., Halfhill, T. R., & Richards, H. (2000). Work groups: From the Hawthorne studies to work teams of the 1990s and beyond. *Group Dynamics, 4*, 44–67.

Tett, R. P., Jackson, D. N., & Rothstein, M. (1991). Personality measures as predictors of job performance: A meta-analytic review. *Personnel Psychology, 44*, 703–741.

Tziner, A., & Eden, D. (1985). Effects of crew composition on crew performance: Does the whole equal the sum of its parts? *Journal of Applied Psychology, 70*, 85–93.

Waung, M., & Brice, T. A. (1998). The effects of conscientiousness and opportunity to caucus on group performance. *Small Group Research, 29*, 624–634.

Williams, W. M., & Sternberg, R. J. (1988). Group Intelligence: Why some groups are better than others. *Intelligence, 12*, 351–377.

CORPORATE CITIZENSHIP IN TEAM-BASED ORGANIZATIONS: AN ESSENTIAL INGREDIENT FOR SUSTAINED SUCCESS

Tjai M. Nielsen, Eric Sundstrom, Sarah K. Soulen, Terry Halfhill and Joseph W. Huff

INTRODUCTION

In striving every day for superior performance and sustained success, many of today's organizations have sought competitive advantage through work teams (Lawler, Mohrman & Ledford, 1998). As team-based organizations (TBOs) become more common, several questions arise: How do team-based organizations ensure that the use of teams continues to pay dividends? What contributes to increased team performance? Once a key, contributing factor is identified, how is it applied and measured? This chapter offers a partial answer for these questions through analysis of one key factor in the sustained success of a team-based organization: organizational citizenship behavior (OCB). Specifically, we propose that OCB provides the fundamental basis for cooperation and effective teamwork necessary for success of a team-based organization. Next, we review current research on OCB and team effectiveness and suggest an agenda for future research. Finally, we offer practical methods for applying and measuring OCB in team-based organizations.

Team-Based Organizing, Volume 9, pages 169–187.

ISBN: 0-7623-0981-4

ORGANIZATIONAL CITIZENSHIP BEHAVIOR AND SUCCESS OF TEAM-BASED ORGANIZATIONS

Organizational citizenship behavior (OCB) has been identified as vital to the success of work teams and organizations (Bateman & Organ, 1983; Nielsen, Sundstrom & Halfhill, 2002; Podsakoff, Ahearne & MacKenzie, 1997; Podsakoff, MacKenzie, Paine & Bachrach, 2000).

The concept of organizational citizenship behavior, first introduced by Bateman and Organ (1983), originated from the work of several people including Barnard (1938), Roethlisberger and Dickson (1964), and Katz and Kahn (1966). The central idea is best expressed by Katz and Kahn (1966) in their discussion of "spontaneous" or extra-role behavior as one of three necessary patterns of behavior elicited by effective organizations. They describe this type of behavior as, "innovative and spontaneous behavior: performance beyond role requirements for accomplishments of organizational functions (p. 337) . . . Within every work group in a factory, within any division in a government bureau, or within any department of a university are countless acts of cooperation without which the system would break down. We take these everyday acts for granted, and few of them are included in the formal role prescriptions for any job" (p. 339).

Organizational citizenship behavior (OCB) refers to a general set of behaviors performed by employees that are helpful, discretionary, and go far beyond normal job requirements. Specifically, OCB has been defined as, "individual behavior that is discretionary, not directly or explicitly recognized by the formal reward system, and that in the aggregate promotes the effective functioning of the organization" (Organ, 1988, p. 4). Some examples include:

- An employee staying late to help a teammate finish his or her part of an important project.
- An experienced manager helping a new manager "learn the ropes," even though this activity is not part of the experienced manager's job description and takes much time.
- An office employee exerting the extra effort to come to work during a snow-storm, even when other employees use the storm as an excuse to stay home.
- A team member spending many hours helping to resolve a conflict between other team members.
- A manager who is willing to adapt to new company human resource policies, rather than complaining about them.

The relationship between OCB and performance at the team level is based on the idea that individual OCB aggregated across people and time will be related to work team performance. There has been some theoretical work attempting to explain why team level organizational citizenship behavior is positively related to work team performance (Podsakoff & MacKenzie, 1997). First, team level OCB represented by team members going out of their way to help each other with work-related problems is thought to decrease the need for manager involvement and promote self-management. Second, team level OCB represented by experienced team members training new ones may increase individual team members' ability to accomplish specific tasks and enhance the team's ability to accomplish overall team goals. Third, team level OCB represented by team members actively participating in team meetings will probably improve work team coordination. Finally, team level OCB represented by team members engaging in helpful and cooperative behaviors will naturally create a more pleasant place to work. This enhanced work environment facilitates performance and may increase the team's ability to attract and keep the most talented employees. These examples suggest a framework for understanding how OCB might improve work team performance and the performance of team-based organizations (see Fig. 1).

First, OCB as a team level variable – partially defined by the extent to which it has been adopted as a team norm – positively predicts work team performance. Second, team level OCB predicts team performance better than individual OCB. Finally, the relationship between team level OCB and work team performance is moderated by the degree to which a work team's tasks are interdependent.

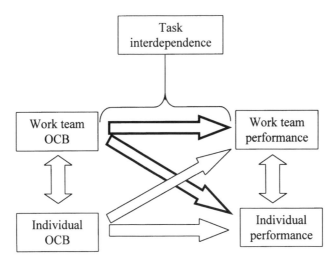

Fig. 1. General Framework for the Relationship Structure of Organizational Citizenship Behavior and Performance.

Teams are the essential foundation on which team-based organizations are built. This has greatly increased the importance of inter and intra-team cooperation. OCB represents the essence of cooperative behavior. Thus, a plethora of research has been conducted on OCB and its relationship with a variety of variables.

CURRENT RESEARCH ON OCB

In recent years there has been an abundance of research conducted involving OCB (Allen & Rush, 1998; Avila, Fern & Mann, 1988; Karambaya, 1991; MacKenzie, Podsakoff & Fetter, 1991, 1993; MacKenzie, Podsakoff & Paine, 1999; Nielsen et al., 2002; Podsakoff et al., 1997; Podsakoff & MacKenzie, 1994, 1997; Randall, Cropanzano, Bormann & Birjulin, 1999; Shore, Barksdale & Shore, 1995; Walz & Niehoff, 1996). Much of this research has attempted to identify the antecedents of OCB (Bateman & Organ, 1983; George, 1991; Podsakoff, Niehoff, MacKenzie & Williams, 1993; Schnake, 1991; Smith, Organ & Near, 1983). The majority of this work was presumably conducted with the assumption that OCBs promote organizational and/or work team performance.

Antecedents to OCB. The empirical research examining antecedents to OCB has concentrated on four primary categories including individual characteristics (e.g. employee attitudes; personality), task characteristics (e.g. task feedback & routinization), organizational characteristics (e.g. reward structure, perceived organizational support, organizational formalization), and leadership behaviors (e.g. transformational leadership; high performance expectations).

Consistent with the theoretical foundation of OCB, many researchers have explored job satisfaction (i.e. individual characteristic) as a predictor of OCB (Bateman & Organ, 1983; George, 1990; Karambaya, 1991). The strength of this relationship appears intuitively plausible and has been empirically supported (Organ & Ryan, 1995; Podsakoff et al., 2000). A variety of other antecedents have also been examined. Such as:

Individual Characteristics. Fairness – (Farh, Podsakoff & Organ, 1990; Niehoff & Moorman, 1993).
Organizational commitment – (Kidwell, Mossholder & Bennett, 1997).
Personality – (Barrick, Mount & Strauss, 1992).
Affect – A recent review of this literature (Organ & Ryan, 1995) indicated satisfaction, fairness, organizational commitment, leadership, and conscientiousness to be the best predictors of OCB. However, each relationship was only moderately well supported.

Task Characteristics. The majority of research in this category originates from the substitutes for leadership literature (i.e. Podsakoff & MacKenzie, 1995; Podsakoff, Niehoff, MacKenzie & Williams, 1993). A review of this literature (Podsakoff et al., 2000) revealed that task feedback and intrinsically satisfying tasks were positively related to OCB while task routinization was negatively related to OCB.

Organizational Characteristics. The relationship between organizational characteristics and OCB is somewhat tenuous. Organizational formalization, organizational inflexibility, advisory/staff support, and spatial distance were not consistently related to OCB (Podsakoff et al., 2000). Only group cohesiveness demonstrated a positive relationship with OCB (Kidwell, Mossholder & Bennett, 1997).

Leadership Behaviors. Transformational leadership behaviors were positively related to OCB (MacKenzie, Podsakoff & Rich, 1999). Leader supportiveness was also related to OCB (Schnake, Dumler & Cochran, 1993).

In the discussion sections of many articles examining antecedents to OCB are qualifying statements related to the need for research exploring the relationship between OCB and work group or organizational performance. For example, Organ and Ryan (1995) state, "And we should note that a key assumption in the rationale for studying OCB [antecedents] is the notion (Organ, 1988) that ultimately, aggregated across time and individuals, it contributes to organizational effectiveness. With notable exceptions. . . little effort has been given even to heuristic indicators that this assumption is viable" (p. 797). In addition, Bolino (1999) states, ". . . in contrast to the numerous studies exploring the antecedents of OCB, there is a paucity of research examining the outcomes of citizenship behaviors in organizations" (p. 82). More research on the OCB-performance relationship has been at the individual, rather than team level.

Individual Level OCB. Several studies at the individual level of analysis used OCB as a predictor (Allen & Rush, 1998; Avila, Fern & Mann, 1988; MacKenzie, Podsakoff & Fetter, 1991, 1993; MacKenzie, Podsakoff & Paine, 1999; Podsakoff & MacKenzie, 1994, 1997; Shore, Barksdale & Shore, 1995). Shore, Barksdale, and Shore conducted a study involving employees from a large multinational organization located in the Southeast. While assessing organizational citizenship behavior (OCB) and performance at two points in time, the authors found correlations above 0.50 for all relationships (i.e. the authors defined OCB as altruism and compliance). In a study examining computer salespeople, Avila, Fern and Mann found OCB to be positively related to sales performance. Similarly,

MacKenzie, Podsakoff and Fetter explored the relationship between OCB and performance (i.e. subjective and objective) within a large insurance company. Their findings indicated significant, positive correlations between components of OCB and subjective performance, but not objective performance. In another study involving over 900 insurance agents, OCB was positively related to supervisor ratings of performance (MacKenzie, Podsakoff & Paine; Podsakoff & MacKenzie). Randall et al. (1999) examined OCB by dividing it into OCB that benefits the organization (i.e. OCBO) and the individual (i.e. OCBI). OCBO and OCBI were both positively correlated with performance. However, because predictor and criterion ratings were both made by the same supervisors, common method variance could partially account for the results. Similar to the previous studies, Allen and Rush (1998) found OCB to be positively related to task performance and overall performance. The relationship between individual OCB and performance highlights the potential synergistic effects when examined in teams.

Team Level OCB. There is a significant need for research examining the link between OCB and performance at the team level (Bolino, 1999; Organ & Ryan, 1995). To date, only a limited number of studies have attempted to meet this need (Nielsen et al., 2002; Podsakoff & MacKenzie, 1994; Podsakoff et al., 1997). Specifically, these studies assessed team level OCB and work team performance (i.e. multiple types of teams, insurance agency teams, and paper mill work crews, respectively). These studies produced contradictory findings, but provide strong support for a relationship between team OCB and team performance.

A study involving paper mill work crews yielded contradictory results (Podsakoff et al., 1997): a positive relationship between sportsmanship, helping behavior and the quantity of output, but a negative relationship between helping behavior and the quality of output. Podsakoff and MacKenzie (1994) studied the relationship between team OCB and insurance agency performance. While these researchers obtained a large sample and objective ratings of performance, results were mixed. They found sportsmanship and civic virtue to be positively related to agency performance, while helping behavior and agency performance demonstrated a negative relationship. Nielsen et al. (2002) conducted a longitudinal field study and found a positive relationship between OCB and concurrent and subsequent team performance. Moreover, these researchers found that team norms of OCB accounted for 31% of the variance in concurrent team performance and 16% of the variance in subsequent team performance. These studies differ from research that has examined OCB and performance at the organizational level (Karambaya, 1991; Walz & Niehoff, 1996).

Karambaya (1991) and Walz and Niehoff (1996) assessed performance at the organizational level (i.e. work units and limited menu restaurants, respectively).

Karambaya (1991) examined the relationship between organizational level OCB and work unit performance and found them to be positively related. However, limitations suggested by small sample size and subjective performance ratings of work units from different organizations reduce the level of confidence that can be placed in the results. Walz and Niehoff (1996) assessed the relationship between organizational level OCB and organizational level performance in limited-menu restaurants. Results indicated that OCB accounted for 29% of the variance in overall restaurant performance. Other research has focused on specific components of OCB like helping behavior.

A key component of organizational citizenship behavior is helping behavior. Researchers have explored the relationship between helping behavior directed at customers and team performance (George, 1990; George & Bettenhausen, 1990). Team customers can be defined as anyone who receives that team's products, services, information, or decisions.

George and Bettenhausen (1990) explored the relationship between the helping behavior (i.e. customer service) and performance of sales people from 33 retail stores that were part of a national chain. Results indicated that customer service was related to sales performance. George (1990) also studied helping behavior defined as customer service. Results demonstrated a significant, negative correlation between customer service and negative affective tone (i.e. criterion variable). Nielsen, Sundstrom and Halfhill (2001) and Nielsen et al. (2002) investigated the relationship between OCB and customer-rated performance. Results indicated that team OCB and customer-rated performance were strongly related. The mixed results from research on OCB and performance highlights the need to examine other factors that may play a part in this relationship. Some researchers have suggested that a key factor in the team OCB-performance relationship is task interdependence (Podsakoff et al., 1997).

Task Interdependence and OCB. Researchers have suggested that many of the inconsistent results in OCB research may be due to a failure to examine key moderating factors in the team level OCB-work team performance relationship (Podsakoff et al., 1997).

One factor that could moderate the relationship between work team OCB and team performance is *interdependence,* or the extent to which team members' individual task performance, goal achievement, or outcomes depend on timely cooperation by teammates. Interdependence has been identified as a key predictor of the formation, motivation, and performance of work teams (Campion, Medsker & Higgs, 1993; Mintzberg, 1979; Wageman, 1995). Specifically, interdependence may increase cooperative behavior (Shea &

Guzzo, 1989), promote the reward value of group accomplishments, and enhance group effectiveness (Guzzo & Shea, 1987).

Among the main forms of interdependence, much research has focused on task interdependence (Wageman, 1995), or "... the degree to which an individual's task performance depends upon the efforts or skills of others" (Wageman & Baker, 1997, p. 141). Studies of this form of interdependence found it associated with measures of group effectiveness (Saavedra, Earley & Van Dyne, 1993). Research on outcome interdependence, the extent to which team members share outcomes of team efforts, such as team-based rewards, also found it associated with indices of team performance (DeMatteo, Eby & Sundstrom, 1998).

Interdependence may have a role in the relationship between work team OCB and team performance (Podsakoff et al., 1997). The more team members depend on each other to perform tasks, the greater the importance of joint, cooperative efforts. OCB represents the essence of cooperative behavior and may have a more significant impact on performance for work teams with a high degree of task interdependence. Thus, work team interdependence might be a powerful moderating variable in the relationship between OCB and performance at the team level of analysis. This hypothesis was supported by Nielsen et al. (2002) in their study on team level OCB and performance. Their findings indicated that task interdependence moderated the relationship between team OCB and performance such that the relationship increased with greater levels of task interdependence.

The research on team OCB and performance leaves some questions unanswered. Does OCB in teams contribute significantly to team performance? Does task interdependence moderate this relationship? What comes first, OCB or good performance? These questions and others suggest several future directions for OCB research.

FUTURE RESEARCH ON OCB AND TEAM PERFORMANCE

While past research provides evidence of a strong correlation between OCB and team effectiveness, many questions remained unanswered about the OCB-team performance relationship. Key areas that future research should address include: (1) OCB as a team and/or organizational norm; (2) Interpersonal and motivational dynamics of the OCB-team performance link; (3) OCB as a predictor or criterion; (4) OCB at the individual, team, and organizational levels; (5) Recipients of OCB; (6) Factors promoting OCB; and (7) OCB and virtual teams.

OCB as a Team and/or Organizational Norm. Norms are informal rules implicitly adopted by a group that have powerful effects on group behavior (Hackman, 1976). Norms may contribute to or detract from group performance depending on their structure (Seashore, 1954). The key role norms play in the functioning of teams indicates they may be essential ingredients in the measurement of team level variables including OCB. One method for measuring the degree to which OCB is a team norm involves the use of multiple measures. For example, OCB might be assessed from different perspectives (i.e. current levels and consistency over time) and from different stakeholders (i.e. team members and customers). Combining all of these measures into an index may yield more accurate results when assessing OCB as a team norm.

This methodology may also be appropriate for the assessment of other team level variables. For example, would the measurement of team conscientiousness be more accurate by operationalizing conscientiousness as a team norm and utilizing an index score to represent the level of team conscientiousness? Would conscientiousness be a better or worse predictor of team performance if it were assessed using this methodology?

Interpersonal and motivational dynamics of the OCB-team performance link. Among the questions left unanswered by prior research, many concern the nature of the link between OCB and team performance. Because most empirical studies of OCB so far have relied on correlational methods, they have not addressed the question about causal links: Does OCB promote team performance, or does performance promote citizenship, or both? What dynamics underlie these linkages? Prior research suggests several different dynamics. For example, high team performance could boost individual members' motivation to work toward team goals (Hackman & Helmreich, 1987), resulting in more discretionary efforts to help teammates and/or team customers. Similarly, extra help in the form of team OCB might lead to improved individual motivation and effort, or simply to better performance as a result of improved coordination among team members.

OCB as a performance criterion. While past research has treated OCB mainly as a predictor variable and potential contributor to performance, some researchers have also identified OCB as a type of performance (Borman & Motowidlo, 1997). As organizations make teamwork an essential part of evolving job descriptions, OCB may change from "discretionary" (as Organ, 1988, suggests it has been) to expected and required. Future research might explore the changing nature of performance expectations in team-based organizations, and the possible transformation of OCB into a performance requirement.

OCB and Levels of Analysis. The OCB-performance relationship has been examined at the individual, team, and organizational levels. Most studies used subjective indicators of performance. Future research needs to examine the relationship between OCB and performance at multiple levels of analysis and with both subjective and objective performance criteria. This will aid in determining whether this relationship systematically varies across levels of analysis and criterion type.

OCB Recipients. Future research might address responses to OCB in key recipient groups, such as teammates, co-workers who belong to other teams, and customers. Some research suggests that customer-focused OCB represents a significant predictor of team performance (George & Bettenhausen, 1990). Future research might explore whether the same kind of relationships hold for teammate focused OCB or cross-team OCB. Especially in a TBO that depends on cooperation among multiple, interdependent teams, research might find that cross-team OCB can become a source of competitive advantage.

Factors Promoting OCB. Future research should examine specific team and organizational variables that promote employee OCB. Creating an environment where OCB is fostered and expected due to work team norms or organizational culture will likely lead to improved performance and satisfaction.

OCB and Virtual Teams. Finally, future research should address the role of OCB in virtual teams. Is OCB more or less important for virtual teams than for co-located teams? Because virtual teams depend on electronic links instead of the face-to-face interaction that supports cohesion in co-located teams, OCB could play a more central role in virtual teams. For example, developing a norm of having members volunteering help for those who fall behind in individual tasks could boost cohesion more in a virtual team than in a co-located team. Future research on OCB in virtual teams might address the link of individual OCB with team OCB norms as well as the links of team OCB with team cohesion, performance, and longevity.

PRACTICAL METHODS FOR PROMOTING AND APPLYING OCB IN TEAM-BASED ORGANIZATIONS

The research may indicate that OCB contributes to the performance of teams and team-based organizations (TBOs), but this is of little value without methods for implementation and measurement. Successfully applying OCB in TBOs requires a multi-faceted approach. Successful TBOs must lay the proper foundation to establish the proper context that promotes more effective teams (Sundstrom & Associates, 1999). Regarding OCB, the foundation includes staffing, training and development, and measurement and feedback systems.

Staffing. Putting the right people on the right teams at the right time is difficult but essential to promote performance excellence (Campion, Papper & Medsker, 1995; Cohen & Bailey, 1997; Halfhill, Sundstrom, Lahner, Calderone & Nielsen, 2002). There are many factors involved in the effective staffing of teams (e.g. necessary KSAOs, type of team, type of task, team goals, etc., Klimoski & Zukin, 1999) that are beyond the scope of this chapter, but one key factor involves selecting team members who will cooperate and help each other. In other words, team members with high levels of OCB.

The importance of selecting team members with high levels of OCB suggests that one component of the assessment-for-selection process is measuring candidate's level of OCB. This process should focus on assessing behaviors representing high levels of OCB such as: (1) An employee staying late to help a teammate finish his or her part of an important project; (2) A team member spending many hours helping to resolve a conflict between other team members; (3) A manager who is willing to adapt to new company human resource policies, rather than complaining about them. Measuring these behaviors could be done in several ways. First, people who work closely with the candidate could provide OCB ratings (e.g. as part of a 360 feedback process). Second, the candidate could complete a self-report assessment on their level of OCB. Finally, another option would involve combining all of the above into an index measure of OCB.

Training and Development. A focus on people development has been identified as vitally important to organizations for keeping talented employees and maintaining competitive advantage (McCall, 1998; Peters & Waterman, 1982; Senge, 1990). Equally as important, but often overlooked is a focus on team development (Stevens & Yarish, 1999). The importance of team development becomes even more paramount in team-based organizations.

Individual team members may have a variety of competency areas that must be developed to excel in their organization. However, these individual needs are not identical to those of the team. For example, there are five members of a department store sales team, two of which need work on being more responsive to customers, two others need to work on communicating more openly with their team-mates, and the last member needs to develop more product knowledge. While these are individual areas needing improvement, they will likely become barriers to team performance. If this situation is viewed at the team level, the key development need of the team may be in the area of helping behavior. Each team member might improve his or her specific areas of weakness, but this will not necessarily translate into an increase in team performance. However, several of the individual developmental needs could be met if the team were to collectively work on their helping behavior. In addition, this process might result in improved team functioning and performance.

Measurement and Feedback. Just as a business utilizes key metrics to assess financial performance and viability, so too must a business measure key metrics involving human performance. Specifically, team-based organizations must measure the critical elements of team performance and provide this information to the team in the form of feedback (Jones & Moffett, 1999). Without this, teams have little hope of knowing how they are doing or how to improve. A key element that should be measured is the teams' level of OCB. The measurement of team OCB requires a comprehensive approach which will be discussed more thoroughly in the next section.

Successfully applying OCB to a team-based organization requires establishing the proper context that will support high performing teams. Three important components necessary for supporting the establishment of OCB as a team norm involve staffing, training and development, and measurement. Team-based organizations must: (1) staff teams with individuals who will engage in OCB; (2) train and develop teams on the essential components of citizenship behavior like cooperation and helping; and (3) measure the degree to which individuals and teams engage in OCB and provide them with feedback. Measuring OCB presents its own set of challenges, especially at the team level.

MEASURING OCB

Measuring OCB in research or in practice as an organizational metric, is crucial in understanding the extent to which it is perceived by team members, team leaders, or even customers. A team-based organization has no way of identifying the degree to which OCB is a part of the culture without a valid and reliable measurement tool. There are different conceptualizations of what behaviors comprise OCB and how to measure them (LePine, Erez & Johnson, 2002).

The OCB Construct. The OCB construct was originally divided into five factors (Bateman & Organ, 1983). They included altruism, conscientiousness, sportsmanship, courtesy, and civic virtue. They may be defined as follows: (1) altruism – discretionary behaviors that have the effect of helping a specific other person (e.g. supervisor, teammate & customer); (2) conscientiousness –

discretionary behaviors on the part of an employee that go well beyond the minimum role requirements of the organization, in the areas of attendance, obeying rules and regulations, taking breaks, and so forth; (3) sportsmanship – willingness of an employee to tolerate less than ideal circumstances without complaining; (4) courtesy – discretionary behavior on the part of an individual aimed at preventing work-related problems with others; (5) civic virtue – an individual's behavior indicating that he or she responsibly participates in, is involved in, or is concerned about the life of the organization. Recent research (e.g. MacKenzie et al., 1991, 1993; Podsakoff & MacKenzie, 1994) has indicated that participants have difficulty distinguishing altruistic and courteous behaviors. This led to Podsakoff et al. (1997) combining these two factors into a single "helping behavior" dimension. Measures of helping behavior, sportsmanship, and civic virtue have received strong empirical support for reliability with coefficient alphas (Cronbach, 1951) of 0.95, 0.96, and 0.88, respectively (Podsakoff et al., 1997).

Behavioral examples of these specific dimensions include:

Civic Virtue – A team member risks the disapproval of peers in order to express his or her beliefs about what is best for the team; team members actively participate in team meetings.

Helping – A team leader helps a new team member "learn the ropes," even though this activity is not part of the team leader's job description; one team member helps another finish his or her part of an important team project.

Sportsmanship – Team members adapt to new company human resource policies, rather than complaining about them.

While there are different conceptualizations of the OCB construct, some valid and reliable measurement tools exist.

Tools for Measuring OCB. A questionnaire established by Podsakoff et al. (1997) is very versatile and reliable. This questionnaire contains three sub-scales measuring helping behavior, sportsmanship, and civic virtue. Each scale represents a dimension of organizational citizenship behavior previously established as reliable (Podsakoff et al., 1997). There are 13 items, with seven tapping the dimension of helping behavior, three tapping sportsmanship, and three tapping civic virtue. Each item includes a statement about the behavior of the individual or work team and is followed by a list of responses indicating the level of agreement. The response format contains a 5-point scale of agreement including, 1 = strongly disagree, 2 = disagree, 3 = neutral, 4 = agree, and 5 = strongly agree. This scale can be used to assess individual level OCB, team level OCB, and the consistency of team level OCB over time (Nielsen et al.,

2002). To customize each measure, a stem is used to place the items in the appropriate context. Multiple stems can be used such as, "When I work with my team I . . .", "Members of my team . . .", "Consistently, over time, members of my team . . .", and "Members of the _____ team . . .." Items can be worded differently depending upon the specific stem, but generally include the following ("R" indicates a reversed scored item):

(1) Help out other team members if someone falls behind in his/her work.
(2) Willingly share my expertise with other members of the team.
(3) Always focus on what is wrong with the situation, rather than the positive side (R).
(4) Take steps to prevent problems with other team members.
(5) Willingly give my time to help team members who have work-related problems.
(6) Touch-base with other team members before initiating actions that might affect them.
(7) Consume a lot of time complaining about trivial matters (R).
(8) Provide constructive suggestions about how the team can improve its effectiveness.
(9) Am willing to risk disapproval to express my beliefs about what's best for the team.
(10) Always find fault with what other team members are doing (R).
(11) Try to act like a peacemaker when other team members have disagreements.
(12) Encourage other team members when they are down.
(13) Attend and actively participate in team meetings.

This measurement tool can be used in a variety of contexts and is flexible in its application. However, the measurement of OCB at the team and organizational levels presents some dilemmas. Specifically, systematically avoiding errors of aggregation.

Measuring OCB as a Team Norm. Individuals in human resource departments need to measure a variety of team level variables. These variables may range from team satisfaction and team sensitivity to diversity and team citizenship behavior. Typically, this type of assessment is done through the aggregation of individual data on the variable in question. Several researchers have identified that aggregation can be misleading (James, Demaree & Wolf, 1984; Roberts, Hulin & Rousseau, 1978; Rousseau, 1985). One method to gain accuracy may involve conceptualizing specific team level variables as team norms and measuring them accordingly. Norms are informal rules implicitly adopted by a group that have powerful effects on group behavior (Hackman, 1976). Norms may contribute to or detract from group performance depending on their structure (Seashore, 1954). If a work team has positive and functional norms such as helping behavior and sportsmanship, then the team's norms will likely facilitate performance. However, if a work team has established negative performance norms such as low performance goals, then the team's norms will likely be deleterious to performance. The key role norms play in the functioning of teams indicates they may be essential ingredients in the measurement of team level variables.

OCB represents a relatively straightforward set of behaviors, but when OCB is assessed at the team and/or organizational level several key measurement issues are created. It may not be enough to simply aggregate individual scores from an OCB measure and then label this mean or aggregate score as representative of team level OCB. For example, a work team that has a high degree of variability on individual OCB is not likely to realize the full benefits of OCB. That is, a team that has only a few members frequently engaging in OCB will realize some performance benefit, but not compared with the synergy realized from a team where a majority of members carry out citizenship behaviors. If most members of a team frequently engage in organizational citizenship behavior, it is an expected form of behavior, and is explicitly related to how the team is perceived – or in other words, if it is a team norm – then performance may increase exponentially.

Accurately measuring team level OCB may require it to be conceptualized as a team norm and team norms cannot be assessed through the simple aggregation of individual scores. Measuring OCB as a team norm may be more accurate if four key steps are followed. First, within-team variability must be assessed to determine the level of agreement between team members. Second, individual team member OCB scores need to be aggregated. Third, the extent to which team OCB is consistent over time should be assessed to determine stability. Finally, the perception of team level OCB as seen by team members (change in referent from the individual to the team), team leaders, and those external to the team (e.g. customers) must be assessed. Integrating each of these steps will result in an index measure of team level OCB. This index will facilitate measurement of team level OCB and may represent a qualitatively different and potentially more accurate approach to the assessment of other team level variables (Nielsen et al., 2002). While this methodology may yield more accuracy, it also takes more time and money to execute. These drawbacks must be weighed against the advantages for specific organizations.

OCB IN TEAM-BASED ORGANIZATIONS

In summary, organizational citizenship behavior plays a pivotal role in team-based organizations. It is the fundamental basis for cooperation and teamwork. Successfully applying OCB in team-based organizations requires a multi-faceted approach including staffing, training and development, and measurement and feedback systems. These essential support systems for team effectiveness are important to sustain the positive impact of OCB.

Competition is rapidly increasing, more organizations are moving to team-based structures, and employees are increasingly being required to become more adaptable. All of these factors highlight the importance of helping behavior, sportsmanship, and civic virtue for achieving high levels of success. It is not enough to be technically efficient and task focused. The category of organizational citizenship embodies many of the behaviors and skills that will be required of employees, teams, and organizations now and in the future.

REFERENCES

Allen, T. D., & Rush, M. C. (1998). The effects of organizational citizenship behavior on performance judgments: A field study and a laboratory experiment. *Journal of Applied Psychology, 83*, 247–260.

Avila, R. A., Fern, E. F., & Mann, O. K. (1988). Unraveling criteria for assessing sales people: A causal analysis. *Journal of Personal Selling and Sales Management, 8*, 45–54.

Barnard, C. I. (1938). *The functions of the executive.* Cambridge, MA: Harvard University Press.

Barrick, M. R., Mount, M. K., & Strauss, J. P. (1992). Big Five and ability predictors of citizenship, delinquency, and sales performance. Paper presented at the Seventh Annual Conference of the Society of Industrial and Organizational Psychology, Montreal.

Bateman, T. S., & Organ, D. W. (1983). Job satisfaction and the good soldier: The relationship between affect and employee "citizenship." *Academy of Management Journal, 26*, 587–595.

Bolino, M. C. (1999). Citizenship or impression management: Good soldiers or good actors? *Academy of Management Review, 24*(1), 82–98.

Borman, W. C., & Motowidlo, S. J. (1997). Task performance and contextual performance: The meaning for personnel selection research. *Human Performance, 10*(2), 99–109.

Campion, M. A., Medsker, G. J., & Higgs, A. C. (1993). Relations between work group characteristics and effectiveness: Implications for designing effective work groups. *Personnel Psychology, 46*, 823–850.

Campion, M. A., Papper, E. M., & Medsker, G. J. (1995). Relations between work team characteristics and effectiveness: Replication and extension. *Personnel Psychology, 49*, 429–452.

Cohen, S. G., & Bailey, D. E. (1997). What makes teams work: Group effectiveness research from the shop floor to the executive suite. *Journal of Management, 23*(3), 239–290.

Cronbach, L. J. (1951). Coefficient alpha and the internal structure of tests. *Psychometrika, 16*, 297–334.

DeMatteo, J. S., Eby, L. T., & Sundstrom, E. (1998). Team-based rewards: Current empirical evidence and directions for future research. *Research in Organizational Behavior, 20*, 141–183.

Farh, J., Podsakoff, P. M., & Organ, D. W. (1990). Accounting for organizational citizenship behavior: Leader fairness and task scope vs. satisfaction. *Journal of Management, 16*, 705–722.

George, J. M. (1990). Personality, affect, and behavior in groups. *Journal of Applied Psychology, 75*, 107–116.

George, J. M. (1991). State or trait: Effects of positive mood on prosocial behaviors at work. *Journal of Applied Psychology, 76*, 299–307.

George, J. M., & Bettenhausen, K. (1990). Understanding prosocial behavior, sales performance, and turnover: A group level analysis in a service context. *Journal of Applied Psychology, 75*, 698–709.

Guzzo, R. A., & Shea, G. P. (1987). Group effectiveness: What really matters. *Sloan Management Review*, (Spring), 25–31.

Hackman, J. R. (1976). Group influences on individuals. In: M. D. Dunnette (Ed.), *Handbook of Industrial and Organizational Psychology* (pp. 1455–1526). Chicago, IL.: Rand-McNally.

Hackman, R. J., & Helmreich, R. L. (1987). Assessing the behavior and performance of teams in organizations: The case of air transport crews. In: D. R. Peterson & D. B. Fishman (Eds), *Assessment for Decision. Rutgers Symposia on Applied Psychology* (Vol. 1., pp. 283–313).

Halfhill, T., Sundstrom, E., Lahner, J., Calderone, W., & Nielsen, T. M. (2002). Personality composition and group effectiveness: A meta-analysis. In: T. M. Nielsen & T. Halfhill (Co-chairs), *Work Group Composition and Effectiveness: Personality, Diversity, and Citizenship.* Symposium conducted at the 2002 Society for Industrial-Organizational Psychology Conference, Toronto-Ontario, Canada.

James, L. R., Dameree, R. G., & Wolf, G. (1984). Estimating within-group interrater reliability with and without response bias. *Journal of Applied Psychology, 69*, 85–98.

Jones, S., & Moffett, R. G. (1999). Measurement and feedback systems for teams. In: E. Sundstrom (Ed.), *Supporting Work Team Effectiveness: Best Management Practices for Fostering High Performance* (pp. 157–187). San Francisco: Jossey-Bass.

Karambaya, R. (1991). Contexts for organizational citizenship: Do high performing and satisfying units have better citizens? Unpublished manuscript, York University, Ontario, Canada.

Katz, D., & Kahn, R. L. (1966). *The social psychology of organizations.* New York: Wiley.

Kidwell R. E., Jr., Mossholder, K., & Bennett, N. (1997). Cohesiveness and organizational citizenship behavior. A multilevel analysis using work groups and individuals. *Journal of Management, 23*(6), 775–793.

Klimoski, R. J., & Zukin, L. B. (1999). Selection and staffing for team effectiveness. In: E. Sundstrom (Ed.), *Supporting Work Team Effectiveness: Best Management Practices for Fostering High Performance* (pp. 63–91). San Francisco: Jossey-Bass.

Konovsky, M. A., & Organ, D. W. (1996). Dispositional and contextual determinants of organizational citizenship behavior. *Journal of Organizational Behavior, 17*(3), 253–266.

Lawler, E. E., III, Mohrman, S. A., & Ledford, G. E. (1998). *Strategies for high performance organizations: Employee involvement, TQM, and reengineering programs in Fortune 1000 corporations.* San Francisco: Jossey-Bass.

LePine, J. A., Erez, & Johnson, D. E. (2002). The nature and dimensionality of organizational citizenship behavior: A critical review and meta-analysis. *Journal of Applied Psychology, 87*(1), 52–65.

MacKenzie, S. B., Podsakoff, P. M., & Ahearne, M. (1998). Some possible antecedents and consequences of in-role and extra-role salesperson performance. *Journal of Marketing, 62*, 87–98.

MacKenzie, S. B., Podsakoff, P. M., & Fetter, R. (1991). Organizational citizenship behavior and objective productivity as determinants of managerial evaluations of salespersons' performance. *Organizational Behavior and Human Decision Processes, 50*, 123–150.

MacKenzie, S. B., Podsakoff, P. M., & Fetter, R. (1993). The impact of organizational citizenship on evaluations of salesperson performance. *Journal of Marketing, 57*, 70–80.

MacKenzie, S. B., Podsakoff, P. M., & Paine, J. E. (1999). Effects of organizational citizenship behaviors and productivity on evaluations of performance at different hierarchical levels in sales organizations. *Journal of the Academy of Marketing Science, 27*, 396–410.

MacKenzie, S. B., Podsakoff, P. M., & Rich, G. A. (1999). Transformational and transactional leadership and salesperson performance. *Journal of the Academy of Marketing Science, 29*(2), 115–134.

McCall, M. W. (1998). *High flyers: Developing the next generation of leaders.* Boston, MA: Harvard Business School Press.

Mintzberg, H. (1979). *The structuring of organizations: A synthesis of the research.* Englewood Cliffs, NJ: Prentice Hall.

Niehoff, B. P., & Moorman, R. H. (1993). Justice as a mediator of the relationship between methods of monitoring and organizational citizenship behavior. *Academy of Management Journal, 36*, 527–556.

Nielsen, T. M., Sundstrom, E., & Halfhill, T. (2001). Work teams and their customers: The role of OCB. Paper presented at the 13th annual American Psychological Society convention. Toronto, Ontario, Canada.

Nielsen, T. M., Sundstrom, E., & Halfhill, T. (2002). Organizational citizenship behavior and work team performance: A field study. In: T. M. Nielsen & T. Halfhill (Co-chairs), *Work Group Composition and Effectiveness: Personality, Diversity, and Citizenship.* Symposium conducted at the 2002 Society for Industrial-Organizational Psychology Conference, Toronto, Ontario, Canada.

Organ, D. W. (1988). *Organizational citizenship behavior: The good soldier syndrome.* Lexington, MA: Lexington Books.

Organ, D. W., & Ryan, K. (1995). A meta-analytic review of attitudinal and dispositional predictors of organizational citizenship behavior. *Personnel Psychology, 48*, 775–800.

Peters, T. J., & Waterman, R. H. (1982). *In search of excellence: Lessons from America's best-run companies.* New York, NY: Harper & Row Publishers.

Podsakoff, P. M., Ahearne, M., & MacKenzie, S. B. (1997). Organizational citizenship behavior and the quantity and quality of work group performance. *Journal of Applied Psychology, 82*(2), 262–270.

Podsakoff, P. M., & MacKenzie, S. B. (1994). Organizational citizenship behavior and sales unit effectiveness. *Journal of Marketing Research, 31*, 351–363.

Podsakoff, P. M., & MacKenzie, S. B. (1995). An examination of substitutes for leadership within a levels of analysis framework. *Leadership Quarterly, 6*, 289–328.

Podsakoff, P. M., & MacKenzie, S. B. (1997). The impact of organizational citizenship behavior on organizational performance: A review and suggestions for future research. *Human Performance, 10*, 133–151.

Podsakoff, P. M., MacKenzie, S. B., Paine, J. B., & Bachrach, D. G. (2000). Organizational citizenship behaviors: A critical review of the theoretical and empirical literature and suggestions for future research. *Journal of Management, 26*(3), 513–563.

Podsakoff, P. M., Niehoff, B. P., MacKenzie, S. B., & Williams, M. L. (1993). Do substitutes for leadership really substitute for leadership? An empirical examination of Kerr and Jermier's situational leadership model. *Organizational Behavior and Human Decision Processes, 54*, 1–44.

Randall, M. L., Cropanzano, R., Bormann, C. A., & Birjulin, A. (1999). Organizational politics and organizational support as predictors of work attitudes, job performance, and organizational citizenship behavior. *Journal of Organizational Behavior, 20*, 159–174.

Roberts, K. H., Hulin, C. L., & Rousseau, D. M. (1978). *Developing an interdisciplinary science of organizations.* San Francisco: Jossey-Bass.

Roethlisberger, F. J., & Dickson, W. J. (1964). *Management and the worker.* New York: Wiley Science Editions.

Rousseau, D. M. (1985). Issues of level in organizational research: Multi-level and cross-level perspectives. In: B. M. Staw & L. L. Cummings (Eds), *Research in Organizational Behavior* (pp. 1–37). Greewich, CT: JAI Press.

Saavedra, R., Early, P. C., & Van Dyne, L. (1993). Complex interdependence in task-performance groups. *Journal of Applied Psychology, 78,* 61–72.

Schnake, M. (1991). Organizational citizenship: A review, proposed model, and research agenda. *Human Relations, 44,* 735–759.

Schnake, M., Dumler, M., & Cochran, D. (1993). The relationship between "traditional" leadership, "super" leadership, and organizational citizenship behavior. *Group and Organization Management, 18*(3), 352–365.

Seashore, S. E. (1954). *Group cohesiveness in the industrial work group.* Ann Arbor, MI: University of Michigan Press.

Senge, P. M. (1990). *The fifth discipline: The art & practice of the learning organization.* New York, NY: Currency Doubleday.

Shea, G. P., & Guzzo, R. A. (1987). Groups as human resources. In: K. M. Rowland & G. R. Ferris (Eds), *Research in Human Resources and Personnel Management* (Vol. 5, pp. 323–356). Greenwich, CT: JAI Press.

Sherif, M. (1936). *The psychology of social norms.* New York, NY: Harper & Row.

Shore, L. S., Barksdale, K., & Shore, T. H. (1995). Managerial perceptions of employee commitment to the organization. *Academy of Management Journal, 38*(6), 1593–1615.

Smith, C. A., Organ, D. W., & Near, J. P. (1983). Organizational citizenship behavior: Its nature and antecedents. *Journal of Applied Psychology, 68,* 655–663.

Schnake, M., Dumler, M., & Cochran, D. (1993). The relationship between "traditional" leadership, "super" leadership, and organizational citizenship behavior. *Group and Organization Management, 18*(3), 352–365.

Staw, B. M. (1975). Attribution of the "causes" of performance: A general alternative interpretation of cross-sectional research on organizations. *Organizational Behavior and Human Decision Processes, 13,* 414–432.

Stevens, M. J. & Yarish, M. E. (1999). Training for team effectiveness. In: E. Sundstrom (Ed.), *Supporting Work Team Effectiveness: Best Management Practices for Fostering High Performance* (pp. 126–156). San Francisco: Jossey-Bass.

Sundstrom, E., & Associates (1999). *Supporting Work Team Effectiveness: Best Management Practices for Fostering High Performance.* San Francisco, CA: Jossey-Bass.

Sundstrom, E., De Meuse, K. P., & Futrell, D. (1990). Work teams: Applications and effectiveness. *American Psychologist, 45,* 120–133.

Sundstrom, E., McIntyre, M., Halfhill, T., & Richards, H. (2000). Work groups: From the Hawthorne studies to work teams of the 1990s and beyond. *Group Dynamics, 4*(1), 44–67.

Wageman, R. (1995). Interdependence and group effectiveness. *Administrative Science Quarterly, 40,* 145–180.

Wageman, R., & Baker, G. (1997). Incentives and cooperation: The joint effects of task and reward interdependence on group performance. *Journal of Organizational Behavior, 18,* 139–158.

Walz, S. M., & Niehoff, B. P. (1996). Organizational citizenship behaviors and their effect of organizational effectiveness in limited menu-restaurants. In: J. B. Keys & L. N. Dosier (Eds), *Academy of Management Best Papers Proceedings* (pp. 307–311).

TEAM LEADERSHIP AND COORDINATION IN TRAUMA RESUSCITATION

Seokhwa Yun, Samer Faraj, Yan Xiao
and Henry P. Sims, Jr.

ABSTRACT

This study investigates team leadership and coordination during a trauma resuscitation. A trauma resuscitation team is an emergency cross-functional medical team, which includes several specialists such as a surgeon, an anesthesia provider, and nurses. The main purpose of the team is to perform a resuscitation; treatment to a patient who experiences a trauma (e.g. car crash, stabbing, gunshot) and has a life-threatening injury. The trauma team can be seen as a type of crisis team since the need for treatment is quite intense and urgent. Team members must treat and stabilize the patient within minutes and without much information about his/her condition and medical history. As a result, this team is working in an intense and highly stressful situation. We used focused ethnography in order to gain an understanding of leadership and coordination during a trauma resuscitation. Over a period of six months, we observed admissions, shadowed teams, and interviewed specialists as a primary data collection method. Our findings suggest that the effectiveness of leadership differs depending on: (1) the severity level of patient condition; and (2) the level of team experience. Directive leadership is more effective

Team-Based Organizing, Volume 9, pages 189–214.
© 2003 Published by Elsevier Science Ltd.
ISBN: 0-7623-0981-4

when a patient is severely injured, whereas empowering leadership is more
effective when a patient is not severely injured. Also, directive leadership
is better when a trauma team is inexperienced, but empowering leader-
ship is better when a trauma team has a high level of experience.

INTRODUCTION

Over the past two decades, teams have emerged as a critical organizing structure in the United States (Aldag & Fuller, 1993; Dumaine, 1990, 1994). The study of teams has become increasingly important in recent years as more and more organizations are turning to team methods of organizing (Dumaine, 1994). "One clear message from all the recent interest [in teams] is that there is a strong need for a better understanding of team functioning and team leadership in a wide variety of contexts" (Hollenbeck, Ilgen & Sego, 1994, p. 4).

Many of those teams are empowered and have a high degree of authority and responsibility vested within the team. A recent survey found that most Fortune 1,000 firms use teams with at least some employees, and that teams are one of the fastest growing forms of employee involvement (Lawler, Mohrman & Benson, 2001). Another recent trend is that teams are increasingly becoming a dominant form of organizing in knowledge intensive work settings. Knowledge teams are teams of individuals who apply "theoretical and analytical knowledge, acquired through formal education" to solve team-related tasks (Janz, Colquitt & Noe, 1997, p. 878). Empowered knowledge teams are frequently used in situations requiring a high degree of specialization and interdependence such as in management consulting and in software development. One example of these empowered knowledge teams is a trauma resuscitation team, which is the focal interest of this paper.

This paper is composed of four parts. First, we describe a trauma resuscitation team, its organizational context, and its conduct of a resuscitation. Second, we discuss a research method that we utilized in order to understand the leadership phenomenon in a trauma resuscitation team. Third, we report the results of our detailed examination of team leadership during a trauma resuscitation and develop specific propositions. Finally, we discuss our findings, limitations, implications, and contributions.

A TRAUMA RESUSCITATION TEAM

A trauma resuscitation team is a medical team that provides treatment to a patient who experiences a trauma. A trauma is defined as "physical injury caused by violent or disruptive action, or by the introduction into the body of a toxic substance" (Glanze, Anderson & Anderson, 1990, p. 1189). Typically this involves serious, possibly life-threatening, injuries to the person who is involved in the trauma event such as car crash, stabbing, gunshot, and the like. Without proper and timely treatment, the patient may expire. Proper treatment must be provided to a trauma patient within a very limited time period. As a result, this team is a *high reliability team*, which is not allowed to make mistakes and places reliability as a priority over any other organizational objectives because of the criticality of failure. In this section, we describe a trauma center, where trauma resuscitation teams work, and the composition of a trauma resuscitation team. Then we discuss the characteristics of a trauma resuscitation team, which is followed by an illustration of a typical example of a trauma resuscitation.

A Trauma Center

This research is conducted in a Trauma Center (TC), which is located at a mid-Atlantic Medical Center in the United States. A trauma center is "a service providing emergency and specialized intensive care to critically ill and injured patients" (Glanze, Anderson & Anderson, 1990, p. 1189). It is a particular type of emergency medicine delivery system that is especially characterized by self-sufficiency in that it has all the facilities (e.g. trauma resuscitation unit, operating room, post anesthesia care unit, intensive care unit, intermediate care unit, etc.) necessary for trauma treatment within itself. It can provide most of the medical services that a trauma patient needs until he/she is discharged.

Most of the patients are admitted through the Trauma Resuscitation Unit (TRU)[1], a main part of the TC. We mainly focused on the TRU, where patients first arrive for treatment and a trauma resuscitation is conducted. The TRU is a type of "emergency room" that admits patients who have suffered some type of "trauma," or sudden severe injury. The treatment of a patient is typically called a resuscitation. A resuscitation is often an intense, crisis-like event, because it deals with human life. Sometimes the patients die during the resuscitation.

The TRU has ten bays, which is shared workspace where trauma resuscitation team members work together to treat a patient. Each bay has a bed and the facilities (e.g. monitors, ventilator, etc.) necessary for most of the trauma treatments. Normally, a patient is assigned to an empty bay. However, under exceptional circumstances, when there are more than 10 patients, two patients can be lodged within a bay. Thus, the TRU can treat up to 20 patients at the same time. Other necessary facilities, such as a CAT Scan, are located next to the TRU.

Team Composition: A Cross-Functional Professional Taskforce

A trauma resuscitation team is composed of several individuals who have
different expertise and professional affiliations. In a generic sense, it is a specific
type of a cross-functional professional taskforce or knowledge team. Those
individuals include surgeons, anesthesiologists, medical residents, TRU nurses
and TRU technicians. In most cases, a surgeon is the team leader (Cicala &
Murphy, 1993). The typical roles and responsibilities of the individual trauma
resuscitation team members are presented in Table 1. Figure 1 provides a typical
example of trauma team configuration.

   An attending surgeon is in charge of a trauma resuscitation. He/she is a leader
of a surgical team[2] as well as the trauma resuscitation team. The attending
surgeon has responsibilities to supervise and coordinate team members' activities

Table 1.   The Trauma Team Hierarchy: Typical Roles and Responsibilites.

Trauma Team Role	Responsibilities
Attending Surgeon	• Supervision and coordination of the team activity • Formulation of care plan • Charge of the resuscitation and patient • Perform primary and secondary survey

Surgery Fellow	• When an attending surgeon is not present
	  • Taking his/her responsibilities
	• When an attending surgeon is present
	  • Supervision and coordination of surgery residents
	  • Assisting an attending surgeon
	  • Performing surgical procedures

Surgery resident	• Perform primary and secondary survey • Assist surgeons • Perform surgical procedures
Anesthesia provider	• Airway management • Intubation • Insertion of endogastric tubes
Trauma nurse	• Intravenous access • Assist with surgical procedures • Getting vital signs • Document resuscitation • Taking care of the patient after resuscitation
Trauma technician	• Assist with nurse • Transport of patient

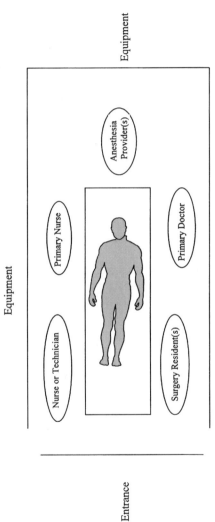

Fig. 1. An Example of Trauma Team Configuration. The Primary Doctor could be a Surgery Resident, a Surgery Fellow, or an Attending Surgeon.

and decide and approve a final plan of care. As a leader, an attending surgeon conducts a trauma resuscitation with the help of other services such as anesthesia. As described later in the section of qualitative findings, an attending surgeon is considered the ultimate authority. He/she is the one who is ultimately responsible for the care and well being of the patient. An attending surgeon may not be in the bay during the resuscitation for several reasons (e.g. performing his/her rounds or a surgical operation), but he/she is still regarded as the responsible authority and the team leader.

A surgery fellow is one who has finished his/her residency, but decides to be trained in a specific area before practice. In other words, he/she could become an attending surgeon in any other hospital, but wants to learn more in a specialty area. Often, the surgery fellow plays a role similar to an attending surgeon. When the attending surgeon is not in the bay, a surgery fellow is responsible for the supervision and the coordination of the team activities, and for the formulation of care plan. Then, later, when the attending surgeon is available, the fellow reports to the attending surgeon. However, when an attending surgeon is in the unit, the fellow's role is somewhat unclear. He/she is "in between" an attending surgeon and other team members. Usually, when an attending surgeon is in the bay, a surgery fellow's role is supervising and coordinating surgery residents and assisting the attending surgeon.

Another role in a trauma team is surgery residents who typically stay less than several months in the TC. Surgery residents are under training after graduation from a medical school. Their main responsibilities are performing initial physical examinations, assisting an attending surgeon or a fellow to perform surgical procedures. When a patient is admitted in the TRU, typically a surgery resident picks up the patient, becomes a primary doctor for the patient, follows the patient, and reports to the attending surgeon and the fellow about the patient until the patient is discharged.

One of the major services necessary for most trauma patients is anesthesia. A typical trauma patient may have a problem in his/her airway and experience very high levels of pain. The main responsibilities of an anesthesia provider are managing the patient's airway and pain. Sometimes, anesthesia providers need to intubate a patient, because: (1) the patient has a serious problem breathing him/herself; or because (2) the patient is not cooperative so that the team has difficulty in conducting their resuscitation. Typically, at least an anesthesia resident participates in a trauma resuscitation and an attending anesthesiologist supervises him/her. Sometimes, a certified registered nurse anesthetist (CRNA) participates in a resuscitation.

The last two roles in a trauma resuscitation team are the TRU nurse and the TRU technician. The nurses have more professional training than the technicians and are higher than them in the status hierarchy. During a trauma resuscitation, a primary nurse typically stands by the right ear or right hand side of the patient. The main responsibilities of a primary nurse is putting intravenous lines in, assisting physicians with surgical procedures, and getting the vital signs such as blood pressure. The TRU nurses take care of a patient while in the TRU from the time of admission, even after finishing the trauma resuscitation. The main responsibility of TRU technicians is in assisting TRU nurses. They are sometimes called nursing extenders.

Technically speaking, these last two roles, the TRU nurse and the TRU technician, are full time TRU staff. In contrast, the physicians treat trauma patients but are not specifically assigned to the TRU. Physicians generally have patients in other units including the operation room, intensive care unit, and intermediate care unit. They come to the TRU when their expertise is needed. For example, an attending surgeon may be taking care of his/her patient in another unit such as the intensive care unit when he/she receives a call from the TRU, notifying the imminent arrival of a new patient for trauma resuscitation. The physicians generally follow their patients across and between units until the patients are discharged. In contrast, the TRU staff (e.g. TRU nurses) does not follow patients. They care for patients only while they are staying in the TRU.

Characteristics of a Trauma Resuscitation Team

Based on our observations, we noticed several characteristics of a trauma resuscitation team, which differ from a traditional work-team. In the following section, these characteristics are discussed.

A high reliability team. The main purpose of the team is to provide appropriate treatment and thus save the life of a trauma patient. Typically a trauma patient has serious and multiple, possibly life-threatening, injuries. A trauma team works in a very intense, time-constrained, high velocity, and high-risk situation. Without proper and timely treatment, the patient may suffer severe organ damage or die. As a result, the team needs to consistently perform without errors and place reliability above any other organizational objective because of the criticality of failure.

Empowerment. The team as a whole is typically highly empowered. That is, it basically conducts its task (i.e. providing high quality trauma treatment) on its own, subject primarily to professional standards, policies of, and professional review of the organization. During an emergency treatment of a patient, the team conducts its own task without direct external influence. The team leader and members on their own undertake the timely decision and medical interventions that constitute the treatment of the patient.

Short duration of a team existence. A trauma team exists for only a very short period of time, from half an hour to several hours. In the TRU, a new trauma team is formed each time a patient arrives for treatment (i.e. the admission of an emergency patient in a trauma center). Then, after the team provides emergency treatment to the patient, the team dissolves. Typically, this period lasts less than one hour.[3] In other words, a team in the TRU is a short cycle intense task force. Since it exists for only a short period of time, the team does not have enough time to engage in lengthy development of interpersonal relationships while conducting the task.

Flexible boundary of a team. Membership of teams is fluid, in that new members can come into or emerge from the treatment task. For example, while the team provides a trauma treatment to a patient, new patient(s) may be admitted. Often, the TRU has several admissions within one hour. For instance, we observed five admissions during a one and half an hour period on one Friday evening. When there are several admissions, some of the team members may leave their current patient and treat other patients. Members can also join a treatment of another patient after they have stabilized their own patient. In addition, the team may need to rapidly integrate a needed specialist such as neurologist, who is typically not a team member. Therefore, the team membership is fluid and changes, depending on the need.

Uncertainty, or lack of information. In order to formulate a proper care plan and provide a quality medical care, a trauma team needs information on the patient. First, they need to know what exactly happened that caused the injury or "trauma". In addition, the patient's medical history, such as allergies, is necessary. Unfortunately, the patient is often unable to give an adequate account of the traumatic event, and, moreover, is often unable to supply any medical history, because they often arrive unconscious. A trauma team mainly relies on the paramedic's[4] explanation, an overall visual assessment of the patient's status, primary survey, and so on. However, the team may not receive enough information regarding the patient's status. Therefore, the basic premise of "assuming nothing until disproved" should be foremost in decision making (Parr & Grande, 1993). They may be able to get more accurate information from the patient or the patient's family later, after the resuscitation treatment, but this information is not always available. Thus, the team functions with uncertain or missing information. Also, continuous and multifaceted patient monitoring is an important part of resuscitation, which helps to reduce the unknowns about the patient's status and increase the team's ability to judge and adjust the treatment plan.

Urgent, multiple, and concurrent tasks. Typically, the need for treatment is quite intense and urgent, and the trauma team can be viewed as a type of crisis team. A severely injured patient's fate can change for better or worse depending on how well and how fast he/she is treated. Many patients have serious and multiple injuries that require the team to perform multiple necessary tasks and examinations concurrently in order to save time and perhaps save a life. For instance, an attending surgeon needs to conduct the primary and secondary survey, while an attending anesthesiologist intubates the patient and a nurse obtains vital signs.

Different goal/orientation among team members. The primary goal of a trauma team is providing high quality health care. However, a third or a half of trauma team members are surgery residents. A surgery resident is a physician in one of the postgraduate years of clinical training and is not yet board-certified. Surgery residents have a different orientation compared to other roles in a trauma team. They come to the hospital to learn how to run a trauma resuscitation and to practice what they learned in medical school while they provide high quality treatment to a trauma patient. Sometimes, surgery residents cause the resuscitation to take longer, because they, in general, have less experience and expertise than other team members. However, without the residents, a trauma team has a smaller number of team members, which may result in a shortage of hands, and can make resuscitation take longer. Therefore, because of this tradeoff effect, we cannot conclude whether a surgery resident is necessarily detrimental or helpful in conducting a trauma resuscitation. However, this characteristic makes the situation more complex.

A Typical Procedure of a Trauma Resuscitation

Typically, a trauma event starts with a call and information delivered through Dispatch between the field and the TRU. Usually a TRU nurse or a TRU technician receives the call and sometimes puts it on speaker so that other staff may hear, while writing information on a "grease board" so that other team members can be notified. A physician rarely takes the phone, even though he/she is next to the phone. A clerk then pages all trauma resuscitation team members (i.e. surgeons, anesthesiologist, nurses, residents, and technicians). The page includes some beginning information on the new patient such as mechanism of injury.

Dispatch rarely provides sufficient information for the trauma resuscitation team to completely prepare for the new patient. Often, the team gets an update call from the field. Again, a TRU nurse or a TRU technician takes the phone and updates the information on the grease board next to the phone. A clerk again pages all team members with updated information. In most cases, the trauma team has basic information on the new patient such as priority level, age, sex, blood pressure, heart rate, respiration rate, and, most importantly, estimated time arrival.

Meanwhile, the TRU charge nurse assigns one of the available nurses and one of the available bays to the patient. He/she also may assign himself/herself to the patient instead of another nurse. Team members check the bay to make sure everything in the bay ready for the new admission in order to provide trauma treatment as soon as the patient arrives. Often, the patient comes to the TC by air (e.g. helicopter) and the assigned nurse and the TRU technicians go to the heliport (on the roof of the building) to take the patient down to the TRU.

When the patient arrives, one of the residents takes the role of primary doctor who will follow the patient and report to the attending surgeon until the patient is discharged. The paramedics verbally report the patient's condition to the team and trauma treatment starts. First, team members visually assess the trauma patient's status and interview the patient. However, since many of the trauma patients are unconscious, the team usually may not be able to receive important facts (e.g. AMPLE, which stands for Allergies, Medications, Past illness and surgery, Last meal, and Events preceding accident; Parr & Grande, 1993) from the patients. Following overall visual assessment, a primary survey is conducted. The primary survey is a phase to check ABC (Airway, Breathing and Circulation) in order to identify life-threatening conditions. In this primary survey phase, the team also assesses neurologic function and completely undresses the patient for a thorough examination, assessment, and intervention.

The secondary survey begins after the primary survey is completed and while a resuscitation is in progress. It involves the detailed head-to-toe evaluation of the patient. The primary survey aims at basic physiologic support and resuscitation. The secondary survey should result in a complete list of injuries that allows the formulation of a treatment plan.

Conceptually, a resuscitation treatment is divided into several phases. But practically, these activities are often conducted simultaneously. For example, the team may begin certain treatments while the visual, the primary survey and/or the secondary survey is in progress. This whole process usually takes less than half an hour.

The team is then dismissed once they provide necessary, initial treatment to the trauma patient. After that, usually an assigned TRU nurse takes care of the patient until the patient is disposed to OR, ICU, general nursing care unit, or discharged home.

RESEARCH METHOD

We utilized a qualitative method in our research. Qualitative methods are particularly useful when describing a phenomenon from the *emic* perspective, that is, the perspective of the problem from the "native's point of view" (Vidich & Lyman, 1994). Qualitative research is usually conducted to explore phenomena about which relatively little is known. A qualitative method should be used in the situation "when little is known about a phenomenon . . . or when the research question pertains to understanding and describing a particular phenomenon or event about which little is known (Morse & Field, 1995, p. 10)." This study examined leadership phenomena in a trauma resuscitation team, which has received little prior research attention. Therefore, we employed a qualitative method, specifically focused ethnography, in order to: (1) explore the richness of the context; (2) understand the leadership phenomenon during trauma resuscitation; and (3) develop propositions that can be tested through a quantitative study in the future.

Focused Ethnography

Historically, ethnography evolved from cultural anthropology. A researcher conducts ethnography to "understand the cultural perspective of the group [the emic perspective]" (Morse & Field, 1995, p. 154). Ethnography allows the researcher to view and understand phenomena in the context in which they occur and to develop a theory that explains the context and may be applicable to another setting. Fieldwork is essential and involves working with people for long periods of time in a naturalistic setting.

Recently, Boyle (1994) classified ethnography into four different categories such as classical/holistic ethnography, particularistic and focused ethnography, cross-sectional ethnography, and ethnohistorical ethnography. In the organizational literature, many studies have used focused ethnography, in that the researchers carefully selected topics before the qualitative data collection commences, and they generally limit observation to the selected topic. For instance, Ancona and Caldwell (1992) limited their qualitative investigation on the external activities of new-product teams. Manz and Sims (1987) focused on the roles, responsibilities, and performance of mature self-managing teams and the team leadership. We used focused ethnography in order to develop insight regarding team leadership in trauma setting.

Data Collection and Data Analysis

We used several data collection methods, including observation, shadowing or following, and interviews. We observed 40 admissions during about 55 hours over six months. Observation hours were chosen initially randomly, and then intentionally. At first, we started observation randomly in order to understand what happens in different time periods. However, the TRU has different workloads at different times. For example, they have high workload on weekend evening and nights (Friday, Saturday, and Sunday). Also, their workload is typically higher around 8–9 a.m. and 4–6 p.m. because of automobile accidents caused by heavy traffic. Based on these basic understandings of the context, many of the observations were conducted on Friday evening, which is one of the busiest times.

Fieldnotes were taken on site during most observations. The fieldnotes mainly describe what we observed and heard, rather than our interpretation or impression. Fieldnotes were typed into a computer as an observation summary, shortly after each observation. While typing fieldnotes of observation summaries, we added our interpretations, impressions, understanding, questions, and tentative themes. This process itself was a part of data analysis in that we tried to understand, conceptualize, and theorize what happened during observation (Morse & Field, 1995).

We also followed or shadowed TRU staff. We followed two attending surgeons, one of the surgery teams, and an attending anesthesiologist while they were on call. Each shadowing session lasted from three to four hours. When we followed/shadowed one of the staff members, we carried a micro cassette in order to record our observations and interpretations. Also the short interviews we conducted during the shadowing were audio-taped with the interviewee's agreement.

In addition, we conducted formal/informal interviews with 30 staff members, who are involved in a trauma resuscitation. Those interviews include four attending surgeons, one surgery fellow, one surgery chief resident, four surgery residents, eight nurses, three attending anesthesiologists, two anesthesiology residents, two observers, two CRNA (certified registered nursing anesthetist), one medical student, one TRU technician, and one X-ray technician. During interviews, we intentionally did not reveal our viewpoint in order to not contaminate the interviewee's opinions. This is important, since one of the goals of a qualitative research is describing phenomena and developing theory from the emic perspective, not from a researcher's perspective (Vidich & Lyman, 1994). Most of the interviews were audio-taped with the interviewee's agreement and transcribed.[5]

FINDINGS: THEMES AND PROPOSITIONS[6]

In this section, the findings are summarized into four main themes. The first theme is an answer to the question of "who is a leader in a trauma resuscitation team?" Though the answer is not entirely straightforward, the attending surgeon is mainly considered the leader of a trauma resuscitation team. The second theme is about the forms of leadership displayed by team leaders. The third and fourth themes are regarding the effectiveness of leadership. Based on the third and fourth themes, we developed three propositions.

Theme 1: A "Duality" of Leadership, but an Attending Surgeon is an Ultimate Authority.

To study leadership in a team, first, there is a need to define the formal authority structure in the team. Normally, in a department or division of a business organization, this is a fairly straightforward process. That is, there is a manager or a supervisor who is the (appointed) formal leader. In a trauma resuscitation team, however, who the leader is may not be so readily apparent. In a team like a trauma resuscitation team, which is composed of several experts, the team leader is not always obvious at a glance, because each team member is responsible for tasks related to his/her expertise or professional affiliations to some degree. For example, a nurse may be responsible for IV insertion and an anesthesiologist may be responsible for airway management. Each team member is required to take initiative in conducting tasks related to his/her expertise.

Moreover, an important element is the special role of the surgical fellow. Surgery fellows are surgeons who have previously finished a surgical residency and decide to undertake special training in a specific area such as emergency (trauma) surgery, before entering practice.[7] For many resuscitation events, the fellow is in charge of the resuscitation. That is, the fellow can be observed to be actively involved, touching and testing the patient, asking questions, and giving directions to other team members. An attending surgeon may delegate his/her responsibilities to run the resuscitation to one of team members, often to a surgery fellow but sometimes to a resident, when the TRU has multiple admissions. Also, if an attending surgeon is not able to be in the TRU when a new admission arrives, a fellow usually is in charge of the resuscitation.[8, 9] Some of the interviewees referred to both attending surgeons and surgery fellows as the team leader in the bay during the resuscitation.

Even though each team member has responsibility for different tasks, there is a formal leader and an ultimate authority that organizes and coordinates team efforts and is responsible for the whole team's performance. This formal leader is the attending surgeon who is in charge of the patient and responsible for the trauma resuscitation. When a new patient comes in, he/she is assigned to the attending surgeon on call, who is legally responsible for the care of the patient until the patient is discharged, because all unlicensed doctors treat the patient under the supervision of the licensed attending surgeon. Even though a surgery fellow or a resident runs a resuscitation, the ultimate authority of the trauma treatment is an attending surgeon. The attending surgeon is the one who makes final decisions and who can disapprove other team members' decision(s). Without his/her permission, the team members cannot run the resuscitation or provide trauma treatment to the patient. This is confirmed from several interviews. (Source of quote is in brackets at the end of the excerpt.)

> ... Certainly the person in charge is attending traumatologists [surgeons] ... they are responsible no matter what ... An attending surgeon usually makes that call ... their patients. Anesthesiologists are there to provide a service for the surgeons. It's surgeon's patient ... it's always attending surgeon's patient ... [a nurse anesthesia].

> ... [I'm the leader] ... I don't think it makes difference where you are ... I will be more or less involved depending on who else is in the room ... [an attending surgeon].

> ... over here it's been accepted trauma surgeon is the leader. He has the patient. A patient is assigned to his name and everybody else should be the consultant to that physician. And trauma surgeon has his own crew of surgery. I mean set of residents ... As an anesthesiologist, I'm a member of the [trauma resuscitation] team. Of course, I will function on the assignment or on the legal aspect of my profession ... we all expect the trauma surgeon on call to be the leader of that team ... [an anesthesiologist].

> In the TRU, or throughout all aspects of the patient's care, the attending surgeon is the primary physician, the way that I like to describe it is with significant input from me ... The trauma attending [is the leader of the bay] ... [an attending anesthesiologist].

> I think, well the first thing as the fellow is that you need to remember that you are not the attending, and you always have to be under the attending. So when he or she tells you that's the way it is, that's the way it is ... [a fellow].

As quoted above, a trauma surgeon or an attending surgeon is considered the team leader. Most of the interviewees referred to an attending surgeon as a team leader in a bay during the resuscitation, regardless of whether or not he/she actively and directly engages in patient care.

An attending surgeon is the one who signs the patient chart, which means that he/she takes care of the patient, is responsible for the treatment, or approves the treatment. This is also partially supported by legality issues. When there is a legal issue, an attending surgeon is the one who has legal responsibility. An attending surgeon mentioned this during the interview:

> Attending D controls things all the time, partly because I think that he has been aware, he's more aware or more affected by the legalities of the business. And he feels that his name

is gonna be going to court anywhere. It's gonna be his decision on every step of the way, because ultimately its gonna be his credit the person is gonna be after . . .

All in all, these imply that an attending surgeon is responsible for the trauma resuscitation and the ultimate authority. First of all, most (virtually all) of trauma resuscitations include surgical activity, which often requires operations. Among surgical team members (i.e. attending surgeons, surgery fellow, surgery residents, and medical students), an attending surgeon is the one who has most experience and highest level of medical skill and hierarchy. Also, as an attending surgeon mentioned, he/she is going to be responsible for legal issues.

Theme 2: Attending Surgeons have Different Leaderships.

One of the initial questions was whether different team leaders (i.e. surgeons) actually do differ in their leadership. Specifically, is there variance between team leaders in regard to their leadership? In fact, many of the TRU staff members mentioned that they have seen different leadership in the bay during resuscitation. For example, one surgery resident stated he had seen different leaderships among the attending surgeons. Some of them have very empowering leadership, and others are very directive. Other TRU staff members also suggested similar phenomena.

We find all attendings different [in leadership] . . . [a nurse].

. . . so residents call me and ask me "what do you want me to do with this patient?" my answer would be what I like you to do is to be a doctor, I want you to go and examine the patient, I want you to consider the possibilities, and I want you to tell me what you think, then we will discuss whether it is a good idea or bad idea. If I just tell you what to do, you are just a secretary. You haven't learned. You haven't thought about it . . . they will come up and say "I'm gonna do this." My first question is "why" and the way I go with this is "what are your choices, why do you, if you have four choices why do you pick that?" I think it's the better way to do it. . . because what I want to teach them is the way of thinking . . . I want you to consider a problem, find what the problem is . . . [an attending surgeon].

. . . it varies a lot from attending to attending. Each of them has a very different style . . . Some of the doctors, I guess Dr. E, very hands off, and when you need something from him, you can ask him and he gives you his opinion and he's there for you. Others like Dr. F. are more hands on, and go forth very well, and I think you just need to not take offense that people have different styles . . . [a fellow].

Dr. A [an attending] is very, he likes to . . . let me work . . . Others of them, like a Dr. B, he likes a kinda stay back. He will come up, you know, what's going on, what he needs to step in, if it's in a rush or whatever, you know because he is the boss, he would say where to stop . . . Basically a lot of them are paying attention to what's going on, but they are not stepping in, unless they have to do, like fellows do what they need to do . . . [a nurse].

... Some of the attendings are very much get in there and do things ... At times ... another attending stands back and let the fellow and residents do what they have to do ... [an anesthesiology resident].

These interviews suggest that there are different forms of leaderships among attending surgeons. The main factor seems to be the difference in leadership among the team leaders in regard to how much autonomy they give the team members, especially the surgical fellow and residents. Some attending surgeons are very directive [hands-on] and run a resuscitation directly. Others are empowering. That is, they stand back and encourage the team members to run the resuscitation.

These two different leaderships, empowering versus directive, were also found in our own observations. Sometimes, at one extreme, an attending surgeon did not show up and delegated all responsibilities to team members while the team conducted trauma resuscitation. In most of these situations, the fellow was in the unit, however there were still some cases when both of them were not present in the unit. When both of them were not in the unit and other team members carried on the resuscitation by themselves, the team members were fully empowered, at least in the short term. They made their own decisions on what to do and how to do it, and carried out their decisions. These are extreme cases of empowering leadership from both an attending surgeon and a fellow. These kinds of situations are observed relatively often in May, when most of the team members (especially residents) have a significant experience in medicine (more than 10 months). Most of the team members also have had previous experience with similar situations several times at this point in the year, so the team leader has more confidence in empowering team members to conduct the resuscitation without him/her.

In most cases, either a fellow or an attending surgeon is in the unit during resuscitation. However, they are not always *directly* involved in the resuscitation. Sometimes they may not be in the bay or near the bay and other team members run the resuscitation, or they may be watching the team working on a case from a vantage point outside the bay. For instance, during one of our observations, the residents and other team members were running a resuscitation and the fellow stayed outside the bay seeming to do other things when the team was informed of a new admission. One of the residents came and asked the fellow, "Can I take the patient?" The fellow responded, "Sure." This showed that the fellow displayed empowering leadership by providing the resident with opportunities to run the resuscitation.

Similar behaviors were observed during shadowing/following an attending surgeon and a surgical team on call in early July. Both the attending surgeon and the fellow were in the unit, when a new patient was admitted. However, they let the primary resident and the team run the examination and resuscitation, while standing by the bay. They allowed the team to decide what they needed to do, and then asked the team "What is your plan?" The entire team discussed the plan with the attending surgeon and fellow and then the team carried out the plan. Both the attending surgeon and the fellow empowered the team to assess the patient and to make decisions on the resuscitation plan. When the attending surgeon and the fellow asked the questions and discussed the plan, they wanted to be assured that the team had the right resuscitation plan. The cases described above show a limited or quasi-empowering leadership, in that the team members were empowered to make decisions, but the team's plan was not decided until the attending or fellow confirmed it.

In contrast, in some cases, either an attending or a fellow did not allow other team members to run a resuscitation. The attending surgeon made decisions on his/her own and ordered other team members what to do. This kind of behavior was also found in our observations. In one case, there were two patients from the same motor vehicle accident. One of them was a priority level 1 patient.[10] Before the patient arrived, the team was ready and waiting for the patient. The fellow was in charge of the resuscitation, and about ten team members were in the bay. However, shortly after the patient arrived, the attending surgeon came to the unit and assumed direct "hands on" control over the resuscitation. He ordered a couple of team members to "get out of there." Then he made most of the decisions himself and gave orders to other team members. He told the team what he needed and the fellow repeated what the attending surgeon wanted. After the initial examination and resuscitation, he said, "X-ray . . . get out of here . . ." This meant that he wanted all of the team members to leave the bay so that the radiologist could shoot the X-ray. Right after the X-ray, they took the patient to an operating room and the attending surgeon pointed to a resident and told her, "You go and see the X-ray. Don't wait here . . ." Also, he stated very specifically what he wanted her to see and report to him. During this resuscitation, the attending surgeon basically made and carried on all necessary decisions with other team members' assistance. This was an extreme case of directive leadership. The leader basically took total control and did not allow or empower any of the team members, including the fellow, to make decisions.

Theme 3: Empowering Leadership is, in General, More Effective Than Directive Leadership.

Several interviewees suggested that empowering leadership, in general, was more effective in coordinating and performing a trauma resuscitation than directive leadership. For example, one of the anesthesiology residents said that an effective leader is one who allows a lot of autonomy to the team members to run the resuscitation. He also gave several examples of effective leaders, who are considered empowering leaders among the TRU staff. A surgery resident also offered a similar opinion. An effective leader is one who is confident, quiet, not yelling, and empowering. Others also provided similar viewpoints:

> ...I say the [effective] fellows I work with are ones who stand back and observe and let the residents and the designated physician who's running the trauma code run the trauma code and give guidance and trust the physicians to make their own decisions . . . And I think the burden on [leader] is less . . . [an anesthesiology resident].

> ...[an effective leader] is someone who . . . obviously as a nursing staff, we prefer that if the attending chooses to stay out of the room and allow the residents or the fellow to run the resuscitation or the admission that they've been at least prepared somewhat . . . there are better team leaders [in coordinating and performing a trauma resuscitation] . . . [a nurse].

> ...Leadership should be knowledgeable, should keep track of all things that are going on, should not be hands-on, should be away from any resuscitative procedures occurring . . . [a surgery resident].

In summary, many interviewees considered empowering leadership to be more effective than directive leadership. They believe, in general, a leader needs to empower team members to coordinate and run the resuscitation. In this way, he/she can manage his/her own workload and provide team members with opportunities to learn how to lead the resuscitation.

There are two possible reasons that support these opinions. First, a leader can get information or knowledge that he/she does not have, but another team member has (information effect). A trauma resuscitation team is composed of several experts in different specialties that participate in trauma resuscitation in order to provide their professional knowledge and opinions. An attending surgeon may not have information or knowledge that an anesthesiologist or a nurse has. Without other professionals' help, an attending surgeon may misinterpret symptoms of a patient and/or cannot recognize problems, which can cause serious results. Durham, Knight, and Locke (1997) found such an information effect in a laboratory experiment on leadership.

Also, even though an attending surgeon has knowledge and information, he/she may not be able to thoroughly examine a trauma patient, especially, one who has multi-system injuries, given that the team should provide treatment within a very short period of time. He/she may have to focus on a part of a patient, which is most severely injured and/or is most related to his/her physicians in the team are strong, well rounded, have been through a lot of situations, can come in here, pick up the way we do things . . . so B team, they are clinically very strong, very aware, like a unit aware, team awareness, so if one of their guys is really busy, somebody else will pick up and help him out in a true team concept, whereas there are other teams [which are clinically weak] . . . You have to have element of stepping in and taking charge, if you have to. You kind of need to have a couple of different styles, whatever the situation carries for you . . . [a nurse].

. . . If you have a critically ill patient and a resident who is a mainly not as strong or having difficulty in a certain situation, I will expect the attendings and fellows jumping and doing things. But I think it depends on . . . If there is less acuity, there are more leeways to do things . . . [an anesthesiology resident].

. . . That really depends on skill or capability of primary doc. There are all different levels of physicians. We have senior surgical residents. And we have first year emergency medicine resident. So there are different levels of training. And they all get a patient, because it's busy enough where the workload has to work that way. So experienced person, experienced doctor I can trust, I do very little in terms of intervening. He can just do everything himself. I will just stand back and make sure everything is appropriate. If he is a more junior person, he might need a lot more guidance. So I often end up actually doing more of the interviewing of the patient or examining the patient, and directing the care of the patient. Because this inexperienced doctor would not have done the correct things as in correct time. So depending on the skill level or training level of that primary doctor, I need to be more or less involved in that patient . . . [an attending surgeon].

. . . If you have a very junior team, you might need to help some of lines with procedures, with ordering, whatever. You may have to do that . . . [a surgery resident].

. . . If my fellows are there, post-graduate fellow, everyplace else would be the attending, right . . . that doesn't mean I walk away and have a donut. It means I stand in the corner and because in the end it's my medical, legal, and ethical responsibilities to put my care for that person . . . my name is on the nameplate . . . It's depending on which fellow it is, which chief resident it is; I may be more or less involved. In July when everybody's all of sudden smarter, I'm a lot more likely to be there [in the bay] than I am at the end of June . . . [an attending surgeon].

e interviewees' opinions can be theorized into a leadership contingency ory. That is, an effective leader needs to use different leaderships depending the situation. There are two main situation factors mentioned that impact dership: the severity level of the patient injury and the level of the team perience in emergency medicine.

The first situation factor is the severity level of a patient's condition. As a ient's condition becomes more and more severe/critical/urgent, a trauma team s less time to provide proper treatment. If the team leader displays powering leadership in this situation, the treatment typically takes longer, ich may be detrimental to the patient. In addition, when a patient is severely

profession/specialty, as other team members examine othe
to provide timely, comprehensive care within a limited time |
ering team members to run or to actively participate in resus
can utilize the team's resources (e.g. time, profession, kno'
effectively.

Second, an empowering leader may produce a motiva
members of a trauma resuscitation team are experts who ty|
level of professionalism and need for autonomy. An attend
to deal with their needs to effectively lead them. If he/she ig
team members' needs, the team members are less likely to
him/her. When an attending surgeon does not allow a team
his/her opinion that might be different (and/or better), the
not be motivated or devoted to run a resuscitation. When ar
does not allow team members to actively participate in rest
members do not have sufficient opportunity to satisfy
professionalism. In other words, the team member may not
their best for a team leader who totally controls a resusci
when a leader respects a team member's professional opinio
is more willing to get totally involved in the resuscitation.

Proposition 1: Empowering leadership is, in general,
coordinating and performing a trauma resuscitation than c

Theme 4: The Effectiveness of Leadership Differs, Dep Situation.

Even though empowering leadership is generally considere
coordinating team efforts and in providing quality health ca
resuscitation than directive leadership, some interviewe
different leadership might be more effective under diffe
some situations, directive leadership was considered bette
leadership. For example, when the trauma team members k
experience in trauma medicine, the leader needs to be more c
are quotations from several interviewees, who expressed th
of leadership differs depending on the situation.

> . . . Effective leadership is one who steps back when they can and jur
> ation requires that . . . [an attending surgeon].

> . . . It [effective leadership] really depends on how sick a patient is, v
> done with the patient, how strong or weak the [trauma resuscitation] te

injured, team members may be overwhelmed or may experience very high stress level, which can create difficulty in making decisions and fully utilizing their cognitive capabilities (George, 1980). In this situation, the most skillful and experienced personnel who have been in similar situations before, typically an attending surgeon, need to take charge of the resuscitation to provide a proper trauma treatment. In sum, directive leadership is more effective when a patient is severly injured, whereas empowering leadership is more effective when a patient is not severly injured.

Proposition 2: Directive leadership is more effective in coordinating and performing a trauma resuscitation when a patient is severely injured, but empowering leadership is more effective when a patient is not severely injured.

The interview data also imply that the effectiveness of leadership depends on the level of team experience. An inexperienced team may not have sufficient knowledge, skill, or experience to properly manage a trauma resuscitation. When the team leader empowers an inexperienced team to run the resuscitation without his/her direction, the patient is exposed to higher risk levels, which may cause a serious problem. Thus, a team leader needs to be more directive and involved when he/she leads an inexperienced team.

Also, an inexperienced team is more likely to be overwhelmed or to experience high stress levels, compared to an experienced team. The high stress level may be detrimental to a full utilization of the team's resources, or might retard decisions. In order to avoid a breakdown of teamwork, a leader needs to take control of the situation. In other words, rather than relying on other team members, a team leader with a high level of experience (an attending surgeon) needs to be more involved in resuscitation, makes decisions, and directs and instructs the team members in order to run a resuscitation efficiently. However, an experienced team may experience less stress and may know how to cope with such a situation. Thus, an attending surgeon leading an experienced team may be more effective when displaying empowering leadership, because he/she is able to utilize team members' capabilities and team's resources more fully. In sum, a leader needs to be directive when the team is inexperienced, but empowering when the team is highly experienced.

Proposition 3: Directive leadership is more effective in coordinating and performing a trauma resuscitation when a trauma resuscitation team is inexperienced, but empowering leadership is more effective when a trauma team is experienced.

DISCUSSION

In this research, we examined leadership in coordinating a trauma resuscitation, utilizing focused ethnography. Considering the importance and criticality of the trauma team's performance, it is rather surprising that there are not many studies of the trauma team. In this research, we attempted to take an initial step in understanding the leadership phenomenon in coordinating and performing a trauma resuscitation.

Qualitative findings were summarized into four themes. On the basis of these qualitative findings, we developed three propositions regarding the effectiveness of leadership. First, empowering leadership is, in general, considered more effective than directive leadership. However, our findings also suggest that the effectiveness of different leadership is contingent on the situation. Two main situation factors are the severity level of a trauma patient injury and the experience level of a trauma team. Directive leadership is more effective in coordinating and performing a trauma resuscitation when a patient is severely injured, whereas empowering leadership is more effective when a patient is not severely injured. Also, directive leadership is considered more effective in conducting a trauma resuscitation when a trauma team is inexperienced, but empowering leadership is more effective when a trauma team has a high level of experience.

These findings can be theorized into a leadership contingency theory in that the effectiveness of leadership depends on the nature of the situation. Our findings generally support the main argument of leadership contingency theory. However, the contingency theory developed in our study is significantly different from traditional leadership contingency theories (e.g. Fiedler, 1967; House, 1971; Vroom & Yetton, 1973).

Fiedler's (1967) contingency theory was the first to introduce situational variables into leadership research. This theory proposes that the success of a leader depends on the matching of the leader's trait and the situation. It also assumes that an individual's leadership is fixed. However, our study mainly links the leader behaviors, not leader's traits, with team coordination and performance. Also, we do not assume that leadership is fixed and our findings suggest that leaders often adapt their behaviors depending on situations.

House's (1971) path-goal theory proposes that environmental contingency factors (formal authority system, task structure, and work group) and the subordinate contingency factors (locus of control, experience, and perceived ability) moderate the effect of leadership on follower job satisfaction and performance. However, the theory and propositions developed in this research relate to the effects of team leadership on team coordination and performance, not individual follower satisfaction or performance.

Vroom and Yetton (1973) proposed another leadership contingency theory focusing on a leader's decision procedure. They suggested that various aspects of the situation moderate the effect of the decision procedures on the decision quality and decision acceptance by the subordinates. The theory is operationalized as a prescriptive model in the form of a decision tree, which helps a leader determine appropriate decision processes. Their theory focuses on specific aspects of leadership or intervening variables, rather than final outcome of the behaviors of a leader (Yukl, 1998). However, the contingency theory proposed in this study focuses on not only group process variables (coordination) but also the final outcome of leadership.

This study can contribute to the improvement of emergency health care by helping a leader in a trauma resuscitation team develop and improve his/her leadership. The results suggest that a leader in a trauma resuscitation team needs to change his/her leadership depending on the situation. First of all, an attending surgeon needs to change his/her leadership behaviors (as discussed in the "Findings" section of this chapter), contingent on the severity level of a trauma patient. When the patient is severely injured and has life-threatening injuries, the leader needs to display directive leadership. In contrast, when the patient is not severely injured, the leader needs to utilize empowering leadership in order to provide high quality health care to the patient.

Also, the experience level of a trauma resuscitation team requires an attending surgeon to change his/her leadership. Empowering leadership is more effective when a trauma resuscitation team has a high level of experience. On the contrary, directive leadership is more effective when an attending surgeon leads an inexperienced team.

Our findings can be also applied to other empowered knowledge teams. Those teams include software development teams, management consulting teams, operating teams, and the like. However, we need to be cautious since those teams may have different characteristics that a trauma team does not have. Therefore, future research needs to test our propositions in different teams before we apply our findings to those other empowered knowledge teams.

This study also has some limitations. First, our study was conducted in only one organization, which can limit the generalizability of our studies. Currently, we are designing a quantitative study that will include many trauma centers in the U.S. in order to test the generalizability of our findings. Second, this study attempts to understand a trauma resuscitation team and to develop a theory to explain the leadership phenomena in a trauma setting, rather than testing a theory. Therefore, we utilized a qualitative method, which is useful to explore and understand phenomena about which little is known (Morse & Field, 1995). Currently we are conducting a quantitative study to test the propositions developed on the basis of the qualitative findings of this study. By employing a quantitative method as well as a qualitative method, we will be able to triangulate the findings (Morse & Field, 1995). Third, a qualitative study requires that researchers are heavily involved in both data collection and analysis, which brings the issue of subjectivity. We were very careful in order to avoid this issue, as we held several meetings with three other researchers[11] in order to verify our interpretation and understanding. We believe that this approach helped us understand and interpret the situation more objectively. Also, as mentioned above, we are conducting a quantitative study to test our qualitative findings. This quantitative study will help reduce the concern for the subjectivity.

Despite these weaknesses, this is one of the first studies that examined a trauma resuscitation team and leadership phenomenon during a trauma resuscitation. Even though many studies have been conducted on teams and leadership, little is known about trauma resuscitation teams and team leadership during a trauma resuscitation. Therefore, this research improves our understanding of team leadership in an empowered knowledge team operating in an intense situation. However, there are more unknowns than knowns in this area. We hope that more research will be conducted so that we can further enrich our understanding of teams operating in an intense and highly stressful situation.

NOTES

1. TRU is also called Admitting Area, since most patients are admitted through TRU.
2. The surgical team typically includes the attending surgeon, a surgery fellow, medical residents, and medical students.
3. Medical practitioners called the first sixty minutes after a trauma event the golden hour. This period could make the difference between life and death, depending on whether a patient receives the right kind of care (Gerwirtz, 1994).
4. The paramedic is the emergency medical technician called to the site of the injury and provides initial treatment to the patient and transports the patient to a hospital.
5. Unfortunately, two interviews were not taped because of a technical problem (i.e. breakdown of tape recorder). For those two interviews, we recorded notes and recollections, shortly after the interviews.
6. In this section, many quotations are made. Names are concealed to protect subjects.
7. The length of a fellowship varies. A couple of interviewees referred to the fellowship as a post doctoral program.
8. Sometimes, the context is more complex when both the attending surgeon and the fellow are not able to be in the TRU. They both delegate the responsibilities to a resident. In these situations, some of the other team members are typically more experienced and may, in fact, tell the resident what to do.

9. The situation is, in fact, more complex, in that the attending anesthesiologist is typically a physician more experienced than the fellow; or the anesthesiologist may be an anesthesiologist fellow, an anesthesiologist resident, or a CRNA (certified registered nursing anesthesiologist).

10. A priority level 1 patient is a patient who has a life-threatening injury.

11. They included two nursing Ph.D. students and one management Ph.D. student. All three researchers are familiar with the context.

ACKNOWLEDGMENTS

This research was funded by a grant from the National Science Foundation (IIS-9900406, PI: YX). We would also like to thank Sharyn Gardner, Jaqueline Moss, and Caterina Lasome for their contributions. We would also like to thank all of the surgeons, anesthesiologists, nurses, and other care providers who participated in the data gathering and observation part of this study. The views expressed here are those of the authors and do not reflect the official policy or position of the funding agency.

REFERENCES

Aldag, R. J., & Fuller, S. R. (1993). Beyond fiasco: A reappraisal of the groupthink phenomenon and a new model of group decision processes. *Psychological Bulletin, 113*, 533–552.

Ancona, D. G., & Caldwell, D. F. (1992). Bridging the boundary: External process and performance in organizational teams. *Administrative Science Quarterly, 37*, 527–548.

Boyle, J. (1994). Style of ethnography. In: J. M. Morse (Ed.), *Critical Issues in Qualitative Research Methods* (pp. 159–185). Thousand Oaks: Sage.

Cicala, R. S., & Murphy, M. T. (1993). Trauma centers, systems, and plans. In: C. M. Grande (Eds), *Textbook of Trauma Anesthesia and Critical Care* (pp. 56–70). St. Lois, Missouri: Mosby.

Dumaine, B. (1990). Who needs a boss? *Fortune*, (May 7), 52–60.

Dumaine, B. (1994). The trouble with teams. *Fortune*, (September 4), 86–92.

Durham, C. C., Knight, D., & Locke, E. A. (1997). Effects of leader role, team-set goal difficulty, efficacy, and tacit on team effectiveness. *Organizational Behavior and Human Decision Processes, 72*, 203–231.

Fiedler, F. E. (1967). *A theory of leadership effectiveness*. New York: McGraw-Hill.

George, A. (1980). *Presidential decision making in foreign policy*. Boulder, Colo: Westview Press.

Gerwirtz, A. R. (1994). Split working well for emergency systems. *Baltimore Business Journal, 11*(48), 16–17.

Glanze, W. D., Anderson, K. N., & Anderson, L. E. (1990). *Mosby's medical, nursing, and allied health dictionary* (3rd ed.). St. Louis: Missouri: The C. V. Mosby Company.

Hollenbeck, J. R., Ilgen, D. R., & Sego, D. J. (1994). Repeated measures regression and mediational tests: Enhancing the power of leadership research. *Leadership Quarterly, 5*, 3–23.

House, R. J. (1971). A path-goal theory of leader effectiveness. *Administrative Science Quarterly, 16*, 321–339.

Janz, B. D., Colquitt, J. A., & Noe, R. A. (1997). Knowledge worker team effectiveness: the role of autonomy, interdependence, team development, and contextual support variables. *Personnel Psychology, 50*, 877–904.

Lawler, E. E., Mohrman, S. A., & Benson, G. (2001). *Organizing for high performance: Employee involvement, TQM, reengineering, and knowledge management in the Fortune 1000: The Ceo report*. San Francisco: Jossey Bass.

Manz, C. C., & Sims, H. P., Jr. (1987). Leading workers to lead themselves: The external leadership of self-managing work teams. *Administrative Science Quarterly, 32*, 106–128.

Morse, J. M. (1994). Emerging from the data: The cognitive processes of analysis in qualitative inquiry. In: J. M. Morse (Ed.), *Critical Issues in Qualitative Research Methods* (pp. 159–185). Thousand Oaks: Sage.

Morse, J. M., & Field, P. A. (1995). *Qualitative research methods for health professionals* (2nd ed.). Thousand Oaks, CA: Sage.

Parr, M. J. A., & Grande, C. M. (1993). Concepts of trauma care and trauma scoring. In: C. M. Grande (Ed.), *Textbook of Trauma Anesthesia and Critical Care* (pp. 71–92). St. Louis, Missouri: Mosby.

Vidich, A. J., & Lyman, S. M. (1994). Qualitative methods: Their history in sociology and anthropology. In: N. K. Denzin & Y. S. Lincoln (Eds), *Handbook of Qualitative Research* (pp. 23–59). Thousand Oaks, CA: Sage.

Vroom, V. H., & Yetton, P. W. (1973). *Leadership and decision making*. Pittsburgh: University of Pittsburgh Press.

CREATIVITY IN SCIENCE TEAMS

Karen Blansett

ABSTRACT

Advances in science, through the development of new products, processes, or theories, have a significant impact on today's society. Generating these breakthrough discoveries is a creative process that can be helped or hindered by a number of individual and contextual factors. Because of the complexity and scope of the work, much scientific investigation is done in teams; thus, team dynamics as well as individual characteristics help shape the quality of creative output. As teams do not operate in isolation within an organization, team leader behaviors and organizational factors also contribute to team creativity. When organizations and managers value, support, and reward creativity, a climate conducive to innovation is more likely to result.

INTRODUCTION

The products of scientific investigation are becoming increasingly important in today's society. In the form of conceptual theories, these products advance the frontiers of knowledge in a specific area and add to the overall body of scientific understanding. On the other hand, the products of research can be very practical and tangible, such as new medicines or more sophisticated cell phones. In both cases, successful outcomes depend on the ability of scientists to be creative and innovative in their thinking.

Team-Based Organizing, Volume 9, pages 215–232.
© 2003 Published by Elsevier Science Ltd.
ISBN: 0-7623-0981-4

In the business world, the pressure on research and development (R&D) teams is intensifying. New, innovative products may not only enhance a business' profitability, they may also be essential to its survival in a highly competitive environment (Dallenbach, McCarthy & Schoenecker, 1999; Harmsen, Grunert & Declerck, 2000; Kerssens-van Drongelen & Bilderbeck, 1999). As organizations from private industry to government-funded research labs are being increasingly driven by the bottom line, research departments are being held more accountable for delivering profitable outcomes. Thus, companies that are most adept at fostering creativity and channeling it into the development of new products are best able to keep themselves a step ahead of their competitors.

Aside from business pressures, there are other factors driving the need for scientific innovation and discovery. On a macro scale, a nation's economic competitiveness in a worldwide market can hinge on its ability to identify and capitalize on new ideas and unforeseen opportunities. From a strategic standpoint, technological advances have the potential to change people's conceptions about what is accepted as standard in their day-to-day lives (Sapienza, 1995). For example, e-mail and cell phones have significantly altered the way people communicate with each other. In addition, the capacity to envision and implement new technologies contributes significantly to a country's military strength (Sapienza, 1995). Further, in an age of heightened security concerns and potential biological threats to society, there is a compelling need for science to take a prominent role in public safety issues. Cutting-edge thinking is necessary for the development of advanced recognition and identification measures as well as highly sensitive devices for detection of hazardous materials. Thus, society as a whole has a vested interest in the cause of advancing scientific technology.

In both research and applied settings, the work of creating and innovating is often done by teams. Projects are often too complex to be completed by a single individual, and the compressed time frames dictated by competitive pressures frequently make collaboration necessary. The high costs often associated with the development of new technologies may necessitate shared responsibilities across different departments or even multiple organizations. Further, large, complicated projects typically overlap several fields of knowledge. Using cross-functional teams leverages the knowledge and expertise of various groups, leading to greater efficiency and higher quality output. In certain circumstances, government regulations and guidelines mandate collaboration, or collaboration may be required in order to obtain government funding (Sapienza, 1995). Given the scope of most R&D efforts, it is highly likely that the work of generating and implementing innovative ideas involves teams at some point in the process.

DEFINING CREATIVITY

Achieving breakthroughs in science, industry, or any other endeavor is a creative process. Whether it involves finding different ways to apply old knowledge or generating new solutions, creativity requires the ability to combine and reorganize concepts to produce unique ideas (Mumford, 2000). Originality alone, however, is not sufficient to establish creativity. As multiple researchers have pointed out (Amabile, 1998; Ford, 1996; Mumford, 2000; Pelz & Andrews, 1976), an idea must be both novel and useful in order to have value as an innovative discovery.

Within the scientific realm, Mansfield and Busse (1981) further define creativity as having the power of transformation. Thus, to be creative, a scientific discovery must not only be new and have practical value, it must also force people to transform their perceptions and view reality in a new light. Mansfield and Busse also propose that the highest levels of creative output are characterized by the quality of condensation. In other words, the full meaning and impact of the discovery are not immediately evident. Rather, there are subtle nuances that are revealed each time the output is scrutinized, resulting in new knowledge with each examination.

Individual Creativity

New products, processes, and breakthrough discoveries all start as ideas, and the creativity to spark these ideas begins at the individual level. Over the years, much research has been conducted in order to identify the inherent traits and characteristics associated with high levels of individual creativity. The findings from these studies suggest that individual capacity for creative thinking is influenced by intellectual, motivational, and work style factors.

Certain cognitive capabilities appear to be a prerequisite for creative thinking. A certain threshold of intelligence is required; however, beyond this level, more is not necessarily better (Ford, 1996; Mumford & Gustafson, 1988). Regarding the process of thinking itself, several researchers have identified the ability to combine and reorganize concepts as being key to creative thought (Dunbar, 1997; Mumford, 2000; Woodman, Sawyer & Griffin, 1993). This type of conceptual thinking requires analogical reasoning to isolate key elements and perceive new relationships (Mumford, 2000). Dunbar (1997) also described the use of analogies as an important factor in the thought process of creative scientists. Thus, the ability to recognize parallels between seemingly disparate concepts enables people to make leaps in their thinking toward more novel solutions. Fluidity and flexibility of thought are important to divergent thinking

(Woodman et al., 1993), which is, in turn, critical to the generation of multiple ideas and alternatives (Ford, 1996).

High intellectual capacity aids people in assimilating new information, and the accumulation of knowledge is an important precursor to creativity (Ford, 1996). Creative people possess a high level of knowledge, giving them a strong foundation for producing new ideas. Knowledge and experience may also streamline the path toward innovative idea generation by providing both a frame of reference and an efficient problem-solving process that has evolved over time (Mumford, 2000). Innovative scientists, for example, have extensive knowledge about procedural methods and the skill to apply these methods to a variety of problems.

Research also suggests that creative individuals are achievement oriented, and their motivation comes from within (Amabile, 1998; Dunbar, 1997; Sethia, 1993). Internally driven, creative people work independently toward goals and do so for the personal satisfaction of achieving them rather than for external rewards (Amabile, 1998; Sethia, 1993). They find their work to be intrinsically interesting, enjoyable, and satisfying in its own right (Sapienza, 1995). With independence of thought and action, they work autonomously and prefer to prove facts for themselves rather than take information at face value (Sethia, 1993). Mansfield and Busse (1981) found that commitment to work was another hallmark of highly creative people. They worked harder and longer than their less creative peers, resulting in greater productivity.

Because creative work involves identifying and solving ambiguous problems, individuals who have the flexibility and self-discipline necessary to work effectively in the absence of structure are most likely to be successful (Mumford, 2000). They display openness to new experiences (Dunbar, 1997; Mansfield & Busse, 1981) and have a high tolerance for ambiguity and uncertainty (Mansfield & Busse, 1981; Sapienza, 1995). The creative scientists studied by Dunbar (1997) were distinguished by their willingness to take risks in order to achieve new levels of understanding. In their work, these scientists explored challenging topics where answers were complex and difficult to extract, often requiring the invention of new techniques in order to fully investigate possibilities. A high self-image was also found to be important, providing the individual with the confidence needed to take risks (Sapienza, 1995; Sethia, 1993).

Context for Creativity within Organizations

Amabile, Conti, Coon, Lazenby and Herron (1996) have drawn a distinction between creativity (the generation of new, useful ideas) and innovation (the successful implementation of these ideas). From this perspective, individual creativity is merely a starting point. Though necessary, it is not enough by itself to bring about innovation. For creative potential to be realized, the environment in which the work is being carried out must be conducive to not only generating creative ideas, but also successfully implementing them. In Ford's (1996) systems view, people, processes, and places are intertwined elements that provide the context for creative output. Thus, the dynamics within each team or work group, the management practices and leadership behaviors of the individual responsible for the team's work, and the structure, policies, and values of the organization all have an impact on creativity.

Creativity in Teams

In organizations, work is increasingly being done by teams, and this holds true for creative efforts as well as more routine projects. The complex nature of many projects and the need to have a variety of resources that can be applied to problem solving often necessitate the use of teams (Mumford, 2000). For example, the variety of tasks, skill sets, and areas of knowledge needed for successful completion of a large research endeavor requires the efforts of more than one person. Teaming, then, allows for a more efficient combination of resources, both material and intellectual (Kraut, Egido & Galegher, 1990), leading to greater productivity with less cost.

As mentioned previously, creativity involves the ability to generate many ideas about a single topic or problem. Because collaboration involves the efforts of multiple people, it can spur creativity through the resulting increase in volume of ideas and options. The rich database of possibilities generated by a group provides more of the potential combinations and unique juxtapositions of existing elements that lead to creative thought.

Because many creative ideas are formed by drawing connections between seemingly disparate concepts, a broad foundation of knowledge is another key to creativity. Viewing the team as a collection of many individual knowledge bases, the breadth and depth of expertise available within a group provides more intellectual resources to draw upon. Further, team members bring to the group not only factual knowledge about multiple topics, but also a variety of thinking and problem-solving skills (Amabile, 1998). The greater the number of ways in which a problem can be taken apart and reconstructed, the more likely a creative solution is to be the result.

In addition to the varied frames of reference and areas of expertise that multiple perspectives provide, diversity within a group can add to creativity by generating useful conflict. According to Tjosvold (1991), group creativity results from productive controversy during the problem-solving process. Differences of opinion and conflict among diverse points of view enable group members to see problems from other perspectives and allow new possibilities to emerge. The discussion and defense of individual ideas sparks the formation of new concepts as people consider different alternatives and reorganize their thinking accordingly.

The group problem-solving process itself, including open debate on controversial ideas, helps to shape more creative solutions. In essence, the group serves as a laboratory where ideas can be analyzed, tested, and examined from multiple perspectives. By challenging conclusions and offering different points of view, the process of discussion acts as a feedback mechanism. Constructive criticism from team members aids in refining ideas, resulting in higher overall quality of solutions (Kraut et al., 1990).

Beyond the technical, knowledge-based advantages to teamwork, the interpersonal aspects of working in a group can also boost creativity. Teams provide the social context in which creativity occurs (Woodman et al., 1993). Teams provide more opportunities for interaction with others – the type of informal information sharing, casual observation of others' work, and snippets of overheard conversation that spark ideas. In addition, when team members feel supported and encouraged by the group, they are more comfortable taking the type of risks necessary to challenge existing thinking and pursue new ideas. Support from team members also helps create an open, intellectually challenging environment where entrepreneurial behavior is encouraged (Mumford, 2000) and the freedom to fail is supported (Thomke, 2001). Finally, people often find collaboration more enjoyable than working alone, so their intrinsic motivation, commitment to the task, and overall job satisfaction may be enhanced in a group setting (Kraut et al., 1990).

In summary, creativity is dependent on the number and quality of ideas generated, the number of diverse views, and the ability to bring a broad range of expertise to bear on a problem. Because of the multiple individuals involved, all of these factors are present to a greater degree in a team than within a single person. Consequently, there is high potential for enhanced creativity in teams.

SCIENCE TEAMS

Innovations and new discoveries are the products of science, so creativity plays an important role in productivity and teams help facilitate the creative process. Especially important in scientific work are open debate and flexibility in problem-solving options, and teamwork creates a favorable environment for both of these. Creativity in an R&D climate involves risk, as scientists must venture into unknown territory in order to make technological advances (Bain,

Mann & Pirola-Merlo, 2001). Consequently, properly functioning teams provide the security necessary for people to feel comfortable engaging in the risk-taking behavior needed for innovation (Johnson & Johnson, 1994).

Within the R&D function, some researchers make a distinction between research (R) and development (D) based on the nature of each group's work and the expectations for their output Bain et al., 2001). In turn, the different creativity demands suggest that the optimal structures and systems for the research arm of the department may not be appropriate for the area focusing on development. Further, the focus for collaboration may differ between the two groups.

Research scientists have the responsibility of generating new ideas, theories, and avenues for further exploration. Through their work, they have an opportunity to make a significant contribution to general scientific or technical knowledge. Research scientists typically operate under a wider scope for innovation, with fewer constraints and less emphasis on quantifiable metrics such as deadlines and budgets (Bain et al., 2001). When scientists are in the initial phases of exploring new ideas or avenues for research, formal rules, procedures, and structures constrain their thinking. Because the primary emphasis for collaboration in this phase is in the generation and refinement of new ideas, structures and systems should be set up to encourage close social relationships, informal communication, and constructive debate. Thus, the best conditions for creativity occur when scientists work within small groups that are horizontally structured, an arrangement that provides for greater role flexibility and more peer-to-peer interaction than hierarchical structures based on traditional superior/subordinate relationships (Sapienza, 1995).

On the development side, the group's objectives are more narrowly defined (Bain et al., 2001). The development phase mostly involves refinement and implementation of existing ideas, and the responsibility of the development team is to translate a creative idea into a tangible outcome. Because creativity in these circumstances is limited to the boundaries of the current project, scientists have fewer opportunities to produce major, impactful scientific innovations (Bain et al., 2001). As development projects tend to be large and complex, collaboration spreads out the workload and helps ensure smooth implementation. Within this framework, established rules and procedures make for a more efficient process. Consequently, larger groups with a more vertical, hierarchical structure may be more appropriate (Sapienza, 1995).

Kraut, Egido and Galegher (1990) suggest that collaboration changes the research process for scientists in a positive and desirable way. They are able to work on larger, more significant research projects as a result of their involvement with others. The quality of the finished product is likely to be higher due to the concentration of knowledge, synthesis of ideas, and opportunities for feedback afforded by multiple scientists working together. Thus, their efforts are likely to have greater impact on the scientific field, their professional reputations, and their personal development. From an interpersonal standpoint, the scientists interviewed in the Kraut et al. study felt that working in partnership with others was more fun than working alone. Collaboration provided them with an opportunity to stay in touch with others, share experiences, and socially connect in both formal and informal ways, thus enhancing their enjoyment of the research process.

In contrast to the volumes of research dedicated to teams in general, there is comparatively little that specifically targets science or research teams, especially in regard to their potential for innovation and creativity. One exception is a study of R&D departments in the biotech industry by Judge, Fryxell and Dooley (1997), in which they found that highly innovative R&D units were distinguished by a sense of community that was not present in low innovation units. This sense of community was characterized by honest communication, deep personal relationships that included allowing others to see their real selves, a genuine desire to reach agreement, and the absence of hidden agendas and barriers between people. Scientists in the highly innovative units described their group as being like an extended family; they felt a strong sense of trust in their coworkers and cared about them as people. Another study by Mumford (2000) found that the prevailing climate in a group can have an impact on technical innovation. Scientists who share diverse, yet related, backgrounds develop more threads of ideas and bring a broader range of experiences to a problem. Both of these contribute to creative thinking and subsequently to higher levels of innovation.

Much of the existing research into science team creativity is focused on new product development teams within industry. For example, the use of crossfunctional teams for new product development has been positively associated with performance, as measured by speed of bringing new products to market, meeting budgetary goals, developing high-quality products, and team member satisfaction (McDonough, 2000). Other research on cross-functional new product development teams has identified a number of behavioral factors associated with higher performance. These include the presence of trust, effective interpersonal relationships, and effective communication among group members as well as the existence of common goals to focus the team's efforts (McDonough, Kahn & Barczak, 2001).

Team Member Behaviors

Science is a social process, as the day-to-day work of scientists involves frequent contact with others (Kraut et al., 1990). When scientists work in teams, their interactions with other group members have an impact on the team's functioning. Thus, interpersonal behaviors are important, as the social dynamics of the group set the tone for positive, productive working relationships.

Risk taking and having the freedom to fail without repercussions are often cited as being essential to creativity (Bain et al., 2001; Sapienza, 1995; Thomke, 2001). Many studies point to the importance of perceived psychological safety in establishing a comfortable climate for risk taking in groups (Smith, 1993). Without this element of safety (i.e. individuals feel that their opinions will be openly received and their ideas will not be criticized or dismissed), people are reluctant to share the controversial, out-of-the-mainstream ideas that provide the foundation for creativity. In an "unsafe" environment, people are more likely to offer "safe" solutions that are less likely to provoke negative reactions. The quantity of ideas generated is also likely to suffer under conditions of psychological insecurity. Smith (1993), for example, found that groups in which an individual's ideas were deliberately discounted produced significantly fewer ideas than groups in which no discounting occurred. Further, control groups that were trained to avoid discounting produced the greatest number of ideas of all. Overall, the degree to which individuals feel comfortable within a group and secure in expressing their thoughts can have a significant impact on creativity.

A key element in establishing this psychological safety net is the level of trust that individuals within the team feel in one another. When members trust that all are contributing to the group's goals and have the group's best interests (rather than personal gain) at heart, their level of cooperation is increased (Johnson & Johnson, 1994). Trust among team members also promotes the open expression of ideas, thoughts, and opinions, even those that are likely to be controversial. This facilitates information flow, as team members are more likely to speak up and share knowledge and ideas when they know that their input will be positively received. The likelihood of constructive conflict is also enhanced if people feel comfortable saying "what needs to be said" rather than "what other people want to hear," thus the potential for creativity is enhanced.

Commitment to the group and its purpose also contributes to team effectiveness. Commitment has been defined as "a sense of duty that the team feels to achieve the project's goals and . . . the willingness to do what's needed to make the project successful" (McDonough, 2000, p. 226). If people have confidence in the capabilities of their fellow team members, they are more likely to believe that the group can be successful and thus their commitment to the task is likely to be increased.

Ownership is a concept that takes commitment a step further. Not only is the group committed to its goal, but the team members themselves tie their identities to the project's outcome (McDonough, 2000). The likelihood for ownership to develop is greater when the team has the autonomy to decide how they will accomplish tasks. This increases the team members' intrinsic motivation, leading to feelings of ownership and greater propensity for creative output (Amabile, 1998).

In one study, members of successful, highly innovative R&D units exhibited a strong personal connection to each other that was not present in lower performing units (Judge et al., 1997). They described their group as being like an "extended family" (p. 75), where people cared about each other on a deeper level than in a typical working relationship. The personal relationships not only made work more enjoyable for them, but also created a safe haven that let them be themselves and behave naturally, without fear that their words or actions would be criticized. As noted earlier, this is a critical step in establishing a work environment that allows creativity to naturally emerge.

Creative tension within a group arises from team member diversity. With a wide-ranging spectrum of individuals present within a group, its members are exposed to a greater number of unique ideas and perspectives, thus setting the stage for creative thinking (Tjosvold, 1991). The task-related conflict that surfaces among team members stimulates the type of divergent thinking that is essential for generating creative ideas (West & Anderson, 1996). Constructive conflict not only improves the quality of ideas (Tjosvold, 1991), but also increases intrinsic motivation by fostering a positive sense of challenge in the work (Amabile et al., 1996). Constructive controversy occurs in a group environment that is cooperative, not competitive, where people are working toward mutually beneficial goals and all members have equal influence (West & Anderson, 1996). The foundation for constructive controversy is team member trust, respect, and honesty.

Leadership Behaviors

Rarely is a group completely autonomous in that it has no accountability to another individual or entity outside its own boundaries. In most settings within organizations of any type, the research team falls under the oversight of one or more managers. The behaviors and practices of these managers have a significant impact on innovation, whether through their interactions with the team members or their influence on the group's work environment (Amabile, 1998; Mumford, 2000).

Managers can facilitate creativity by creating an appropriate structure for the team to operate within. This includes clearly defining boundaries for the team and establishing where the lines of responsibility are, while simultaneously allowing the team autonomy of movement within these boundaries (McDonough, 2000). The most effective leaders for creative teams adhere to a participative leadership style (McDonough, 2000) that is democratic and collaborative (Woodman et al., 1993). They openly discuss ideas, share information broadly, allow the team to make its own decisions (McDonough, 2000), and permit the team to have discretion in the structuring of work activities (Mumford, 2000). Further, they keep an open mind to new ideas generated by the team. They are encouraging and supportive, praising creative efforts rather than focusing solely on successes (Amabile, 1998).

The presence of group goals is the factor found to most often contribute to group effectiveness and creativity (West & Anderson, 1996), and managers play a key role in establishing the objectives for the team. Research has shown that effective R&D units are goal directed and working toward strategic objectives developed by management, yet are given the freedom to work independently within that context (Judge et al., 1997). The most innovative research teams have a clear sense of the end results being sought and are able to work toward reasonable goals without a strong emphasis on deadlines. When group members collectively understand what they are trying to achieve, they are able to focus and combine their work efforts most effectively. Clear objectives enable innovative thinking by providing a focal point for the development of new ideas and greater precision in the evaluation of ideas (West & Anderson, 1996). Goals that the group members understand and commit to also provide a rallying point that keeps the team moving forward in the face of resistance.

Once goals have been established and understood, managers who provide autonomy to the team in deciding how to reach the goal are more likely to see creative results emerge. Previous studies have shown that people produce more creative work when they believe they have a choice in how to accomplish the work (Amabile et al., 1996). Further, team member participation in decision making has been associated with less resistance to change, thus creating a favorable climate for innovation (West & Anderson, 1996). Autonomy also increases team member commitment to the task and ownership of results, so team members are more invested in the project and more likely to suggest improvements. Freedom allows people to leverage their expertise and skills in a way that makes the most sense to them (Amabile, 1998), adding to their work challenge and enjoyment. Leaders help team members control their work situation (and thus feel greater commitment, investment, and ownership) by providing the appropriate preparations and environment (e.g. resources, clear goals) and allowing team members to work without interference (Norrgren & Schaller, 2001).

Effective managers also provide team members with the appropriate resources for doing creative work. Time is one such resource that can have a significant impact on creativity. Creative work does not always fit neatly into a schedule; it requires ample time for exploration, incubation, and reflection on ideas as well as examination of multiple options and potential solutions. Thus, deadlines that are overly tight can smother creativity. When a schedule is virtually impossible to meet, time to think and reflect is compromised. Further, people may feel overcontrolled and helpless to achieve what is expected of them. As a result, their intrinsic motivation suffers, lessening their interest in the work and the creative challenge it offers (Amabile, 1998). Thus, effective managers allow and encourage time for thinking and reflection (Mumford, 2000).

Beyond time, team members need sufficient physical and intellectual resources in order to put forth their best efforts. Effective managers ensure that groups have these resources, so that team members' creativity is not exhausted by efforts to obtain the needed tools, equipment, funding, or expertise (Amabile, 1998; Mumford, 2000). Finally, a lack of resources can also impact the team's functioning in more subtle ways. When team members are not given the necessary resources to do their work, they may infer that their work is not important to the organization or respected by management (Amabile et al., 1996). Again, this affects their intrinsic motivation and ultimately their creativity.

Managers also serve as the bridge between the team and senior management. In this capacity, they take on the role of lobbying for resources (McDonough, 2000), relieving team members of this burden. They also protect the team, shielding it from outside interference from other parts of the organization (Norrgren & Schaller, 2001), managing the impressions of outsiders (McDonough, 2000), and buffering group members from extraneous distractions (Mumford, 2000). In risk-averse organizations, the buffering role of the manager helps ensure that initial failures are not viewed in a negative light by higher management (Sapienza, 1995), thus protecting the team from consequences that may hamper their creativity.

Managers also ensure that team members find their niche within the group and have appropriately challenging work. Matching people to the right assignments (Amabile, 1998), ensuring that people "fit" within the group not only technically but socially (Judge et al., 1997), and keeping team members individually and collectively challenged while maintaining a positive attitude toward the project (McDonough, 2000) keep individuals' enthusiasm and motivation high and foster creativity.

Effective managers also evaluate team performance in a planful, helpful way. They give frequent feedback and review work progress in an ongoing manner rather than as part of a yearly performance review (Mumford, 2000). They recognize both individual and group successes and provide personalized, intrinsic rewards that are tailored to individual team members (Judge et al., 1997). They evaluate progress rather than outcomes, as imposed, rigid goals can inhibit creativity (Mumford, 2000).

Organizational Support

Perhaps ironically, the beginnings of many organizations are rooted in creativity (Schumann, 1993). Start-up companies are often launched by the creative vision of their founders. An imaginative individual envisions a unique product or service, and a new organization is born. Other entrepreneurs find novel ways to capitalize on current products and services in order to fill existing gaps in the marketplace. However, as organizations become more successful, they also expand and become more complex (Schumann, 1993). The increasing productivity demands brought about by growth require more standardized processes in order to streamline operations and maximize efficiency. In the initial stages of a company, it is often easy for ideas to move from conception to finished product in a fluid manner, nurtured by a small core of individuals from beginning to end. Within the bureaucracy of a large organization, responsibility and ownership of ideas are diffused, and accountability for timely, measurable results often overrides the importance of creativity. At its best, the creative process is messy, unorganized, and ambiguous – characteristics that are at odds with the need of large organizations to measure exactly, manage toward metrics, stay on schedule, and minimize risks. This makes it even more important that organizations recognize creativity as a critical asset and design their structures and systems to accommodate it.

Both individual and team efforts are shaped by the organization around them. Behaviors that facilitate creativity can be reinforced and rewarded by the organization's culture and practices, thus increasing the likelihood that they will be repeated. Conversely, if these behaviors are met with punishment or indifference, innovation is likely to be suppressed. In essence, organizations foster innovation when their structures and systems are constructed in a way that reinforces the team member and leadership behaviors that enhance creativity.

The organizational climate is the primary foundation. When the organization's values and culture are supportive of innovation and teamwork, group creativity benefits (Amabile et al., 1996; Mumford, 2000). Mumford and Gustafson (1988) describe supportive climates for innovation as those that encourage interaction, autonomy, and knowledge production. In their view, a supportive organizational climate is defined as one that embraces innovation and demonstrates the value attached to it by reinforcing creative endeavors with personally meaningful rewards. At the same time, the organization must ensure that employees are not constrained in their attempts to achieve these rewards, whether by lack of knowledge, resources, or any other impediment. Environments that encourage creativity have also been characterized as those that are open to new ideas (Amabile et al., 1996; Pelz & Andrews, 1976), supportive of risk taking (Amabile et al., 1996; Pelz & Andrews, 1976), encourage teamwork and open communication (Sapienza, 1995; West & Anderson, 1996; Woodman et al., 1993), and allow autonomy in decision making (Sapienza, 1995). Further, Bharadwaj and Menon (2000) propose that organizations that explicitly set up structures, processes, and systems to facilitate creativity send unspoken signals to their employees about the value of innovation, implicitly reinforcing its importance. Along these lines, when organizations incorporate innovation into their strategic objectives, employees get a clear message about its importance (Mumford, 2000).

While organizational practices do not ensure creativity, they can encourage it (Mumford, 2000) and can remove barriers that stand in its way. However, simply removing obstacles to creativity is not always enough. In every situation, individuals have a choice whether to take action in a creative or noncreative way, and the organizational context can affect which choice is made. Even when the environment is conducive to creativity, the natural inclination of most people is to choose comfortable, habitual actions. Therefore, creative actions are not likely to emerge unless individuals perceive that there are rewards (either on an individual or a team level) for doing so that are more personally desirable than the consequences for continuing familiar behaviors. Attempts at innovation will be abandoned if taking the "safe" road remains a more attractive option (Ford, 1996).

To create an optimal climate for creativity, organizations should encourage risk taking (Mumford, 2000; Woodman et al., 1993). When people are supported and rewarded for taking risks rather than being punished for failures, they are more likely to explore less fail-safe ideas and approaches. If support for risk taking permeates the organization and is present at all levels of management, there is both implicit and explicit permission given for employees to take chances and explore creative alternatives (Amabile et al., 1996). The sense of psychological safety needed to feel comfortable taking chances or making risky decisions is magnified within the larger organizational context. The same feeling of freedom from repercussions must be present on an organizational level, not just the team level, in order to promote creative thinking.

Organizations that encourage ongoing development have been shown to be more likely to produce innovative products. This encouragement includes opportunities to learn new skills as well as organizational support for external education, conference attendance, and professional involvement (Mumford, 2000). All of these promote new skill development and the acquisition of knowledge, both of which provide additional fodder for the generation of creative ideas. Further, an organization that emphasizes opportunities for development is more likely to appeal to creative people because of their interest in acquiring knowledge and mastering new challenges. Thus, a development culture can feed the intrinsic motivation of its current employees as well as serve as a recruitment tool to attract other creative individuals.

A key component of organizational support is the organization's system for rewarding performance. Even though creativity is not enhanced by external rewards (and can in fact be hindered by them), a reward that appears to be an "extra" does not decrease the individual's intrinsic motivation to achieve (Amabile et al., 1996). Likewise, rewards that validate the individual's competence or importance to the organization, or ones that enable the individual to do more interesting and challenging work enhance creativity (Amabile et al., 1996). In one research study, the most highly innovative R&D units used personalized rewards, tailored to the individual, whereas less innovative units relied on impersonal, extrinsic rewards such as money or stock options (Judge et al., 1997). Overall, organizations that explicitly reinforce the value of innovation by recognizing creative work and providing meaningful, personalized rewards for accomplishments are most likely to reap the benefits of their employees' creativity.

RESEARCH AGENDA

Given its economic and strategic importance and the scarcity of research in this area, scientific creativity is a topic ripe for investigation. Understanding the factors that support the creative process and the conditions that underlie creativity in research teams can assist organizations in providing an optimal environment for breakthrough thinking. The opportunities for additional research are extensive and varied, as individual, team, leadership, and organizational factors all play a part in science team creativity. Personal characteristics such as the degree to which individuals are intrinsically motivated, flexible in their thinking, and comfortable with risk taking could contribute to group creativity. Variables such as group size and group composition could potentially affect the social dynamics of the team. In addition, the emergence of virtual teams raises further questions about a team's ability to maintain social ties and sustain a sense of community in the absence of frequent face-to-face interaction. The impact of leadership behaviors on team creativity might have implications for self-managed work teams. In particular, the team's ability to negotiate for resources and interface with upper management might be affected by the lack of a formal leader. Because of their impact on intrinsic motivation, organizational reward systems could be a fruitful topic for future research. The type and frequency of feedback and rewards may influence a team's creative output. Further, the organization's use of individual or team-based recognition systems may be an important variable to investigate. Finally, providing training for team members in skills that support effective team dynamics, such as listening skills or conflict management could pay dividends in the form of increased team creativity.

SUMMARY

The optimum conditions for creativity within an organization or research lab do not exist in isolation. Rather, the ability to produce creative output is dependent upon individual, group, and organizational factors that combine in such a way as to facilitate breakthrough thinking. In Ford's (1996) systems view, the context for creativity is supplied by the overlap of the individual, the field of people with whom the individual interacts, and the rules and practices that govern the individual's domain. Similarly, Bain et al. (2001) propose that individual, group, and organizational creativity are intertwined. Thus, an organizational climate that fosters creativity sets an expectation for team creativity, which in turn serves as a model for individual experimentation and creative thought. Thomke (2001) envisions creativity as being the byproduct of a smoothly running machine, where all parts function in synchronization with each other. For creative ideas to be born, nurtured, and brought to fruition as tangible outcomes requires a system that lends itself to experimentation, testing, and refinement of ideas through a feedback loop of constructive criticism and readjustment.

The ideal environment for breakthrough thinking begins with creative people – that is, people who are motivated, confident, flexible, and intellectually curious. These individuals carry out their work in teams whose members respect and care about each other. This provides the intellectual stimulation, diversity of thought, freedom to take risks, and immediate support that are necessary for high levels of creative thinking. The supportive team environment is maintained by the manager, who provides clear goals and expectations, empowers the team to take action on its own, and buffers it from outside distractions. Further, the actions and methods of the manager and team members are reinforced by an organizational environment that supports open communication, ongoing learning and risk taking, and appropriately rewards creative behavior.

REFERENCES

Amabile, T. M. (1998). How to kill creativity. *Harvard Business Review*, (September–October), 77–87.

Amabile, T. M., Conti, R., Coon, H., Lazenby, J., & Herron, M. (1996). Assessing the work environment for creativity. *Academy of Management Journal, 39*, 1154–1184.

Bain, P. G., Mann, L., & Pirola-Merlo, A. (2001). The innovation imperative: The relationships between team climate, innovation, and performance in research and development teams. *Small Group Research, 32*, 55–73.

Bharadwaj, S., & Menon, A. (2000). Making innovation happen in organizations: Individual creativity mechanisms, organizational creativity mechanisms, or both? *Journal of Product Innovation Management, 17*, 424–434.

Dallenbach, U. S., McCarthy, A. M., & Schoenecker, T. S. (1999). Commitment to innovation: The impact of top management team characteristics. *R&D Management, 29*, 199–208.

Dunbar, K. (1997). How scientists think: On-line creativity and conceptual change in science. In: T. B. Ward, S. M. Smith & J. Vaid (Eds), *Creative Thought: An Investigation of Conceptual Structures and Processes* (pp. 461–493). Washington, D.C.: American Psychological Association.

Ford, C. M. (1996). A theory of individual creative action in multiple social domains. *Academy of Management Review, 21*, 1112–1142.

Harmsen, H., Grunert, K. G., & Declerck, F. (2000). Why did we make that cheese: An empirically-based framework for understanding what drives innovation activity. *R&D Management, 30*, 151–166.

Johnson, D. W., & Johnson, F. P. (1994). *Joining Together*. Boston: Allyn and Bacon.

Judge, W. Q., Fryxell, G. E., & Dooley, R. S. (1997). The new task of R&D management: Creating goal-directed communities for innovation. *California Management Review, 39*, 72–85.

Kerssens-van Drongelen, I. C., & Bilderbeck, J. (1999). R&D performance measurement: More than choosing a set of metrics. *R&D Management, 29*, 35–46.

Kraut, R. E., Egido, C., & Galegher, J. (1990). Patterns of contact and communication in scientific research collaborations. In: J. Galegher, R. E. Kraut & C. Egido (Eds), *Intellectual Teamwork: Social and Technological Foundations of Cooperative Work* (pp. 149–172). Hillsdale, NJ: Lawrence Erlbaum Associates.

Mansfield, R. S., & Busse, T. V. (1981). *The psychology of creativity and discovery*. Chicago: Nelson-Hall.

McDonough, E. F., III (2000). Investigation of factors contributing to the success of cross-functional teams. *The Journal of Product Innovation Management, 17*, 221–235.

McDonough, E. F., III, Kahn, K. B., & Barczak, G. (2001). An investigation of the use of global, virtual, and colocated new product development teams. *The Journal of Product Innovation Management, 18*, 110–120.

Mumford, M. D. (2000). Managing creative people: Strategies and tactics for innovation. *Human Resource Management Review, 10*, 313–351.

Mumford, M. D., & Gustafson, S. B. (1988). Creativity syndrome: Integration, application, and innovation. *Psychological Bulletin, 103*, 27–43.

Norrgren, F., & Shaller, J. (2001). Leadership style: Its impact on cross-functional product development. *Journal of Product Innovation Management, 16*, 377–384.

Pelz, D. C., & Andrews, F. M. (1976). *Scientists in organizations: Productive climates for research and development* (Rev. ed.). Ann Arbor, MI: Institute for Social Research, The University of Michigan.

Sapienza, A. M. (1995). *Managing scientists: Leadership strategies in research and development.* New York: Wiley-Liss, Inc.

Schumann, P. A., Jr. (1993). Creativity and innovation in large organizations. In: R. L. Kuhn (Ed.), *Generating Creativity and Innovation in Large Bureaucracies* (pp. 111–130). Westport, CT: Quorum Books.

Sethia, N. K. (1993). Leadership for creativity in organizations: A prototypical case of leading multidisciplinary teams of professionals. In: R. L. Kuhn (Ed.), *Generating Creativity and Innovation in Large Bureaucracies* (pp. 385–391). Westport, Connecticut: Quorum Books.

Smith, B. L. (1993). Interpersonal behaviors that damage the productivity of creative problem solving groups. *Journal of Creative Behavior, 27,* 171–187.

Thomke, S. (2001). Enlightened experimentation: The new imperative for innovation. *Harvard Business Review,* (February), 67–75.

Tjosvold, D. (1991). *The conflict-positive organization.* Reading, MA: Addison-Wesley.

West, M. A., & Anderson, N. R. (1996). Innovation in top management teams. *Journal of Applied Psychology, 81,* 680–693.

Woodman, R. W., Sawyer, J. E., & Griffin, R. W. (1993). Toward a theory of organizational creativity. *Academy of Management Review, 18,* 293–321.

MERGERS AND ACQUISITIONS AS COLLABORATIVE CHALLENGES

Lori Bradley

INTRODUCTION

There are very few events that have as transforming an effect on organizations, for better or worse, as mergers and acquisitions (M&As). This chapter will begin with a brief overview of the recent history of M&As in the United States and will discuss what research says about the very low success rate of mergers and acquisitions today. The next section will discuss some of the common mistakes organizations make when going through a merger or acquisition, and the impact of these mistakes on employees. Recent research will be drawn upon to outline some ways to improve the chances for a successful merger or acquisition. These methods include performing cultural assessments, engaging in transition planning, improving communication, recognizing and addressing separation anxiety, offering stress management programs or workshops, and offering outplacement services to displaced employees.

HISTORY OF M&As

Historically, M&A activity has been associated with changes in underlying economic forces (Weston, 1999). The transcontinental railway system, completed at the turn of the last century, allowed regional companies to become national companies, and thus sparked a flurry of corporate M&As. The 1920s saw another merger movement as small local sales areas were extended by

Team-Based Organizing, Volume 9, pages 233–246.
© 2003 Published by Elsevier Science Ltd.
ISBN: 0-7623-0981-4

advances in the auto industry. Antitrust policy had heavily thwarted horizontal and vertical mergers by the 1960s. This resulted in firms attempting to achieve the high growth valued by the stock market through acquisitions outside their core industries. The diversified firms were frequently unprepared and ill equipped to manage the unfamiliar business activities, and many would go through subsequent divestitures in the 1980s to move back to their core activities (Weston, 1999).

Technological advances, accelerating in the 1970s, reduced transportation and communication costs, and began to pave the way for national markets to grow into international markets and, finally, into the global markets of the 1990s (Weston, 1999). M&A activity has steadily increased in recent years. A variety of factors including a strong economy in the United States resulting in investment capital, a strategic imperative to compete globally, numerous regulatory changes and a burst of technological advances have contributed to the amplified M&A activity (Tetenbaum, 1999). In 1998, according to the Securities Data Company (as cited in Tetenbaum, 1999), M&As were worth $2.4 trillion worldwide. Domestically, M&As were worth $1.6 trillion or 11% of the total capitalization of the stock market. Half of the CEOs polled believed they would play an active part in a corporate acquisition during the next 12 to 24 months (Tetenbaum, 1999).

M&A activity did go down, however, in 2001. A weak economy created a slow start, and then the events of September 11th caused many deals to be put on the backburner. This was the first decrease in M&A activity in several years. The Mergers and Acquisition Advisor (January, 2002) reports a 25% drop in the total number of deals from the year 2000. However, the last quarter of the year did show an increase in M&A activity. Mergerstat.com (December 21, 2001) reported that the Broadcasting, Banking and Finance, and Drug, Medical Supplies and Equipment industries were the top three in M&A activity for 2001.

The forces driving M&As appear to be strongly influenced by industry effects. In any given year, more than 50% of M&A activity is accounted for by five or six industries. However, the collective five or six industries changes from year to year, with different industries occupying the top slots (Weston, 1999). The 1998 Mergerstat Review reported that three areas accounted for 49% of the dollar value of M&A activity in 1997. These were: (1) banking and finance; (2) electric, gas, and water services; and (3) communications and entertainment media (Tetenbaum, 1999).

According to Weston (1999), the overall level of M&A activity is reduced by greater stock market volatility, however, strategic transactions will continue to be made in the effort to adjust to the massive change forces dominating the world economy. The current skittish market will be less forgiving of a misstep, however, making successful M&As imperative.

SUCCESS RATE

According to a study conducted by Marks and Mirvis (2000), well over three-fourths of all M&As fail to achieve their financial and strategic goals. Galpin and Herndon (2000) found that CEOs and CFOs routinely cite people problems and cultural issues as the top factors in failed integrations. They also found the following to be true of M&As:

- Only 23% of all acquisitions earn their cost of capital.
- Forty-seven percent of executives in acquired companies leave within the first year and 75% leave within the first three years.
- Productivity may be reduced by up to 50% in the first four to eight months after a merger or acquisition.

It should be noted that it is common for a number of executives to leave following a merger and/or acquisition due to redundancy. It is most often executives in the acquired firm that leave. The problem arises when key talent that the acquiring firm intended to retain decide to leave. It is also common and usually expected that productivity will go down during the transition. Even so, these statistics are not encouraging and make it easy to question why any organization would willingly go down this path. As discussed in the previous section, however, huge numbers of organizations have recently, are currently, or will soon be experiencing a merger or an acquisition. The next section discusses why organizations make this decision.

DRIVERS OF MERGERS AND ACQUISITIONS

Maxwell (1998) lists several "drivers" behind M&As. They include: (1) the belief that M&As will increase growth; (2) the current low cost of entering certain businesses; (3) a desire to increase marketing reach; (4) a need to obtain additional service capabilities and to increase industry expertise; (5) expanding customer bases; (6) the acquisition of competitors; and (7) a way to gain ground in an industry in which they may have "fallen behind."

M&As may have any of a number of motivations, and often simply involve the need to reduce costs and the desire to expand business opportunities and to increase efficiency. Accomplishing these business objectives through a merger or acquisition is appealing because it can involve joining with another organization with an established track record and key executive talent, as well as strategic organizational competencies.

STAGES OF M&As

It is important to remember that M&As are not overnight occurrences. In fact, rather than an event, they might better be described as a process. There are at least three, and perhaps four, stages of the M&A process. There is a pre-M&A stage, during which time the organizations come into initial contact with each other and begin due diligence. This usually requires absolute secrecy and information is not freely shared outside the negotiating parties in order to avoid alerting competitors. Within the organizations, information leaks at this time can spark a wildfire of rumors that must be dealt with in the next stage.

The second stage is the time between the announcement of the intended merger and/or acquisition and the legal finalization of the deal. This stage is rich in anxiety and insecurity for the employees and management. Due diligence continues and business must continue to function, all the while knowing that big changes are about to occur. An integration team, which most research recommends, should be in place during this stage.

The post-merger stage is the third stage and this is, so to speak, where the "rubber meets the road." The companies are integrated and begin to function as one entity.

Some might break the M&A process into four stages: (1) the pre-merger stage; (2) the time between the announcement of the deal and the legal finalization; (3) the actual merge (e.g. moving offices, combining systems, staff changes, etc.); and (4) the post-merger period after the initial merge. Using the step-family model that so many writers on this topic refer to – stage one is when the parents are dating; stage two is the engagement; stage three is the wedding and combination of the two households; and, stage four involves living together as a new family (or, at least, the attempts to do so).

The rest of this chapter is primarily concerned with the post-merger stages, but first it will address what goes wrong in M&As.

WHAT GOES WRONG?

There are numerous factors that contribute to the disappointing results of many M&As. The reasons most frequently cited in the literature include: (1) a failure to consider cultural differences between the organizations involved in the merger or acquisition; (2) failure to address the "people" issues; (3) ineffective communication pre-, post- and during the consolidation; and (4) the lack of a post-merger or acquisition integration plan. Each will be discussed below.

Culture. Culture refers to the norms, values, beliefs, and attitudes that organizational members maintain about the purpose of their work and how they are expected to perform their work (Tetenbaum, 1999). Although culture is not always easy to describe or define, every organization has a unique culture, and this can create problems in M&As. Individuals who choose jobs and organizations that are consistent with their own values, attitudes and beliefs tend to be more satisfied employees who stay with their organizations longer than unsatisfied employees (Cascio, 1998). In the case of a merger or acquisition, an employee or group of employees may find themselves in a situation in which the organization that they chose to work for is no longer their employer. The new combined organization may or may not be a good cultural fit for them. It is easy to see why organizations with extreme cultural differences would experience a great challenge in trying to integrate employee groups. In spite of this fact, those responsible for identifying and negotiating consolidation deals often focus on financial and strategic issues and fail to assess cultural differences. Incompatible cultures, however, head the list of impediments to successful integration (Tetenbaum, 1999). In 1996, the British Institute of Management surveyed executives involved in a number of acquisitions and found that the major factor in M&A failure was underestimation of the difficulties of merging two cultures (Marks & Mirvis, 2000).

People issues. Culture can refer to the informal, sometimes invisible, human aspects of an organization; people issues here refers to the more traditional, formal human resources functions. This may include salary issues, performance appraisal systems, employee contracts, and/or benefits. It may also include tax and labor law compliance issues.

Insufficient attention to people issues may help explain the failure of many M&As to live up to expectations. Between one-third and one-half of all merger failures have been blamed on "employee problems" (Cartwright & Cooper, 1993). A survey of human resources professionals showed that people issues are often overlooked until after the agreement is final (Marks & Mirvis, 1992). Human resource issues are a prominent and difficult aspect of M&As, but these concerns are not dealt with effectively in a high percentage of transactions (Marks & Mirvis, 1992). Human resource issues are capable of derailing alliances that have all the prospects of financial success (Tetenbaum, 1999).

The pre-merger period tends to be very stressful for both the acquiring and acquired company and this stress changes, rather than ceases, in the post-merger period. While less worried about job security, the employees often must negotiate new work processes, new job responsibilities, and new reporting relationships. Employees go through a psychological reorientation from the "old" to the "new" (Marks & Mirvis, 1992). It is common for employees to idealize and mythologize their old jobs and to mourn the loss of laid off workers. This is sometimes referred to as Survivor's Guilt. Marks and Mirvis (1992) identified three primary employee needs during M&As. They are: (1) psychological enlistment – the need to feel wanted and be emotionally invested in their organization's mission; (2) role development – the need for excitement about their new jobs and about the organization's future; and (3) trust and confidence in their co-workers and management.

Communication. Even though it is commonly understood that the rumor mill will fill in the gaps created by an absence of information, many organizations do a poor job of communicating with their employees during a merger or acquisition. There are various factors that contribute to this, including the multitude of contributing factors to the decisions being made, the highly secretive conditions within which these negotiations oftentimes take place, the desire to avoid delivering what will be bad news to some employees, and the failure to recognize and understand the detrimental effects of not providing information to employees in a timely manner.

A study by Fried (1996) provided insight into the importance of communicating effectively with employees whose company has been acquired by another company. This study investigated the ways that locus of control and perceived fairness of termination contributed to psychological withdrawal and intention to leave. In this case, the employees in the acquired company did not receive detailed information on the processes and goals of the acquisition before, during or after its implementation. This company learned the hard way how quickly rumors can circulate and build. Various fictitious stories circulated of unfair practices in determining which employees were retained and which were released, and rumors of favoritism circulated. In Fried's study (1996) belief that employees were treated unfairly was positively related to feelings of helplessness. Psychological withdrawal was heightened when the employees believed that the terminated employees were treated unfairly. Withdrawal heightened one's intention to leave the company and find another job. Obviously, the perception of fair treatment of terminated workers is a crucial factor in determining the attitudes and adjustment to the changes in the remaining employees. For this reason, organizations should focus not only on ensuring fair treatment of terminated employees, but also on a vehicle and method of communicating to survivors how the terminations were decided upon and handled (Fried, 1996). Appelbaum et al. (2000) suggest that setting up specialized in-house centers to help displaced employees find new employment not only assists those employees who need new jobs, but also shows remaining employees that the company cares and is trying very hard to help.

There is strong evidence to suggest that it is the expectancy of change and fear of future survival rather than the actual change, which triggers the most M&A stress (Cartwright & Cooper, 1993). Employees involved in an M&A are likely to find the uncertainty of the pending M&A as stressful, perhaps even more stressful, than the actual changes that follow it. For this reason, it should be remembered that silence breeds fear. Uncertainty may be reduced, or at least managed, by the use of frequent and consistent communication methods. Systematic communication vehicles such as publications and/or regularly scheduled informational meetings between management and employees can go a long way toward enhancing employee's confidence in the future prospects of the merged entity. The message should be conveyed, although it may initially be met with skepticism, that in the long run the merged company may provide greater career opportunities to the employees due to its increased size and resources.

Integration plan. Too often, companies take a "just add water" approach to the post-merger period of time. Organizations desire instant integration and hope it will "just happen" naturally, like love at first sight. As was previously mentioned, M&As create organizational entities that are much more analogous to step-families, with all the challenges this implies. Unfortunately, many organizations enter into these new arrangements without a solid integration plan. There are some exceptions, however. By many reports, Unilever, Bombadier, and Cisco have become M&A specialists (Appelbaum et al., 2000). According to Tetenbaum (1999), integration plans have been shown to improve the odds of M&A success by as much as 50%. In fact, M&A success or failure three years after a deal has been explained by the presence or absence of an integration plan.

IMPROVING THE CHANCES OF M&A SUCCESS

The bad news is that successfully integrating two organizations is very difficult and many M&As fail to live up to expectations; the good news is that it does appear that we are beginning to learn from our mistakes. There has been a significant amount of recent research that both illuminates the causes for the lack of success and offers guidance for future M&As. This section will consider cultural assessments, integration plans and transition teams, and communication as tools to use when weathering M&As. The section will conclude by discussing separation anxiety, employee stress, and outplacement as issues that should be addressed by organizations engaged in a merger or acquisition.

CULTURAL ASSESSMENTS

Research attributes M&A failures primarily to non-integrated, incompatible cultures, which result in lost value and unattained synergies (Maxwell, 1998). There are steps that organizations can take to avoid failure and increase the chances of success.

As early in the process as possible, in every M&A, an assessment of the fit between the two organizations should be carried out. Based on this assessment a judgment should be made as to whether the organizations can realistically be combined. Extensive planning and data gathering, with emphasis on cultural issues, is necessary. The knowledge gained in a cultural assessment will contribute not only to the decision about whether to proceed with the merger or acquisition, but will also assist in designing the eventual integration plan if the merger goes forward.

According to Tetenbaum (1999), a cultural audit should include the following questions: (1) What do the companies value? (2) What do the companies stand for? (3) Who are the company's heroes and heroines? (4) What are the companies' mottos and slogans? (5) What gets celebrated? (6) What gets rewarded? (7) How is leadership expressed? (8) How does each company handle conflict? (9) How do they handle decision making? (10) How do people communicate? (11) What are interactions like? (12) What are the staff's perceptions, attitudes, expectations, needs? (13) How is work monitored? and (14) How are people held accountable? An additional benefit of this exercise is that an organization is forced to take a self-reflective look at its own culture. This self-examination allows the company to identify its own, as well as the M&A partner's, organizational strengths and weaknesses (Buono & Bowditch, 1989). There are many consulting firms that offer their own versions of culture assessments that can be used during M&A activity.

As stated earlier, the sooner in the process that these questions can be answered, the better. However, it may not be possible to conduct a full-blown cultural assessment during the earliest pre-merger stages due to the degree of secrecy and confidentiality that is paramount. The cultural assessment/audit identifies potential barriers and allows the firms to decide whether to proceed or, if significant incompatibilities are surfaced, to walk away from the deal. If the deal progresses, then the organizations should use the cultural assessment collaboratively to begin to plan how the organizations will be integrated.

An integration/transition team should be formed (this will be discussed in the next section). During the transition, historical and cultural artifacts can be used to honor the history of both organizations and to begin to create a blended culture. Symbols can be quite effective and powerful because they convey an image that can be graphically displayed. These might include logos, slogans, pictures, signs, or uniforms (Marks & Mirvis, 2000). It is important that efforts to form a combined culture are authentic and sincere.

TRANSITION TEAMS AND INTEGRATION PLANS

Companies going through a merger and/or acquisition should develop a transition structure when joining forces. This can be a temporary system that lasts three to six months or can extend up to a year or more to provide for coordination and support during implementation of change (Marks & Mirvis, 2000). Some companies have begun to develop and use standardized techniques to assess potential deals and they have developed experienced integration teams to ensure success after the deal is done (Major, 1999). These companies often have templates, processes and mechanics in place.

The absence of an integration plan can result in "post-merger drift" (Marks & Mirvis, 1992). This is a period of decreasing productivity that follows a merger or acquisition during which time employees are expected to maintain productivity while simultaneously undergoing large changes in their work lives. Research has shown, however, a drop in productivity commonly occurs when undergoing any large-scale change (Major, 1999). Post-merger drift, can cause productivity to fall and integration efforts to stall out (Marks & Mirvis, 1992). The greatest productivity drop-off is in the first few months post-merger; however it can take one or more years to fully recover (Tetenbaum, 1999).

Employee anxiety and distraction are also commonly reported during a period of time leading up to and following a merger or acquisition. Role clarification is required before employee commitment and motivation can begin to return to pre-M&A levels. For this reason, the integration team must act quickly and work with management to make decisions about layoffs, restructurings, reporting relationships, and other changes within days after the deal is signed and announced. This information should be communicated to the employees as soon as possible (Maxwell,1998). This helps control post-merger drift and assures employees that there is a plan in place. It also serves the purpose of countering inaccurate rumors. This will be discussed in greater detail in a later section.

The transition team should include members from both organizations. One of the greatest benefits of a transition team is that it creates a relationship-building space within which members of the merging organizations can collaborate to plan the integration. Although challenging, if a collaborative spirit can be established on the transition team, the merger will have a much better chance for success. According to Appelbaum et al. (2000), incorporating employees in the merger process could prove beneficial in eliminating stress, uncertainty, and insecurity. Also, a chartering exercise can help ensure that there is common vision of goals and objectives. The collaborative spirit of the transition team then serves a role-modeling purpose for the rest of the organization.

Most transition structures, or teams, involve three key roles: a steering committee, transition managers, and task forces (Tetenbaum, 1999). It is common to assign someone to be the transition manager in addition to his/her regular job responsibilities; however, given the complexity of the tasks, the amount of time required, and the importance of the role, integration plans are more successful when key people are assigned full-time to the role of transition manager (Galpin & Herndon, 2000; Marks & Mirvis, 2000). GE Capital treats integration management as a full-time position and has discovered that those mergers that did not have integration managers were less successful than those that have them (Marks & Mirvis, 2000).

It is best if the transition team leader has been engaged in the M&A process from the beginning discussions so that he or she is knowledgeable about the strategic intent and the organizational objectives of the consolidation (Tetenbaum, 1999). The leader should be energetic and enthusiastic about the merger and possess high credibility within the organization.

Marks and Mirvis (2000) also recommend the use of steering committees and task forces during the integration period of M&As. The steering committee may be responsible for establishing critical success factors for the merger and defining the decision-making criteria by which to evaluate integration recommendations, among other tasks (Marks & Mirvis, 2000). Task forces are usually cross-company groups who make recommendations on how to structure the combined organization.

COMMUNICATION

Fifty-seven percent of the HR directors surveyed by Hewitt Associates (1998, as cited in Tetenbaum, 1999) cited communication to employees as an important critical success factor bearing on the overall success of a merger or acquisition. In spite of its importance, communication to employees was the least effectively managed aspect of the consolidation, according to the survey. Respondents listed too few resources, communications occurring too late in the transaction, and too little attention to communication paid by senior management as primary issues in the communication breakdowns (Tetenbaum, 1999). This is a particularly disturbing finding since, in the midst of all the uncertainties of M&As, communication is one area over which the company can exercise a good deal of control. The organization has, at its disposal, various methods to communicate with its employees if it should choose to do so.

Inadequate communication results in lower employee motivation and satisfaction, and greater employee anxiety and resistance to the merger. The integration team should make sure that accurate information is conveyed to all employees at every level of the organization in a timely manner (Marks & Mirvis, 2000).

Young and Post (1993) advise that organizations going through a merger or acquisition should communicate not only what is happening, but also why, how, and if possible, when it is happening. As changes happen more frequently and the future is less certain, employees need to know the rationale behind management decisions. Meeting this need is critical to an organization's capacity for implementing change programs. Communication should be continuous during times of change. The cost of not communicating in a timely manner is "disaffection, anger, and loss of trust. In a world where organizations need increasingly high levels of mutual trust among all personnel, the failure to share what you know when you know it is a prescription for trouble" (Young & Post, 1993, p. 42).

Leaders should make use of every method available to communicate with employees. As stated before, information breeds confidence, and silence breeds fear. In large geographically dispersed organizations, this can be a particular challenge, yet the effort that the organization expends to keep its employees informed sends a powerful message, especially to newly acquired employees who are forming their first impressions of the company. Employees who hear news of changes in their company from the media or, perhaps worse, from customers, will feel particularly vulnerable. However, another responsibility of the integration team is to ensure that communication is also moving outward to customers or clients, vendors, the community, and the media (Marks & Mirvis, 2000).

Recognizing separation anxiety. As more research on M&As has become available, separation anxiety has emerged as an issue of which organizational leaders should be aware. Astrachan (1990) defines anxiety as a psychological, social and biological phenomenon resulting from a consciously or unconsciously perceived threat to the individual. Separation anxiety takes place when a relationship with someone or something important to an individual is altered. It encompasses the behavioral and emotional reactions to impending physical or psychological distancing (Astrachan, 1990).

Astrachan (1990) studied separation anxiety in the corporate context of mergers and acquisitions and found that separation anxiety is routinely experienced in organizations before and during mergers and acquisitions.

Additionally, separation anxiety affects both those leaving and those staying in the organization (Astrachan, 1990).

The two most important factors associated with increased stress during mergers are uncertainty and insecurity (Marks, 1982, as cited in Astrachan, 1990). Employees tend to be suspicious and fearful during M&As, which is characteristic of anxiety. Separation anxiety, however, is a specific anxiety that is pivotal to the understanding of how people are affected by M&As. Employees may develop a crisis management orientation similar to the fight or flight response. This orientation can cause employees to become either overly hostile and aggressive, or extremely withdrawn and despondent. Psychological denial, a primary means of coping with anxiety, was also found to be a prevalent coping mechanism for managers going through corporate M&As (Astrachan, 1990).

The strategies for ensuring M&A success that have been discussed so far – dealing with cultural differences, communicating effectively, and having a well-planned integration plan – should help employees who are experiencing separation anxiety. Additionally, some research indicates that companies have had positive results with offering stress management workshops with modules that directly address separation anxiety.

CONCLUSION

If companies are going to be able to increase the success rate of M&As, they must change the way that M&As are managed. A collaborative approach will help achieve this. As soon as is feasible, the organizations should collaboratively carry out a cultural assessment. While the financial and strategic aspects of due diligence are extremely important, in light of current research that cites cultural differences and people issues as the main causes for M&A failure, the results of the cultural audits should be accorded more weight than is currently the case in the decision to proceed.

Once the decision has been made to go forward with a merger or an acquisition, the organizations involved must work collaboratively to form a transition team and design an integration plan. Ensuring collaboration will enhance buy-in from both sides of the union, by providing time to become more familiar with individuals from the other organization, which enables bonds to begin to form and deepens understanding of the culture of other organization. Working closely together might also illuminate obstacles that may prove prohibitive to a merger. If that turns out to be the case, then the time spent was especially valuable in that it enabled the organizations to avoid what probably would have been an unsuccessful venture.

In order to allay employee stress and separation anxiety, organizations must ensure that employees are receiving adequate communication concerning the consolidation. Decisions concerning lay-offs and organizational changes should be made and communicated as quickly as possible. Organizational leaders should consider making stress management workshops, career and personal counseling, and outplacement services available for employees as needed. Designing integration structures that require collaboration between groups of employees from the merged entities may prove challenging at first, but the pay-off will be the genesis of a joint culture. All of these actions should be handled with tact and consideration. The history of each organization and the contributions of each organization's employees should be respected and honored while promoting the message that together, the organizations will be even better.

Although the economy is still recovering from the September 11, 2001 terrorist attacks on the United States and is very unpredictable in light of current recession and turbulent world events, there is nothing to indicate that M&As will NOT continue to be a method of organizational transformation. Industrial/organizational psychologists can draw on their unique expertise in organizational development, organizational theory, group dynamics, and organizational psychology to provide valuable assistance to organizations embarking on the M&A path. The extreme difficulty of M&As and the high failure rate should make this an appealing research area for scientist/practitioners.

REFERENCES

Appelbaum, S., Gandell, J., Shapiro, B., Belisle, P., & Hoeven, E. (2000). Anatomy of a merger: Behavior of organizational factors and processes throughout the pre- during- post-stages (Part 2). *Management Decision, 38,* 674–684.

Astrachan, J. (1990). *Mergers, Acquisitions, and Employee Anxiety: A Study of Separation Anxiety in a Corporate Context.* NY: Praeger.

Buono, A., & Bowditch, J. (1989). *The human side of mergers and acquisitions: Managing collisions between people, cultures, and organizations.* San Francisco: Jossey-Bass.

Cartwright, S., & Cooper, C. (1993). The psychological impact of merger and acquisition on the individual: A study of building society managers. *Human Relations, 46,* 327–347.

Cascio, W. (1998). *Applied psychology in human resource management.* Saddle River, NJ: Prentice Hall.

Fried, Y., Tiegs, R., Naughton, T., & Ashforth, B. (1996). Managers' reactions to a corporate acquisition: a test of an integrative model. *Journal of Organizational Behavior, 17,* 401–427.

Galpin, T., & Herndon, M. (2000). *The complete guide to mergers and acquisitions: Process tools to support M&A integration at every level.* San Francisco: Jossey-Bass.

Major, M. (1999). After the merger: Easing the transition. *TMA Journal, 19*(5), 54–57.

Marks, M., & Mirvis, P. (1992). Rebuilding after the merger: Dealing with "survivor sickness." *Organizational Dynamics, 21,* 18–33.

Marks, M., & Mirvis, P. (2000). Managing mergers, acquisitions, and alliances: Creating an effective transition structure. *Organizational Dynamics*, *28*(3), 35–47.

Maxwell, S. (1998). A merger manual. *Civil Engineering*, *68*(2), 73–76.

Tetenbaum, T. (1999). Seven key practices that improve the chance for expected integration and synergies. *Organizational Dynamics*, *28*(2), 22–36.

Weber, Y. (1996). Corporate cultural fit and performance in mergers and acquisitions. *Human Relations*, *49*(9), 1181–1202.

Weston F., & Jawien, P. (1999). Perspectives on mergers and restructuring. *Business Economics*, *34*(1), 29–34.

Young, M., & Post, J. (1993). Managing to communicate, communicating to manage: How leading companies communicate with employees. *Organizational Dynamics*, *22*, 31–44.

Online resources:
www.maadvisor.com
www.mergerstat.com